Creolizing Practices of Freedom

CREOLIZING THE CANON

Series Editors

Jane Anna Gordon (University of Connecticut) and
Neil Roberts (University of Toronto)

This series, published in partnership with the Caribbean Philosophical Association, revisits canonical theorists in the humanities and social sciences through the lens of creolization. It offers fresh readings of familiar figures and presents the case for the study of formerly excluded ones.

Titles in the Series

Creolizing Rousseau, edited by Jane Anna Gordon and Neil Roberts
Hegel, Freud and Fanon, by Stefan Bird-Pollan
Theorizing Glissant, edited by John E. Drabinski and Marisa Parham
Journeys in Caribbean Thought: The Paget Henry Reader, edited by Jane Anna Gordon, Lewis R. Gordon, Aaron Kamugisha, and Neil Roberts, with Paget Henry
The Philosophical Treatise of William H. Ferris: Selected Readings from The African Abroad or, His Evolution in Western Civilization, by Tommy J. Curry
Creolizing Hegel, edited by Michael J. Monahan
Frantz Fanon, Psychiatry and Politics, by Nigel C. Gibson and Roberto Beneduce
Melancholia Africana: The Indispensable Overcoming of the Black Condition, by Nathalie Etoke, translated by Bill Hamlett
Afrocubanas: History, Thought, and Cultural Practices, edited by Devyn Spence Benson, Daisy Rubiero Castillo and Inés María Martiatu Terry, translated by Karina Alma
Creolizing Rosa Luxemburg, edited by Jane Anna Gordon and Drucilla Cornell
Mabogo P. More: Philosophical Anthropology in Azania, by Tendayi Sithole
Creolizing Practices of Freedom: Recognition and Dissonance, by Michael J. Monahan

Creolizing Practices of Freedom

Recognition and Dissonance

Michael J. Monahan

ROWMAN & LITTLEFIELD
Lanham • Boulder • New York • London

Published by Rowman & Littlefield
An imprint of The Rowman & Littlefield Publishing Group, Inc.
4501 Forbes Boulevard, Suite 200, Lanham, Maryland 20706
www.rowman.com

86-90 Paul Street, London EC2A 4NE

Copyright © 2023 by The Rowman & Littlefield Publishing Group, Inc.

All rights reserved. No part of this book may be reproduced in any form or by any electronic or mechanical means, including information storage and retrieval systems, without written permission from the publisher, except by a reviewer who may quote passages in a review.

British Library Cataloguing in Publication Information Available

Library of Congress Cataloging-in-Publication Data

Names: Monahan, Michael J., author.
Title: Creolizing practices of freedom : recognition and dissonance / Michael J. Monahan.
Description: Lanham, Maryland : Rowman & Littlefield, 2023. | Series: Creolizing the canon | Includes bibliographical references and index.
Identifiers: LCCN 2022034537 (print) | LCCN 2022034538 (ebook) | ISBN 9781538174616 (cloth) | ISBN 9781538174630 (paperback) | ISBN 9781538174623 (ebook)
Subjects: LCSH: Liberty—Philosophy. | Liberty—Social aspects.
Classification: LCC B824.4 .M57 2023 (print) | LCC B824.4 (ebook) | DDC 123/.5—dc23/eng/20220909
LC record available at https://lccn.loc.gov/2022034537
LC ebook record available at https://lccn.loc.gov/2022034538

Contents

Acknowledgments	vii
Introduction: Being, Belonging, and Freedom	1
Chapter 1: Freedom and the Politics of Purity	11
Chapter 2: Recognition and Its Discontents	29
Chapter 3: Recognition, Cognition, and Purity	49
Chapter 4: Toward a Creolizing Freedom	71
Chapter 5: The (We-)Subject of Liberation	93
Chapter 6: On *Human* Liberation	131
Coda: An Opening and an Invitation to a Living Practice of Freedom	165
Notes	169
Bibliography	181
Index	189
About the Author	197

Acknowledgments

While the writing of this book began in earnest in the summer of 2019, on the eve of the outbreak of the global pandemic, the explosion of protests surrounding that *other* global pandemic—white supremacy and state-sanctioned violence against *les damnés de la terre*—and an attempted coup in the US capital, there is a sense in which I have been working on it, on and off, since my dissertation in the early 2000s. It has been frequently interrupted or derailed, by events and crises both professional and personal, only to be gradually re-envisioned and re-assembled. Certainly, what I produced over the last two years is not what I would have produced had I not been side-tracked so often (including the extended "side-track" that was my first book). It is thus with some sense of gratitude that I reflect on the many interruptions of this work, even the ones that were distinctly unpleasant at the time, since I believe what ultimately resulted is an improvement over what I had envisioned in previous iterations in the course of the past two decades. That positive trajectory, of course, owes much to the communities and individuals with whom I have collaborated over the years, which brings me to this profession of gratitude for all their efforts (though certainly any shortcomings in this text are entirely of my own making).

Above all I must acknowledge the support of the Caribbean Philosophical Association (CPA), which has been my intellectual "home" since its inaugural meeting in 2004. The ideas behind the "creolizing" methodology I employ here grew out of the rich discussions hosted by the CPA over the years, and particularly from the work of Jane Anna Gordon and Neil Roberts, both past presidents of the organization. Drucilla Cornell has been an inspirational comrade and fellow-traveler (figuratively and literally). Lewis Gordon, another past president of the CPA, has been a source of support and mentorship vital to my own work, and I hope I have done justice to his thought in my engagement with it in my final chapter of this text. Special thanks also to Derefe Chevannes, Carolyn Cusick, Doug Ficek, Yomaira Figueroa, David Fryer, Erik Garrett, Nathifa Greene, Oscar Guardiola-Rivera, Paget Henry, T Storm

Heter, Victor Hugo Pacheco, Nelson Maldonado-Torres, Thomas Meagher, Mireille Fanon Mendès-France, Michael Paradiso Michau, Dana Miranda, P. Mabogo More, Marilyn Nissim-Sabat, Gregory Pappas, Elisabeth Paquette, LaRose Paris, Peter Park, Andrea Pitts, Stephanie Rivera Berruz, Kris Sealey, Grant Silva, Julia Suárez-Krabbe, Olúfẹ́mi Táíwò, Rosario Torres Guevara, and Hanétha Vété Congolo. The late Charles Mills was also a CPA stalwart, as was Charley Nissim-Sabat, and their absence will be very much present in our future gatherings. The California Roundtable on Philosophy and Race has also been a significant institution in the genesis and development of this project. My deep gratitude to the co-organizers of that community, Falguni Sheth and Mickaella Perina.

My conversations with Jose Medina and Mariana Ortega have also been integral to the development of this project. María Acosta brought me to Bogotá to deliver an early version of chapter 3 in 2010, and I am grateful for the enduring friendship that visit initiated. A conference on the work of Gloria Anzaldúa at the University of Texas, Rio Grande Valley helped to inform much of chapter 5, for which I am most grateful to Mariana Allesandri, Cynthia Paccacerqua, and Alex Stehn. I am grateful as well to my colleagues at both Marquette and the University of Memphis, especially Jim Bahoh, Corinne Bloch-Mullins, Curtis Carter, Yoon Choi, Remy Debes, Shaun Gallagher, Kevin Gibson, David Gray, John Jones, Sebastian Luft, Mary Beth Mader, Tony Peressini, Danny Smith, Nancy Snow, James South, Lindsey Stewart, Theresa Tobin, Deb Tollefsen, Somogy Varga, and Margaret Urban Walker. My students, from whom I learned so much, also deserve my thanks: Alan Chavoya, Morgan Elbot, Reese Faust, D. J. Hobbs, Chad Kleist, Chris Kramer, Jenn Marra-Henrigillis, Keisha Martin, Ashleigh Morales, Melissa Mosko, Sam Munroe, Corey Reed, Jasper St. Bernard, Margaret Steele, Velimir Stojkovski, Greg Trotter, Desiree Valentine, Clark Wolff, Jonathan Wurtz, Marisola Xhelili, and Jim Zubko. Special thanks, as well, to Justin Wooley, who offered valuable feedback and aided in the indexing of the manuscript.

Finally, my deep gratitude to Camille, whose support over the past thirty years has been a constant and astonishing gift.

Introduction
Being, Belonging, and Freedom

The aim of this book is to articulate a theory of freedom and liberation. In particular, I will offer an account of freedom as a *creolizing praxis*, and of liberation as a struggle against what I refer to as the "politics of purity." In the course of laying out and defending this account, I will be dwelling in particular on the underlying metaphysical assumptions that inform, often surreptitiously, so much of literature on these concepts. That project will begin in earnest in chapter 1, but I will take the opportunity in this introduction to situate and motivate the project. Why another text on freedom and liberation?

Primarily, I think another book on freedom is demanded by a context in which oppression in its myriad forms is running rampant, yet within theoretical circles, discourses of freedom and liberation are increasingly viewed with suspicion. Some of this suspicion is warranted, as theoretical accounts of freedom and liberation have often been Eurocentric and colonial—they have, ironically, been oppressive. Indeed, I will explore some of these critiques in the chapters to follow. Yet the resistance to *any* notion of freedom and liberation seems to throw the baby out with the proverbial bathwater. The dismissal of theory in favor of practice does not offer an escape, either. "Practice" must always involve some *understanding* of the problem being addressed, the best means of addressing it, and the results one hopes to realize. Such understanding involves appeals to *meaning*—one cannot identify a problem or a solution absent a *conceptual* framework that enables them to *appear* as such (that is, as "problems" or "solutions"). As a result, it is only by appeal to theory, whether acknowledged or no, that practice is possible in the first place. In a world where there is so much to be done, where the forces and practices of oppression are so varied and sophisticated, our practice must be informed by a *living* theory that is evolving and changing to meet these varied challenges. The approach I take here can thus be understood as a humble effort to breathe life into the gasping lungs of some very world-weary concepts whose value remains nevertheless as critical as ever.

Beyond merely engaging with fundamental questions of freedom and liberation, this book will further transgress the disciplinary norms of political philosophy by offering an explicit appeal to the *metaphysical* underpinnings of these core concepts. For reasons that will become apparent as the text, and my larger argument, develops, questions of freedom and liberation inevitably lead to questions regarding the *subject* of liberation. Is that subject intelligible as an individual outside of her larger social context, or is she to some degree a product of that context? Or is perhaps "the subject" itself an oppressive political/theoretical concept that must be abandoned? In that case, though, what could liberation or oppression even mean without a subject to be oppressed or liberated? Is "liberation," like "the subject," a misguided or even pathological construct as well? Of course, even if this latter view were true, that realization would do little to comfort or address the condition of the enslaved laborer, the refugee displaced by war or economic hopelessness, or those who live in constant and all-too-justified fear of arbitrary police violence. The point in raising all of these questions is to draw important attention to what will become a central preoccupation of this text: in order to treat with concepts like oppression and liberation intelligibly, one ultimately needs an underlying metaphysics. The attempt to avoid or disavow metaphysics that is common in contemporary anglophone political philosophy only ever allows one's inevitable metaphysical presuppositions to operate sub-rosa. Even explicit efforts to dismiss metaphysics only serve to muddy the waters. After all, the only kind of argument one can make for why metaphysics is irrelevant to political theory must ultimately be a *metaphysical* one.

My modus operandi will begin from what I take to be the rather modest premises that oppression is quite real, and that liberation is a worthwhile and meaningful project. From this starting point, the task is to articulate worthy accounts of these fraught concepts, including the metaphysical conditions necessary to render them intelligible. In short, questions of the ontology of the social world within which our struggles for liberation take place and by which they can be rendered meaningful will be front and center throughout this text.[1] The ultimate justification for this approach, for me, is that it is the only way I can see to take seriously the words and deeds of those who struggle and have struggled for liberation. The Haitian revolutionaries were struggling for something real and important. Anti-colonial struggles in the Americas, Africa, and Asia were efforts to gain something worth all of the loss and bloodshed, as were the efforts of those who fought to preserve "the commons"[2] throughout Europe. The civil rights or anti-apartheid struggles, #BlackLivesMatter, resistance to the Dakota Access Pipeline, the effort to thwart the ongoing catastrophe at the southern US border—all these, along with similar struggles in the present and to come, are articulated by those participating in them as liberatory struggles in one way or another. It strikes me as an expression of profound hubris to dismiss that characterization. To honor those present and historical struggles and to support those who follow in their footsteps, it is necessary to begin by taking seriously the claim that these were struggles for liberation and against oppression. That is the central project of this text.

This effort to take seriously and honor those who have struggled and continue to struggle for liberation is not limited to questions narrowly political or metaphysical, however, but is also deeply epistemological. This is a matter not only of what has come to be known as questions of "epistemic justice," but is in fact inextricable from questions of freedom and liberation. Freedom is, regardless of how one ultimately construes it, a question of certain kinds of relations. To struggle for liberation is to struggle to alter relations to other people, relations to one's physical environment, or relations to laws and norms within one's social environment. In all cases, one requirement is an understanding of the subjects and the objects involved in those relations. This raises immediately not only the metaphysical question of what those subjects and objects ultimately are, but what it would mean to adequately *understand* them at all. My ultimate argument here will be that human subjects are constituted in such a way that a particular, and in most ways unorthodox, epistemology is called for in the context of projects of liberation.

One way to see how this relationship between epistemology, the metaphysics of the subject, and liberation works is by turning to Hegel's famous gloss on freedom as "being at home with oneself in the other" (Hegel 1991b, 7z). As I will argue in the course of this text, the insight captured here is one common both to Africana approaches to liberation (even if not phrased in this way) and to certain strands of Latina feminist theory such as Mariana Ortega's account of "hometactics" (Ortega 2016, 201–10; cf. Monahan 2019). I begin, however, with the Hegel quote because, regardless of one's familiarity with his account of freedom, it is a suggestive and provocative way to think about freedom and liberation. In particular, it points precisely toward those questions of relation (between self and home, self and other, other and home), questions of epistemology (what must I know about myself, home, and the other, in order for this condition of "being at home" to be realized?), and of course questions of metaphysics (what are the self, the home, and the other?). If we begin with the idea of "home," it is possible to begin to untangle these different threads of the account I will offer.

There could be many different ways to conceive of *home* as a concept. In the interests of getting the discussion started, however, consider the relatively straightforward sense in which the international traveler can be away, in some sense, from their home.[3] One important insight that emerges from this sort of example is this: in order to better understand our home it is often helpful, even necessary, to leave it. By encountering the strange, the foreign, and the unaccustomed, we are able to encounter our homes, and ourselves, in new ways. By abandoning the familiar, we can come to see the formerly-familiar as the newly-strange even as the formerly strange gradually becomes familiar. Of course, as anyone who has traveled abroad and observed the common instantiations of the genus *tourist* can testify, it is also perfectly possible to cross borders and oceans, yet take, tortoise-like, one's home with them. In extreme cases common to settler colonialism, one is even able to impose one's home on others. Indeed, much of what passes for tourism can be understood as a very concrete instantiation of the "coloniality of Being" (Maldonado-Torres 2007), whereby the world is shaped to cater to the desires and understandings of colonizer (in this case, the tourist). But when the traveler is willing and able to abandon to some extent the comforts of home, and experience their new environment as a stranger and a guest, then it is possible to arrive at a better understanding not only of the larger world, but of one's home, and significantly, oneself. In short, it is in the encounter with what is different that we gain a richer understanding of what is familiar. In more abstract terms, it is through the encounter with difference that identity is constituted and made intelligible.

Part of the process of writing this book took place in Cape Town, South Africa, where I strove (of course, such striving, no matter how successful, is always also to some degree a failure) to manifest the epistemic modesty and openness that will be conducive not only to learning with and from the people I met, but to those moments where I encounter my home, and myself, as strangers. Cape Town is an exceptionally interesting place for such an undertaking. As a largely Anglophone, cosmopolitan, and "developed" city, there are significant aspects of it that are quite familiar indeed to a visitor from the United States. At the same time, my prior experience living and conducting research in the Caribbean also helped to make other aspects familiar (the South African "combi," for instance, is very akin to the Barbadian "ZR" or the Jamaican "Route Taxi"). Learning and exploring those areas of overlap and familiarity are in themselves interesting and important, but it is those moments where the proverbial rug is yanked from beneath our feet that are the most powerful. To be sure, they tend to provide the best stories to tell upon our return home, but more importantly, they offer the best opportunities for growth. The familiar reveals itself as such through the strange, and we can, through this process, gain a deeper understanding of both.

At the same time, there are dangers in over-romanticizing travel and the strange. My travels were voluntary, and undertaken from a position of relative advantage afforded by my gender, my race, my class, and of course my nationality. From such positions of power and relative security, it can often be beneficial to upset the status quo, to shake things up, and have one's expectations unsettled. For the refugee, for the displaced, and for many immigrants, however, the story told here must be a different one in some very significant ways. Too much strangeness, too much rootlessness, or too much unsettling can be alienating and damaging to one's wellbeing, especially when one finds oneself positioned as *other* to a larger societal norm. Mariana Ortega's conception of "hometactics" is an effort to address precisely this troubled relation to home from such a position. Her text works to avoid the pitfalls of nationalism or a kind of mythologized a facile kind of belonging on the one hand, and utter rootlessness and alienation on the other from the position of "a Latina who felt displaced and who often wondered about the question of home ever since revolution transformed my life, and many other Nicaraguans' daily lives" (Ortega 2016, 17). This distinction between a reified sense of belonging and rootlessness is crucial, for I may certainly have been a foreigner in Cape Town, but I knew I would be there only temporarily, and more importantly for present purposes, my basic epistemic position was very much within the *norm* for that context in many of the most significant ways.[4] What this reveals, in part, is that there is a danger on the one hand of being *too much* "at home," which can lead to a kind of epistemic and existential complacency (a deep-seated coloniality, if you will), and on the other hand of being *too much* adrift or displaced, which can lead to a profound and disempowering alienation. Of course, the appeal to "alienation" here is indicative of this complex relationship, for what is alienation at root but the rendering strange of that which would otherwise be familiar, whether it is a place, a practice, or of course one*self*.[5]

This tension between too much and too little familiarity raises the question of how best to navigate a course between these two extremes. How do we articulate a relation between self, other, and belonging to different "worlds" in María Lugones's sense of the term (Lugones 2003, 77–100) that avoids both a facile appeal to some *essential* belonging and a complete lack of rootedness? This is, I submit, at the heart of any serious effort to honor struggles for liberation in the sense that motivates this project. For one key aspect of such struggles is an effort to articulate or re-articulate a sense of belonging, of place, and of new relations between self and other. Sometimes this takes the form of efforts to flee an untenable situation to create the conditions for freedom and a more human life elsewhere, as in the case of marronage (Roberts 2015).[6] Sometimes it requires displacing those who dominate you and prevent you from feeling a sense of belonging, as in cases of struggles for indigenous sovereignty in the face of settler colonialism (Coulthard 2014). At other times it means altering the political and cultural landscape in a way that disrupts pathological senses of belonging (such as white supremacy and US *nativism*) and works toward better accommodating a more inclusive sense of place and community where all (or at least more) can genuinely belong, as in the case with the civil rights struggle in the US. This is surely only one aspect of these struggles, they are also, in many cases, struggles for survival, yet nevertheless they remain always also efforts to secure some sense of *belonging*. What this shows is that the nature of the kinds of relations described above with which liberation is concerned—relations between self and other, and between self, other, and environment or place—are bound up with notions of belonging and being at home, and Hegel's admittedly obscure articulation gestures toward precisely this aspect of freedom and liberation.[7]

This appeal to freedom as a mode of *relation* helps to illuminate the way in which our thinking on the subject of liberation has so often been enmeshed in what I have called "the politics of purity." This is a concept I first developed in *The Creolizing Subject* (2011), and as it will be key to the larger argument I am offering in this book, I will lay out an in-depth articulation of this concept and how it bears on questions of liberation in the first chapter. For present purposes, it will suffice, I trust, to say that the idea of the politics of purity is my effort to capture the general tendency in thought and deed toward clear and distinct boundaries that enable processes of the exclusion of what does not *belong*—of purification. At root, the politics of purity distrusts and disavows ambiguity, such that the presence of ambiguity or indeterminacy is seen as a kind of break-down or failure either in our thinking (we just haven't defined the categories properly/clearly) or in our practical life (we just aren't maintaining the proper order of things, which "proper order" of course is that determined by well-defined and "pure" categories of thought and being). This bears on the question of relation insofar as it demands that relations be *external*. Object A may relate to object B, but the individual objects are themselves self-contained and discrete (if properly understood). But, as I will argue, relations are not always (perhaps never) merely external, but often constitutive of the very objects, ideas, or processes in relation, and this is particularly pertinent to our thought and praxis of liberation.[8] If freedom is a matter of these sorts of constitutive relations between self, other, and place, where liberation is the practice of striving to manifest those relations in a manner conducive to freedom, then the politics of purity, insofar as it demands pure and discrete objects/ideas in external relations, will always fall short of adequately accounting for freedom and liberation.

By way of illustration, consider the question of home and belonging that I have been discussing so far. If we approach it from within the politics of purity, it can manifest quite clearly in varieties of *nativism*. The home is that place to which one belongs in some deep and unquestionable sense—it is at once a primal and a final belonging. If one has a relationship with the home that is in any way ambiguous or tenuous, then this is taken as a kind of failure. Either the individual in question does not or cannot *really* belong, or the place itself is in some way failing to live up to or express its *true* nature or ideals. We see both of these aspects of the politics of purity in the contemporary discourse on immigration and nation in the United States (as one among many possible examples). Those who fail to properly belong do so not by virtue of some failed relationship, but because they are "outsiders" per se. If too many such outsiders enter the "homeland," they will alter it until it is no longer "our" home. When conservative activists announce that they want "their country" back, they are responding to precisely this understanding of events. The politics of purity is present throughout this example. The "real American" is the one for whom "real America" is *home*. Both the nation and the proper subject of that nation are in effect given *a priori* and as pure concepts/categories. Any ambiguity in one's belonging is *prima facie* evidence either that one is not a "real" American in the relevant sense or that America itself has become less "real" (read "authentic") as a result of corruption from "outsiders." If the political landscape of the "home" should begin to shift, then that is always understood as a kind of *pollution* or impurity that demands, from the "real" American, some response in the form of a purification of the homeland. At the same time, however, the move to reject the very idea of home and the concept of belonging in favor of an utterly rootless or "nomadic" self remains likewise beholden to the politics of purity. It posits the ideal of a subject *purified* of any deep or constitutive attachments to place—such a subject is cut off from any place, and belonging nowhere, they in effect belong *everywhere*.[9] Both the naïve and immediate sense of belonging proper to the "nativist" and the absolute rejection of any notion of belonging share exactly the sort of intolerance for ambiguity that is at the heart of the politics of purity.

The implications of approaching questions of freedom in a way sensitive to the politics of purity are, I will argue, wide-ranging and fundamental to our understanding of human agency, of freedom, and of the social world. The tendency of the politics of purity toward positing a world full of discrete, self-contained, and static categories of individual entities that I have described elsewhere,[10] finds, in essence, its antidote in an *ontological dynamism* that I characterize as *creolizing*. If the world is made up not by discrete objects or things *in motion* (a common misunderstanding, in my view, of the appeal to "dynamism") but, rather, by motion *as such*, then much of the bedrock of our analysis of human beings and their place in the world needs to be turned on its head. This has, I will suggest, begun already in theoretical physics, but metaphysics and political theory are lagging far behind that curve. A central element of this book will be to foreground this radical ontological dynamism and take seriously its implications for our thinking about freedom and liberation. This leads to two primary methodological implications.

First, my approach throughout this book will appeal, as much as possible, to the *sonic* both as metaphor and model for our understanding of the dynamic concepts and phenomena that are my focus. Sound is particularly instructive and productive because, as I will argue in more detail later, (a) it is itself fundamentally a kind of movement, (b) it is generated through the dynamic interaction (friction) of various components or elements, (c) it requires a medium that in turn conditions the behavior of the sound wave, and (d) the source and the receiver of sound are connected through the medium, and thus the phenomenon of sound is a kind of indirect *touch*. Thus, at the core of the theoretical framework I will be developing in this text will be concepts like *resonance*, *dissonance*, and *friction*, all of which are utterly incompatible with a *static* system. As I shall show, this shift away from what are typically visual models and metaphors has radical implications that open up profound shifts in how we can think identity and liberation.

The second methodological implication is that rigorous investigation must be open-ended, and actively court difference and what I will call *productive friction*. In the context of philosophical investigation, this means that concepts, ideas, and theories must be taken as ongoing processes that are enriched and further elaborated precisely when they are brought into contact with alternative approaches, methods, and traditions. This is at the core of my earlier discussion of travel, home, and the strange. It is the hallmark of *creolizing* methodologies, where what emerges from the encounter across borders of difference can be more than the sum of its parts (this is what I mean by *productive* friction). For the purposes of this book, it means that I will be drawing from a wide array of sources and approaches to the central topics, not simply so as to "compare" them and thus triangulate a final theory on the model of a static geographic point on a detailed conceptual map (in keeping with a visual metaphor), but rather because what emerges from the encounter will be a shift in the tenor of the theory itself. Through relations of resonance and dissonance, new possibilities are made available that enrich our encounter with the unfolding theory as itself a dynamic and relational process.

I will begin in the first chapter by offering a more detailed account of the politics of purity, and an elaboration of creolizing as a mode of response, focusing on how they inform different approaches to theories of freedom. In chapter 2, I will use contemporary critical discussions of "recognition" to further elaborate the basic framework established in chapter 1, revealing how the politics of purity informs common interpretations of recognition as a way to further elaborate and illustrate my use of the concept of purity. In chapter 3, I will argue that many of these critiques of recognition themselves are implicitly enmeshed in the politics of purity. I offer there an alternative, creolizing interpretation of recognition that at once avoids the politics of purity as well as the powerful critiques of recognition discussed in chapter 2. Chapter 4 will thematize the insights gained from the prior discussion of recognition to articulate a more general account of freedom as "creolizing." It is in this chapter, as well, that I can begin to motivate and account for my turn to the sonic as a metaphor better able to represent the radically dynamic ontology to which have been appealing in the prior chapters. The fifth chapter begins the work of creolizing the account of freedom I am developing in earnest by turning to the work of Steve Biko, and Gloria Anzaldúa. The focus of this chapter is an elaboration of their accounts of agency and identity, in particular their focus on the dynamic elaboration of a *collective* identity—the "we-subject" of liberation. The sixth and final chapter will take up the question of the aim or goal of a creolizing theory of freedom, using Lewis Gordon and Sylvia Wynter's elaborations of "the human" in an anti-Black/colonial context. What emerges will not be a final articulation of a full theory of freedom (indeed, I will argue that this is to already misconstrue what freedom *is*), but an overture toward an ongoing collaborative effort to participate in the open-ended and ongoing articulation of human freedom.

Chapter 1

Freedom and the Politics of Purity

The core argument of this book is that a viable account of freedom, one that can in turn support robust accounts of oppression and liberation, must respond positively to the politics of purity—it must be creolizing. Of course, this raises questions about what I mean by these terms, and so my task in this first chapter is to offer an articulation of the politics of purity, and to describe how it impacts our thinking about freedom and our practices of liberation.[1] The account offered in the first section of the chapter is largely a summary of the more detailed analysis I put forth in *The Creolizing Subject* (2011), though I will be including some of my more recent innovations (renovations?) since that time. Those already familiar with that earlier text, and I flatter myself to think that there might be four or five of you out there, may safely pass over this first section of the chapter (unless, dear past-reader, it's been a while, and you want a refresher, in which case, enjoy!). After setting out what I mean by the "politics of purity," I will make the case that common conceptions of freedom and liberation are bound up in the politics of purity, thus opening up a space for thinking a *creolizing* account of freedom and liberation beginning in chapter 2.

ON THE POLITICS OF PURITY

My earlier articulation of the politics of purity emerged out of my efforts to grapple with questions of race and racism, where I observed that the history of the concept of "race" across the Americas exhibits a consistent orientation toward purity. I observed that, taking the historical view, racial taxonomies and classification schemas are organized around describing and then maintaining discrete categories of racialized being, and this is true even in schemas that appear, on the surface at least, to create room for or even celebrate racial mixture. The recurring pattern is this. A racial taxonomy emerges in a given time and place (seventeenth-century Barbados, or eighteenth-century

Saint-Domingue, or nineteenth-century Brazil, or twentieth-century United States), but the classifications it prescribes are often porous, and "miscegenation," both voluntary and viciously coerced, begins to generate people who do not "fit" into the existing taxonomy. In every case, one of two responses emerges. Either redefine the membership criteria such that those who were ambiguous are (re-)absorbed into an existing category, or create a new category for the new "problematic" individuals. Either way, the *telos* is one of discrete categories where individuals belong to one and only one category, such that the categories are taxonomically *pure*—they contain all and only those individuals who fully and completely (i.e., purely) belong in one and only one category, even where that category is in some sense "mixed."

In the US context, there has been a consistent (but by no means exclusive or universal) employment of the first strategy, which I will call the "absorption" strategy. Many readers will be familiar with the notorious "one-drop rule," which held that the presence of any Black ancestry is sufficient to render a given individual racially Black. There are two important features of this strategy to note from the start. First, it clearly attempts to preserve the purity of the existing taxonomic categories, especially with respect to "white" and "Black." The emergence of the ambiguous "mixed" individual, consequently, poses a threat to the taxonomical purity that demands some response. Through a kind of juridical and symbolic fiat, those with ancestry from both of these categories are simply absorbed into the "Black" category, and consequently no longer appear as ambiguous at all—to have some Black ancestry is understood to simply be (purely) Black with respect to the larger racial taxonomy. Those with ancestry from two or more different nonwhite categories are less strictly juridically controlled but, nevertheless, are often pressured to align with or identify as only one category. To be sure, my claim here is not that this prescription of purity made mixed ancestry utterly irrelevant. The phenotypic differences that typically emerge in such cases often afforded subtle and not-so-subtle advantages in interactions with ("pure") whites, and informed "colorism" within nonwhite communities. Additionally, beyond the Black/white binary there can be a good deal more flexibility in the alleged content of the various taxa. Nevertheless, it remains a constant feature throughout US history that, to the extent that racial ambiguity or mixture appears, it is precisely *as a problem* that needs to be addressed with an eye toward re-establishing and maintaining taxonomic purity. Under no circumstances, within the absorption strategy, can the existence of individuals who belong to multiple categories, or to no category, be tolerated.

The second noteworthy feature of this technique of purity is that, while informal efforts are made to prescribe purity across all categories, the formal and explicit focus is on enshrining and preserving *white* purity. The one-drop rule offers a clear case in which "nonwhite blood" functions as an impurity, thus placing whiteness at the normative and ontological center, tolerating levels of mixture among nonwhites to a degree,[2] but organizing itself principally around and devoting the bulk of its resources and energy to describing and enforcing a hard boundary around whiteness. As Hortense Spillers has emphasized, the one-drop rule served during the antebellum period to prioritize the relation of property over consanguinity, serving at once to make the sexual exploitation of Black women profitable for whites while at the same time preserving the advantages and privileges of whiteness for those who remain *purely* white (Spillers 1987, 74–75). In this way, a regime of racial purity not only reinforces the status of enslaved "Black" people as property but also, following Cheryl Harris (1993), shores up the value of "whiteness" itself as a kind of property. The underlying idea here is that any given individual can belong to one and only one racial category, and that racial purity is a necessary and sufficient condition for membership in the racial category, especially at the pinnacle of the juridically enforced hierarchy.[3]

The second, "generative" strategy of purity was far more prevalent in parts of the Americas beyond the US, where new racial categories were generated to include those emerging forms of mixture that threatened the purity of the prevailing taxonomies. *Creolité* in the Francophone, *mestiçagem* in the Lusophone, and *mestizaje* across the Hispanophone Americas all function to capture this reality of ancestry that crosses racial boundaries in different ways. Even in the Anglophone Caribbean, generative "mixed" categories have emerged in different contexts—indeed, it is principally in the United States that the absorption strategy has been predominant. While examples of the generative strategy differ widely across these different regions and over time, they all share the approach of responding to the emergence of ambiguous individuals by generating a new, yet distinct, category into which these individuals can now be placed. Historically, these systems of categorization have been quite robust, with the eighteenth-century *Sistema de Castas* in colonial New Spain standing as a paradigmatic example. Each possible combination not only of the "pure" racial categories (Spanish, Indian, African) but also combinations of the different "mixed" offspring were assigned their own discrete *casta*.[4] This might seem to break with the politics of purity. However, these new categories, once they have emerged, come to function as "pure" categories over and against all other categories. In other words, they may have emerged from a moment of mixture, but they function as discrete and pure categories within the larger taxonomy. In the *Sistema de Castas*, for example, to be *morisca* was emphatically to *not* be in the same category as either of one's parents (*Español* and *mulata*, according to Miguel Cabrera's 1763 version of the *Sistema*), nor to be in the same category as other varieties of mixture (*albarazado*, or *torna atrás*, for instance). Thus, while the categories of the *Sistema* beyond the original "pure" races are all ways of capturing different kinds of mixture, once established, each distinct *casta* functions as a *pure* category in its own right (where each "mixed" category is comprised of those with pre-determined "quanta" of different ancestries). Within this generative strategy of the politics of purity, the underlying purity of the taxonomy is maintained through the proliferation of new discrete categories that capture the emerging modes of "impurity," thereby rendering them conceptually pure, and maintaining the larger regime of taxonomic purity.

Of course, like the absorption strategy, the generative strategy has adapted over time, and continues to operate today. Throughout most of the contemporary Hispanophone Americas, there typically remain only the various "pure" categories and a single mixed (*mestizo*) category. In some cases, this was part of, or at least linked to, an explicit political project that distinguished Latin America from the US by virtue of the former's more tolerant and democratic racial landscape. This is particularly clear in the case of José Vasconcelos's articulation of *La Raza Cósmica* in Mexico and in the appeal to "racial democracy" in Brazil (Vasconcelos 2007; Freyre 2014). In both cases, the idea, which has been common and recurring throughout the Americas, is that ongoing racial miscegenation will inevitably result in a world where all are "mixed," and so race will in effect be eradicated (and racism along with it). Such ideals have, however, been criticized for appealing to a romanticized and ahistorical view of indigeneity, and for ignoring or disavowing the African contribution to culture and politics altogether. As a result of this "whitewashing" of both Black and contemporary Indigenous participation in the polity, these appeals to a mixed future have been critiqued as, in effect, projects of "whitening" the body politic (*blanquimiento*), despite the explicit appeal to racial mixture. I would agree, arguing that it is a "whitening" insofar as, while the population may have a darker complexion than a "pure" European, the cultural imaginary and epistemic regimes remain very European indeed. Furthermore, in a world that remains deeply structured by anti-Black racism, as Lewis Gordon has argued, there is value in being *distant* from Blackness, and appeals to racial mixture *can* function to create that distance, thus leading to a *whitening* in the sense of generating greater proximity to whiteness (1997b, 51–71).

There is a great deal more to be said about racial politics in Latin America, but for present purposes, a relatively straightforward observation can be made. In all of these complicated cases, from the *Sistema de Castas* to "racial democracy" in Brazil, to be *creole*, *mestiza*, or *pardo* is to *not* be European or Indigenous or African but, rather, something else altogether. In this way, we see the depth at which the politics of purity operates in the very ways we understand racial categorization, despite its many differences across time and place. At its center is a concept of whiteness organized around purity (the absence of nonwhiteness), and whether one places most forms of nonwhiteness into the same category (the "Black" in the antebellum US case, for example) or into any number of other distinct categories, common across all racial taxonomies is the following: to be white is to be purely white—any presence of the nonwhite is sufficient to displace one from that pure category. Every other category, even if it describes a "mixed" subject, still constitutes a pure category insofar as it is discrete from all other categories. The politics of purity in this way always sees the emergence of ambiguity and the transgression of boundaries as illicit, and these two strategies, absorption and generation, are the ways, within the domain of racial taxonomy, this *telos* of purity has tried to eliminate that ambiguity and re-establish a regime of purity.

While this discussion of racial taxonomies offers a clear and concrete example of the basic concept, the politics of purity is not limited to racial taxa, but operates in our thinking about racial ontology more generally. Consider the standard argument for "racial eliminativism" in the context of philosophy of race. The fact of the historical plasticity of racial categorization that I have been discussing so far, along with its variation from place to place, has led many to conclude that "race" is therefore altogether unreal. Eliminativism holds that, if race were real in the relevant sense, then it should be possible to determine empirically justified necessary and sufficient conditions for racial membership. It should be possible, in other words, to articulate empirically-grounded taxonomies that rule out, or at least mitigate against, any ambiguity. For any given individual, in other words, there should be stable and objective means for determining the race of that individual, and racial categories should have more or less clear criteria for membership. Of course, such stable and objective means do not exist. They have changed over time and vary from place to place (they are unstable), and the biological sciences have not identified genotypic or phenotypic markers that could be considered "racial" in any objective (i.e., *purely* empirical) sense. Given the inability of any theory of race to attain this ideal empirical/biological existence, the eliminativist concludes that race is not real. Now, this is an archetype of a general argument, rather than a presentation of a specific version of it. This basic argument has been around for at least the last century. We can see W. E. B. DuBois responding to a version of it in his 1898 "Conservation of Races" (1995, 20–27), for instance. His argument to "conserve" race is couched as a response to the recognition of the lack of reliable and objective biological criteria, and this is why his case for "conservation" ultimately rests upon what Chike Jeffers has called a "cultural theory of race" (Jeffers 2013). Famously, Kwame Anthony Appiah built his own early argument for racial eliminativism as a response to DuBois, arguing that DuBois's account is surreptitiously based on biology, but that there is no biological basis for race, and so race is ultimately an "illusion" (Appiah 1992, 28–46). Similarly, Naomi Zack argued that "race" not only lacks such a biological basis, but has only ever served the political purposes of exploitation and oppression. Consequently, since it is both illusory and ineluctably pernicious, it needs to be actively rejected both as a way of describing the world and as an aspect of individual identity (cf. Zack 1997).

I offer the examples of Appiah and Zack simply to illustrate two different instantiations of the basic archetype I'm attempting to describe. While both of these thinkers have since refined and in some ways attenuated their positions, their early positions on race exemplified this more general type, and in effect became the foil against which a significant proportion of the last three decades of Anglophone philosophy of race has pitted itself. With respect to the politics of purity, what is important to recognize is that this basic argumentative structure is predicated upon a particular account of the *real*. It thus deploys a metaphysical view that is seldom held up to explicit scrutiny. Specifically, the first premise of the general argument as I have offered it here holds that, if race is real, then it would be possible in principle to identify (even if we haven't in fact identified them yet) necessary and sufficient conditions for determining racial membership. In other words, that there would be objective, mind and culture-independent criteria that inscribe our racial taxonomy, so to speak, in the fabric of reality (or, if one prefers, that carves nature at its proverbial joints). If that kind of *real* race existed, then the questions surrounding our use of the concept would be questions about *correct* applications of these objective terms, not questions of their *just* application. The question of *whether* and *how* we should use racial terms and concepts arises, in this view, precisely because races are not real in the relevant sense. As a result, even if they are "socially constructed" and thus have a certain kind of reality, that kind of reality is, precisely because it is social, historical, and contingent, as opposed to empirical/biological, not binding in the way that an objective "biological" reality would be. In a sense, this is a distinction between the *merely* socially constructed reality on the one hand, and the *really* real (scientific/natural reality) on the other—it is an argument that appeals to metaphysics.

This brief discussion of racial eliminativism and its distinction between "social" and "biological" reality exhibits the politics of purity in two different ways. Firstly, consider the key claim that any proper taxonomy will be utterly without ambiguity, such that it would provide necessary and sufficient conditions for racial membership. In taking the indisputable fact that there are individuals who do not "fit" neatly into any particular category as evidence that the categories are "illusory" or to some extent not *really* real, the argument posits an ideal in which a proper taxonomy must be one where each *taxon* is completely discrete from each other, with clear and distinct borders admitting of unambiguous criteria for membership, such that any given individual can be placed or located within a taxonomic category. For the adherents of this kind of argument, the fact that a given individual can be "black" at one time or in one place, and "red" or "*moreno*" in a different time or place shows that the categories are not really "real," precisely because their understanding of reality demands this sort of conceptual/categorial purity—it cannot tolerate ambiguity. Likewise, the fact that there can be individuals who "fit" into more than one category, or rather, as a consequence, do not *really* fit into any category at all, demonstrates the unreality ("illusory" status) of the taxonomy altogether. In short, what is implicitly demanded are fundamentally *pure* categories. Each racial category should pick out all and only members of that race, and if it fails to do so, then that is a sign of its *failure* up to and including its nonexistence. This includes, as I stressed above, members of "mixed" racial categories, insofar as being a member of such a category means precisely that one is emphatically *not* a member of the "pure" races from which those "mixed" categories are understood to be constituted. The politics of purity is expressed here in the metaphysical insistence that any reality we are bound to respect must operate such that it generates or reveals pure categories of being. The absence of purity is thus interpreted as an absence of reality (or at least a failure to properly grasp reality), or as evidence of the taxonomy being at best a "mere" social construct.

The second manifestation of the politics of purity exhibited in the eliminativist argument is a bit more subtle, and can be found in the ways in which eliminativism appeals to a hard distinction between the biological or natural on the one hand, and the social or cultural on the other. If the fact that our conception of race has changed over time, and is thus culturally contingent, is taken as evidence of its lack of reality—or, in some versions, an attenuated reality, then one is operating with a conception of the biological as pure and distinct from the cultural. Even when there is an appeal to race as "social construction," this term has salience precisely because it appeals to a distinction between itself and that which is *not* socially constructed (biological reality, for instance). Thus, even if a given thinker holds that race is a "socially constructed reality," the implication is that this is a kind of reality distinct from some other variety of reality that is not "socially constructed" in this way. To be one is to *not* be the other—the two are *pure* and discrete.

In *The Creolizing Subject*, I offered a much more detailed critique of this view, including a substantial discussion of different approaches to what it might mean for race to be "biologically real" (Monahan 2011, 77–135). Since my task here is only to offer a brief introduction to the concept in order to lay the groundwork for what follows, I will simply refer interested readers to that earlier work. It is worth noting, however, that this appeal to a hard distinction between the cultural or the social and the natural is at the heart of the Husserlian understanding of "naturalism." For Husserl, the "natural attitude" is the typically unquestioned assumption that there is a mind-independent reality made up of objects of consciousness at best only ever accidentally and externally in relation to us as observers (1970, 1–7). That is, they would be the same whether we observed them or not. Husserl, and those who followed in his wake, understood the critique of the natural attitude to be central to any rigorous philosophical project (a project which Husserl and his followers called "phenomenology"). What is most significant for this chapter, however, is simply the point that the *presumption* that nature and culture are pure and discrete categories is a manifestation of the politics of purity.

This point about seeing *proper* taxonomies as carving out pure and discrete categories, including categories like "nature" and "culture," is in fact an expression of the deepest aspect of the politics of purity, and the last general feature I will describe here. Namely, the idea here is that the politics of purity, as it operates within our thinking about nature versus culture, and reality versus illusion and social construction, and about the proper functioning of taxonomic categories, is actually symptomatic of a politics of purity within dominant conceptions of reason and logic themselves. In other words, there is a manner in which the politics of purity conditions our thinking at the most fundamental and abstract level—including our thinking *about* thinking. This will surely strike some readers as a hyperbolic claim. Let me be clear. I am not saying that logic and reason are necessarily pernicious expressions of the politics of purity. Rather, what I am advancing here is the more modest claim that our thinking *about* reason and logic can, and often do, manifest in or express a politics of purity. Consider, by way of illustration, the distinction Lewis Gordon draws between *rationality* and *reason*. Rationality emphasizes, in his account, "instrumental concerns of control and predictability," while reason is characterized by critical and reflexive self-evaluation (Gordon 2006a, 127). "Much of modern European philosophy," he further notes, "has been an attempt to place reason under the yoke of rationality" (127). Rationality values consistency and completeness, such that ambiguity, uncertainty, and incompleteness are all signs of failure and deficiency. For any given rational agent, such deficiencies may ultimately be unavoidable, given the limits of our epistemic capacities, but the *ideal* remains one of conceptual and procedural purity and completeness. The claim here is that rationality, as an ideal, functions such that, given the "correct" principles (which must be consistent and complete) and an exhaustive account of the relevant information, the rational determination will simply *follow* from a logical operation in an unambiguous and complete way.

This general account of rationality is one that we can see informing not only the rational economic agent (*homo economicus*) but also the rational moral agent, whether she be modeled more on a utilitarian or the Kantian standard. The specific account of ideally rational principles may vary among all the economic, utilitarian, and Kantian models, but they all share the view that, once arrived at, correct action is ultimately a matter of acquiring the relevant information and then applying the principles. If *the* correct choice does not emerge as a result, then that is a sign that we either have incomplete information, or that there is some inconsistency or gap in our principles.[5]

In this way, these three archetypes all conceive of reason as aiming at a kind of purity. A given action or decision is either rational or it is not, and ambiguity or indeterminacy are taken to be signs of a failure of rationality that demands some form of redress. Just as the emergence of the racially ambiguous individual demands either absorption into preexisting categories or the generation of new categories in order to preserve taxonomic purity, ambiguity or incompleteness in our systems of reason (including moral reason) demands that we either revise the system or re-describe the offending phenomenon to restore the purity of the rational system. The purity at stake in rationality lies, therefore, in a kind of completeness and consistency. Rationality requires a complete set of principles and relevant information which, when consistently applied, will yield the correct (rational) results.

This appeal to consistency and completeness in our conception of rationality points the way quite clearly to central aspects of logic, which I mean here in the broadest sense. This thus includes not only first and higher-order predicate logics but also relations between fundamental concepts like universal, particular, form, content, essence, accident, and the concept of predication as such. In other words, it would include "logic" as conceived in the ancient and early-modern worlds—as the foundational building blocks of thought. Again, the claim here is not that rationality or logic necessarily exhibit a commitment to purity but, rather, that the politics of purity can, and all-too-often does, demand that any satisfactory systemic account of logic operate in accordance with a *telos* of purity. This ultimately expresses itself at the level not only of our thinking, but our thinking *about* thinking.

Returning to the example of arguments about racial reality, the idea that proper racial categories should be expressed ideally as sets of necessary and sufficient conditions is linked to our thinking about universal/particular and essence/accident, even if this linkage is not always made explicit. The basic claim is that real races would be such that a complete and consistent account of a given racial category would operate so as to place every given individual into one and only one category, so that each category picks out all and only members of that race. It will carve out what is essential, and set aside what is accidental. This is, at root, a process of purification. Likewise, *properly* described categories will function as universals with respect to their members, such that, *qua* member of the category, all particulars lose their particularity (they are identical *qua* members of the category).[6] At the same time, each racial category is a particular with respect to every other such category, since the set of features that constitute the essence of that category must be unique to it, and render it distinct from its fellows. In this way, the universal and the particular function as *pure* categories. The presumption here is one of purity insofar as each underlying idea—essence, accident, universal, particular—is taken to be fully realized and expressed only when it is completely distinct from its opposite, with no blurriness or indeterminacy across their borders. This is precisely what I mean by the politics of purity as in effect a kind of intolerance for or proscription against ambiguity. If there is any ambiguity (inconsistency) or gaps (incompleteness), then that is taken as evidence that the categories (races, in this example) are not real, or at least not yet fully or properly realized and articulated.

So, we can see that the politics of purity may inform our thought and action at the most fundamental levels, such that its manifestation at the level of our social lives (as in political ideologies of racial or national purity, or the distinction between nature and culture) is in effect an expression of that deeper commitment to purity at the level of logic and our conception of rationality as a total commitment to consistency and completeness. Recall, however, that Gordon distinguishes between *rationality* on the one hand, and *reason* on the other, and at this point we are better equipped to grasp his distinction. The problem with this "pure" notion of rationality "is that consistency works well for systems not sophisticated enough to evaluate themselves. For the more complex problems of evaluation, including self-evaluation, a more radical model of reason is needed; one that *cannot* be complete" (Gordon 2006a, 102). In Gordon's view, the key characteristic of reason, as distinct from rationality, is that it is reflexive. Reason raises critical questions about its own operation, and thus requires a kind of open-endedness that is inconsistent with a commitment to completeness as such. He invites us to consider an idealized rational agent, one who is absolutely consistent in the application of her principles, which she takes to be a complete (closed) system or method. With such an exemplar in mind, Gordon muses: "Here we encounter what, for rationality, would be a paradox: maximal consistency is at times unreasonable. In the human world, for instance, a maximally consistent person could not only be an unreasonable person but perhaps also an irrational, maybe even insane, one" (Gordon 2012, 8).

Rather than simply carrying forward the commitment to purity (expressed here as a commitment to consistency and completeness), while perhaps lamenting that human beings are imperfect in their epistemic (incomplete) and rational (inconsistent) faculties, reason, Gordon suggests, demands that we raise the deeper question about whether this commitment to purity is the best ideal to hold in the first place. Reason, in other words, inquires as to the limit and limitations of rationality. What if reason is ambiguous, or at least tolerant of ambiguity? What if it is incomplete, and unrealizable as a closed system not because of our lamentable epistemic incapacities, but because of its very nature?

At this point, it is possible to step back and draw out some broad implications of my account so far. The politics of purity is a kind of drive or imperative mandating the elimination of ambiguity, the demarcation of clear and distinct borders, and the celebration or valorization of purity from its most abstract to its most concrete forms. It informs and conditions our thinking and behavior at the most fundamental levels, such that our conceptions of logic and rationality themselves can (but need not) be expressions of the politics of purity. At this level, the politics of purity can be characterized as a commitment to all-or-nothing, either/or kinds of binary thinking. The individual is either in the taxonomic category or they are not. This is either essence or accident, either universal or particular. The predication is either true or false. All of this in turn informs how we think about reality, including the relation between culture and nature, self and other, and so forth. To be clear, this kind of critique of dualistic, either/or thinking is hardly new or original. It could arguably be traced to Heraclitus, but it is certainly to be found in Nietzsche, Hegel, Édouard Glissant, and Gloria Anzaldúa, for instance (among others), as well as in broader philosophical movements like American pragmatism, Husserlian phenomenology, and poststructuralism. What I do take to be unique to the politics of purity are three features. First, its emphasis on purity as a (political) *project* stresses the way in which ostensive purity is only ever a pretension, often bolstered by deeply embedded myths that require constant re-articulation and re-legitimation. In other words, this is not a celebration of hybridity or impurity as distinct from purity as a condition or state but, rather, the deeper claim that there really never was any purity to begin with, and the problem lies in seeing this absence of purity as somehow unfortunate or tragic. Second, an important feature of the politics of purity is its insistence that this kind of binary thinking must be avoided even in the moment of critique. If one identifies the commitment to purity as problematic, therefore, the response cannot be simply its negation or absence. Some variation on the theme of ~(purity) cannot be the appropriate response, since such a move would be in effect the effort to *purify* one's thinking *of* purity itself, and in so doing appeal to yet another either/or binary of conceptual/logical purity.

Rather, and this is the third important feature, the appropriate response to the politics of purity must be practices of *creolizing*. I have articulated this response elsewhere (Monahan 2011; 2017), and I will develop it yet further as my argument in this text progresses, but for present purposes, I want to make just a few brief points about my use of "creolizing" here. First, I use the gerund form of the term quite deliberately. The response to the politics of purity is not the *creole* as a kind of identity category, or as a final outcome of creolizing processes/practices. To do so would simply be a way of stating

~(purity). Rather, I mean precisely the ongoing process of bringing together disparate elements across, within, and between boundaries and domains, while at the same time recognizing (re-cognizing) that such elements, boundaries, and domains were never as disparate and discrete as they might appear (or pretend). This means, second, that creolizing is distinct from simple hybridity or mixture, both in that it remains more a kind of orientation and process than a product, and because it is, to paraphrase Husserl, an "infinite task" (Husserl 1970, 291). Third, it follows that, because creolizing is this kind of infinite task and ongoing process, borders, domains, and categories cannot be done away with altogether. The aim, in other words, is not the absence of boundaries or limits—in order for there to be creolizing as this drawing together of disparate elements, one needs the boundaries and limits that demarcate, albeit tentatively and ambiguously, those elements. Creolizing does not, simply put, strive for the realization of some final and complete "mixture" where all is *creole* (which would, ironically, be another kind of purity).

In the end, the problem with the politics of purity is that it seeks permanent and fixed boundaries, carving out absolutely discrete domains and categories. It seeks, ultimately, stasis, for it understands "proper" boundaries to be fixed, and thus to carve out a static ontology. Creolizing, as a response to this, demands a kind of attenuation (or, again following the recent work of Lewis Gordon, "suspending") of those commitments to purity, a blurring (but not necessarily eradication) of those boundaries, and an emphasis on dynamism over stasis. I will develop all of this in greater detail in subsequent chapters, but for now, I trust that this will be sufficient as a starting point from which I can begin to articulate implications that the politics of purity has on our thinking about freedom and liberation. Again, the aim in this chapter is to set up the problematic, not to fully spell out the argument. With this in mind, I will now turn to the role of the politics of purity with respect to freedom and liberation, paving the way for my positive account of freedom in chapter 2.

FREEDOM AND PURITY

Of course, philosophers have been writing about freedom for at least two millennia, and thinking about it surely for much longer.[7] We have a wide array of theories to choose from, and can even divide up "kinds" of freedom in different ways. There is, on the one hand, what we might call "metaphysical freedom," characterized in the current moment by debates about determinism, libertarianism, and compatibilism, though still often linked to theological questions regarding divine omniscience and the "problem of evil." On the other hand, there are debates around "political freedom," focused on more macro-scale questions of how best to organize a society so as to give freedom its proper due. Contemporary debates in this latter area tend to construe freedom as the ability to do as one wills (to satisfy one's desires, or maximize one's preferences, etc.) in the liberal tradition, or as the realization of some ideal or end (virtue, self-realization, the beloved community, etc.) in what is typically thought of as the "communitarian" tradition. Ultimately, these distinctions are more often than not only heuristic at best, and one's account of political freedom will inevitably be conditioned by one's understanding of metaphysical freedom, but fortunately, it is possible to draw out some general insights about the politics of purity that can be exemplified along both these lines of thinking about freedom.

Let us begin with the common idea that freedom involves the ability to do what one wills. In the first instance, what matters is whether there are obstacles or impediments to the pursuit of one's desires, but at the deeper level, this approach demands that we give an account of the *self* in order to have a clear measure of whether a goal or desire is properly *of* that self (and thus what one wills). Those familiar with Aristotle's discussion of voluntary and involuntary action in book III of his *Nicomachean Ethics* will see immediately how this works. In his view, what makes an action voluntary is a matter of the action having its source or origin *within* the agent in question, as opposed to outside of that agent. This can be clearly seen in the straight forward example he offers of a ship's captain. If the captain sets a course for a given location and arrives there, then the arrival at that port was voluntary. If, on the other hand, the ship was blown off course by a storm and made landfall at that same port despite the captain's intention to go elsewhere, then the arrival was involuntary. If the storm, which is external to the captain, is the cause of the ship's arrival at the port, then that arrival was *involuntary*. Importantly, what is "internal" or "external" might not always be straightforward at all. When we say things like "I was overcome by rage," or "My need to gamble has gotten the best of me again," we are suggesting that sometimes what we take to have deprived us of our freedom is not some other person or law or force of nature but rather an emotion or a drive or a (psychological or biological) compulsion. However, the very concept of a "compulsion" entails the idea that it forces us to act *against our will* in some relevant sense, and thus such drives are in the relevant sense "external" to one's agency even though they are a psychological feature of the agent themself. There is expressed in these sorts of sayings a distinction between the *self* that is overcome, and the sources of compulsion, which are posited as external to that self. Doing what one wills, therefore, requires a clear distinction between what is genuinely *internal* to the self versus what is external.

Consider, by way of further illustration, debates around freewill and determinism. Materialist determinism places the cause of *all* actions outside of the agent, effectively ruling out the very idea of an agent as such in the sense prominent in so much moral philosophy from Plato to Kant. If every behavior of an individual is determined by some prior causal chain, then in effect there is no "self" in the sense of an independent source of action. Everything is, in effect, external to the self (or rather, there is no self to serve as an "internal" source) in a standard deterministic framework. The Cartesian response to materialist determinism is to in effect locate (metaphorically) the agent herself *outside* of the material world altogether. The Cartesian *ego* as a "thinking thing" (a thing "containing," metaphorically speaking, our thinking faculties) thus clearly and distinctly demarcates what is internal to the agent, and places everything material outside of that agent. Libertarian responses to determinism will thus necessarily take this form of attempting to carve out some metaphorical space for the self from an otherwise determined world. Compatibilism, in its turn, can also be understood as participating in this debate over the internal and the external. For the compatibilist, there is some aspect of the physically determined world that we can nevertheless justifiably call a subject, and if *that* is the source of our action, then we may call it free, even if it took place within a physically determined framework. Unlike the classic libertarian position (*a la* Descartes), the self is in this way not *outside* of the physically determined system, but there is at least something worth calling a self or an agent, and (crucially for my purposes), what counts as free is what originates *in* that agent. This long tradition of philosophical debate about the free or voluntary, including debates about determinism, are thus always centered on the division between the internal and the external with respect to the self.

A similar pattern emerges when we turn to more political approaches to freedom. Consider, as a starting point, Isaiah Berlin's classic distinction between "positive" and "negative" liberty (I will take "liberty" to be synonymous with freedom for present purposes), both of which can be understood to appeal precisely to this internal/external distinction (2002, 166–218). "Negative" liberty as the absence of constraints common to liberal political theory, holds that what is internal to the self is limited to our desires—if no other agents or institutions can impede our pursuit of our desires, then we are free. The free agent is thus the one whose actions are guided by their own desires (understood as their own vision of the good life), such that their actions originate from this *internal* source. The "positive" account, on the other hand, raises the problem of what Jean Grimshaw (1988) calls "the autonomy of desire"—what about those cases where we might think that our desires themselves have been *externally* shaped or even, in effect, implanted? Grimshaw has in mind the ways in which a patriarchal/misogynistic society can condition women to quite sincerely formulate and maintain desires that serve to enhance or legitimate their own oppression—they thus desire that which oppresses them. If we strictly maintained the negative account of liberty, this would be an impossibility, for liberty just is the satisfaction of desire, and so the idea that one can desire one's own oppression is in effect nonsensical.

Berlin's own articulation of positive liberty has something like the Marxian overcoming of alienation more clearly as its model. Positive liberty is the idea that there is some underlying or yet-to-be generated proper or authentic self with its own (proper/authentic) desires, and we are free when our actions originate internally to *that* self. This self may in fact be quite different from our present, alienated self, but crucially for my purposes, we can see that the internal/external distinction lies at the core of this conception of positive freedom every bit as much as was the case for negative freedom. The positive move, given that it seems impossible to offer a coherent account of the concept of "internalized oppression" on the negative model, is therefore precisely to give some positive content to the self or agent beyond the unproblematic assumption of present desires—to describe some true or authentic self, such that one is free only when the origin of one's actions originate from *that* self. Of course, as both Berlin and Grimshaw point out, the positive content of the genuine or authentic self has a way of becoming itself a kind of imposition on the subject, but my aim at this stage is not to enter into this debate, rather it is to make an observation. Namely, I would emphasize that what we see operating in these discussions of political liberty, as was the case with metaphysical debates about determinism, is ultimately a discussion over the boundaries of the self, in order to demarcate what is internal or external to that self.

In this way we come to see the link between metaphysical and political freedom, and the link between freedom and metaphysics generally. For what is free or voluntary, in this general sense, must be a matter of ascertaining what is internal or external to ourselves as agents. We thus need an account of what we *are* in order to make any meaningful claims about our freedom or lack thereof. Indeed, when we look at the broad categories of liberal and communitarian accounts of political freedom, we can see that they are predicated upon quite distinct metaphysical accounts of the self, even when they purport to be eschewing metaphysics altogether (Rawls 1985). Simply put, the liberal tradition tends to see the individual agent as ontologically distinct from their social world, which means that, as external to the self, the social world always stands opposed to individual liberty, and the proper task of political life is to provide a set of rules and procedures that create as much elbow room for as many agents as is feasible. For the communitarian, the social world is to greater or lesser degree constitutive of or internal to the self, which means that the task of political life is to forge a society that best realizes our potential as social beings. Certainly, these are thin sketches, but they serve well enough to illustrate the larger point here—that freedom is at some level about the distinction between self and other (what is internal versus what is external to the self), and in this way the political and the metaphysical are necessarily intertwined.

All of which now allows us to grasp the operation of the politics of purity with respect to our thinking about freedom. If the general approach, common to a wide array of debates and discourses around both metaphysical and political freedom, is to understand freedom as a matter of having an internal source of our actions, then two important consequences follow. First, there must be a clear and well-articulated boundary between what is internal and what is external to the agent. Without such a boundary, then the question of whether an action or agent is free cannot be settled. Again, ambiguity in this regard is seen as a failure that should ideally be overcome, or if this is not feasible, to be tolerated but lamented. This in turn means, second, that liberation, as a project, becomes an effort at *purifying* the self of external influences or impositions. The Kantian account of "enlightenment" as freeing oneself from one's self-imposed tutelage is one clear exemplar of this (Kant 1988, 462). If the true self is our rational self, and thus autonomous or free actions will be those generated by and from that rational self, then the project of liberation will take the form, at the individual level, of erecting and enforcing a strict boundary between our reason and everything else—it will be a project of self-purification. The rational agent, in other words, attempts to purify their will of what is external to reason. What may be "outside" can vary from account to account, of course. Reason may on some accounts include our affective states, or it may not. It may rule out instinct, or it may not. The point with respect to purity is that, once the boundaries of what is rational have been determined, then the rational agent seeks to reinforce those boundaries, and purge or purify her deliberative processes of external (irrational or a-rational) influences. This is a further demonstration of a recurring theme within the politics of purity of generating and maintaining hard and distinct boundaries, which is necessary for determining what is internal and external to those boundaries.

Purity, therefore, becomes the implicit, if not always explicit, aim of liberation. At the level of the individual subject (common to the liberal tradition), one must demarcate the boundary between the internal and the external (the boundaries of the subject/agent), and then begin the work of ensuring that what belongs outside is removed from the inside of that boundary. At the level of a society or community, one must draw the boundaries of the society/community in order to offer a full account of its "proper" content (the common vision of the good), and place individuals inside or outside of that community. To know which community is properly *yours* we must identify the boundaries both of the self in question and of the community to which they do or do not belong. The former (individual/liberal) approach leads to an atomistic conception of the individual fiercely guarding the borders of the self from hostile intrusion, while the latter (communitarian) can lead to homogenizing and deeply colonial accounts of the body politic. Common to both is a conception of freedom as a state of *purity* to be achieved, and of any deficiency in that purity as a failure to be (fully) free. In some accounts, such a state of freedom serves only as a kind of regulatory ideal—as a zero point to be approached only asymptotically—but even in such accounts it remains the case that the ideal of freedom is linked to purity as a goal (even if in principle an unreachable one). There is some end point which we can at best reach, and at worst approximate. Either/or thinking, clear and static boundaries, and imperatives of purity abound as a result in much of the long history of thinking about freedom and liberation. Indeed, even when some effort is made to complicate this picture by articulating freedom as a process, or allowing for "degrees" of freedom, the tendency toward purity more often than not reemerges, even if surreptitiously.

Ultimately, my suggestion here is that theorizations of freedom both past and present tend to reveal, once one digs beneath the proverbial surface, an underlying commitment to purity. From discussions of metaphysical freedom of the will to debates between liberals and communitarians, freedom is understood at root to be a project of purification, where ambiguity and incompleteness are at best a tragic flaw which must be tolerated. To the extent that one views the politics of purity with suspicion, this offers good reason to rethink these approaches to freedom, and thus to our understanding of oppression and liberation. In the next chapter, I will turn to contemporary debates around the politics of recognition to illustrate and further elaborate this relation between freedom, accounts of the subject, and the politics of purity. I will argue that both the critics and the advocates of recognition theory fall back, to varying degrees, into the politics of purity, and that this ultimately undermines their positive projects.

Chapter 2

Recognition and Its Discontents

I have so far offered an account of the "politics of purity," and suggested that many of the standard ways of approaching the theorization of freedom are bound up in the politics of purity in ways that ultimately inhibit our ability to effectively address oppression and engage in liberatory work. There is a tendency to envision freedom as requiring a robust and stable boundary between the self and other (internal/external), and to conceive of liberation as the project of purifying that self of what is external or other to it. This often leads to, on the one hand, an account of freedom that is alienating and atomistic, and a view of liberation that is homogenizing at best and colonial/exclusionary at worst. The realization of these troubling tendencies can lead some thinkers to a rejection of robust notions of freedom and liberation altogether as *inherently* exclusionary and colonial. Such a move may accurately critique this "purifying" account of freedom and liberation, but it in turn undermines and weakens the ongoing and legitimate struggles of the oppressed. As Lewis Gordon has pointed out, such a rejection of the very idea of freedom ends in a de facto conservatism where the status quo cannot be legitimately challenged and "oppression" is deprived of its normative content (2021, 14–15). In other words, without some way to articulate a genuinely liberatory vision, our efforts, in the words of Fanon, to "set afoot" a new humanity will wither on the vine (1963, 316). There is simply too much at stake to allow this state of affairs to continue, and the problem is as much theoretical and philosophical as it is practical and political.

In this chapter, I will turn to recent accounts of the "politics of recognition" to illustrate and elaborate these points. My aim here is twofold. First, by looking at both contemporary critics and proponents of recognition, I can draw out and add greater clarity and depth to my account of the politics of purity as it bears on our understanding of freedom. Second, I will set the stage for elaborating an account of recognition, and freedom, that avoids the pitfalls of the politics of purity in the next chapter. This creolizing *of* freedom will be the principle focus of the remainder of this book, ultimately constituting a theory of freedom *as* creolizing. Before turning to this positive account, however, it is necessary to clear some conceptual ground, and I will use contemporary accounts of recognition to accomplish this.[1]

ON RECOGNITION

Starting in the early 1990s with the publication of Axel Honneth's landmark *Kampf um Annerkennung* (*The Struggle for Recognition*) and Charles Taylor's important essay "The Politics of Recognition," there has been a resurgence of interest in what might broadly be called "recognition theory" (Honneth 1994; 1995; Taylor 1994). Certainly there is a great deal that distinguishes these two texts, but for present purposes, it is their similarities that are most pertinent. To offer a very brief sketch, what they share is the general notion that an essential component of a flourishing political life is having one's particular personhood "recognized" by other members of the polity generally, and by dominant individuals and institutions in particular. By "particular personhood" here, I mean to emphasize that this understanding of recognition is not a simple appeal to an abstract moral status, on the model, for example, of a Kantian recognition of "personhood." There, what is being recognized is a kind of standing as a generic bearer of rights and obligations. This is the kind of recognition common to many forms of liberal discourse, where what is sought is recognition as a person in the relevant moral, legal, or political sense (cf. Darby 2009). Rather than being recognized as a person, however, recognition in the sense intended by Honneth and Taylor, and characteristic of what I am calling "recognition theory" generally, is a demand to be recognized not merely as a bearer of an abstract and universal status but as a concrete and particular individual. Put differently, the kind of recognition pertinent here is not recognition as *a* person but, rather, as *this* person—as a member of particular communities, as a bearer of particular cultures, and so forth. In the broadest terms, I am using "recognition theory" here to capture that subset of political/moral theory in which intersubjective recognition of one's moral/political agency in its particularity (i.e., situated in particular cultures and histories) is a psychological and political good (or even a necessity).

This emphasis on particularity is exemplified by the way Taylor places his original discussion within the context of multiculturalism in education. In his view, teaching African American history, or Latin American literature, is necessary in order to recognize the full and particular personhood of African American or Latinx students within the institution of education. Ignoring their particularity by treating them as students just like every other student, contrary to the liberal appeal to universality, is a kind of (moral, political, or psychological) harm that must be addressed through demands for recognition of that particularity both in one's curriculum and in one's pedagogy (Taylor 1994, 65–73). Honneth, likewise, stresses the way in which one's cultural specificity needs to be recognized as part of developing a healthy psyche and realizing individual autonomy (Honneth 1995, 173–74; 2003, 180–81). In the context of race, one can see this distinction between the recognition of one's particular personhood versus the more abstract recognition of universal personhood in the #BlackLivesMatter movement and the reactionary "all lives matter" response. The universalism of the "all lives" response serves to drown out the efforts to draw attention to the vulnerability of Black people to state-sanctioned violence. As Taylor puts the general point:

> The claim is that the supposedly neutral set of difference-blind principles of the politics of equal dignity is in fact a reflection of one hegemonic culture. . . . Consequently, the supposedly fair and difference-blind society is not only inhuman (because suppressing identities) but also, in a subtle and unconscious way, itself highly discriminatory. (1994, 43)

The struggle of #BlackLivesMatter can thus be understood as a struggle for the recognition of Black (particular) personhood and dignity, while the simple appeal to the (allegedly) universal "all lives matter" effectively washes out Black personhood in a sea of white hegemony. Thus, according to recognition theory, one's autonomy or freedom requires recognition of one's particular personhood, and thus oppression can at least in part be understood as the withholding or inhibiting of that recognition at both the individual and institutional levels.

At the root of Taylor and Honneth's endorsement of recognition is an account of human subjects as fundamentally or constitutively social. In Taylor's words, we are "dialogical," as opposed to "monological" in our constitution (1994, 32), while for Honneth there is an inherently "intersubjective structure [to] personal identity" (1995, 172).[2] We are, in their view, constituted in our individuality (our identity) through concrete social relations. Without social relations that affirm and facilitate this dialogical process of self-formation, we are thwarted in our development. Thus, we need the kinds of social and intersubjective conditions that nurture this development in order to fully realize ourselves as individuals, because our individuality is constituted as such through these social and intersubjective processes.

In the liberal tradition, the individual is understood to be logically prior to the social, in the sense that individual subjects can be accounted for independently of a given social context, and the social is understood to be in effect reducible to the sum of its individual parts. By stripping away what is merely socially contingent in the hypothetical original position, one can describe the political subject in its *pure* state, and then begin to articulate the kind of social relations and institutions proper to that (pre-social) subject. Hence, the individual is prior to the social. The approach advocated by recognition theory reverses this relation, taking the social to be prior to the individual, such that we individuate ourselves from and through a set of social relations and institutions that set the conditions for that process of individuation. What Taylor and Honneth are calling "recognition" is thus a way of capturing this vital aspect of our development as subjects—namely, that we achieve our subjectivity intersubjectively. Who we are as political, moral, and social agents is a function of the varieties of recognition we give and receive. Agency—who we are qua moral/political *subjects*—is thus bound up with recognition, and since, as I discussed in the previous chapter, freedom is necessarily understood in terms of agency and its boundaries, we find that recognition is an essential component of freedom. Taylor and Honneth's respective theories of recognition, therefore, express the ways in which ineluctably social agents work together either to realize or to thwart each other's freedom understood as a kind of process of self-realization and expression.

Furthermore, for both Taylor and Honneth, the turn to recognition serves as part of a larger critique of liberal political theory. Liberalism is "inhospitable to difference," according to Taylor, "because it can't accommodate what the members of distinct societies really aspire to, which is survival" (1994, 61). The survival to which he is referring here is not mere survival as an individual organism (or at least, not strictly as such), but rather as a member of a kind of collective culture in and through which one understands one's identity. My survival, in the relevant sense, is thus intrinsically bound up with *our* survival.[3] Here we see the way in which this dialogical account of the subject works itself out in Taylor's thinking. I understand myself (my identity) through the relations I bear to different communities, and thus threats to those communities are also threats to my identity, and consequently to me *as me* even if not to me qua individual organism. If my survival (not just as *a* person, but as *this* person) is dependent upon the survival of my community(ies), and the survival of those communities is dependent upon the larger acknowledgment not only of their existence but of their "worth" (Taylor 1994, 64), then it is incumbent upon me to seek recognition of that worth in order to secure my (our) survival. In other words, Taylor's view holds that liberalism, despite the central, even defining role that individual liberty plays in it, serves to undermine the very conditions by which we come to understand ourselves as individuals, which is through our membership and participation in distinct communities. By taking the existence of individual subjects for granted, as prior to the social in the sense I described above, rather than seeing them as profoundly social achievements, and by seeing group affiliations and identities as inimical to individual liberty, liberalism undermines the social conditions of genuine freedom precisely because it valorizes a monological, as opposed to dialogical, vision of the individual.

Honneth, likewise, holds that public life must "be regarded not as the result of the mutual restriction of private spheres of liberty, but rather the other way around, namely, as the opportunity for the fulfilment of every single individual's freedom" (1995, 13). Like Taylor, Honneth holds that recognition is a necessary condition for self-realization. The self, in other words, is a social achievement that can be advanced or frustrated by the kinds of relations and institutions within and through which this project of self-realization necessarily takes place. This recognition is expressed in different ways in different spheres, being expressed as love in I/thou relations, as respect in the juridical context, and as solidarity in the relations within and among communities in a larger polity. All three of these kinds or modes of recognition develop self-esteem and self-realization, and the lack or disruption of any of them causes psychological, emotional, and material distress and harm. In Honneth's words, "Since individuals must know that they are recognized for their particular abilities and traits in order to be capable of self-realization, they need a form of social esteem that they can only acquire on the basis of collectively shared goals" (1995, 177–78). This link between recognition, self-realization, and "autonomy" is maintained through Honneth's later work (2012, 46), as he expands his use of Hegel beyond the early Jena-period writings and responds to critics like Nancy Fraser (Fraser 1997; Fraser and Honneth 2003).

It is no coincidence that the re-emergence of recognition theory happened amid increasing interest in and concern over multiculturalism and "identity politics." The triumphant march of European Enlightenment humanism was seen as under threat from forces that sought to dethrone the allegedly universal categories of "citizen" or bearer of "human rights" with appeals to the valorization of particular identity categories that were either ignored or actively denigrated by the inheritors of that humanistic enterprise. Those universal values and institutions, it turned out, were in fact quite particular, and in service of the interests not of humanity simpliciter, but of the conquerors, the colonizers, the slavers, and their descendants. At its heart, identity politics was the effort to critique the false universalism of liberal Enlightenment values by drawing attention to those individuals and communities marginalized and silenced within the larger, allegedly just polity. Of course, this point was hardly new. Ottobah Cuguano pointed out the ways in which Enlightenment values were not universal, but particular in their application to Europeans in his 1787 *Thoughts and Sentiments on the Evil and Wicked Traffic of the Slavery and Commerce of the Human Species* (1999, 1–111). This critique of universalism was not limited to the liberal tradition, either. In 1928, José Mariátegui was raising questions about the universal applicability of Marxism in his *Seven Interpretive Essays on Peruvian Reality* (1971). We can see the same questions regarding European humanism being raised in the aftermath of the Second World War by Aimé Césaire's *Discourse on Colonialism* (2000). At the close of the twentieth century, however, the ostensive fall of socialism had brought forth a reinvigorated faith in the triumph of (neo)liberalism, and the calls for multiculturalism and identity politics were part of a resistance to that growing triumphalism.[4] Recognition theory provided a way of framing the calls to attend to and value specific communities as related to, but distinct from, the dominant culture that many found to be a powerful theoretical tool, but which also came under considerable critique.

CRITIQUES OF RECOGNITION

I will return to Honneth, Taylor, and Fraser toward the end of this chapter. To draw out my larger point regarding recognition theory and the politics of purity, however, I wish to begin my critical analysis by examining some important trends in the critical literature on recognition theory. This is because taking up these critiques will at once invite a further elaboration of the details of recognition theory as offered by these key figures, and make clear how such critiques are informed in different ways by the politics of purity. My aim here is to engage with what I see as larger trends in the critical encounters with recognition theory over the past twenty-five years, though for the sake of exposition I will be focusing in particular on Patchen Markell's *Bound by Recognition* (2003). This is because it exemplifies these trends in the kinds of arguments it offers, and because those arguments are offered in such a clear and compelling way. Where appropriate, I will draw from other critics, but I do not wish to become bogged down in literature review, so I will not be performing a close reading of each of the major critics, but rather focusing on these general trends and themes, as exemplified largely by Markell, in order to support my broader argument about the politics of purity.

The first of the general trends in the critique of recognition has to do with the marked tendency in the recent literature on recognition to refer to discrete acts of recognition as moments of exchange, where recognition is given and received. This can be implicit, as in Nancy Fraser's "status model" of recognition, which links recognition to justice as a kind of equity in the form of "parity of participation," or it can be explicit, as it often is in Markell (Fraser and Honneth 2003, 29–33; Markell 2003, 6, 16, 88, 153). The basic model here holds that the relevant agents (who may be individuals, groups, or in some cases institutions) *exchange* recognition through the performance of what can be understood broadly as discrete communicative acts. Everything from the passing of a law to the tipping of a hat become moments were recognition is given and received through acts of exchange. Social injustice, on this model, is thus a matter of the inequality of these exchanges—some give more or less than they ought, and some receive more or less than they are due. There are myriad problems with this exchange model of recognition, some of which Markell takes to task explicitly in his critique of recognition. It treats the subject of recognition as a distinct bearer of an identity that stands as a complete and fixed *fait accompli* (Markell 2003, 14), and for which the other must give some quanta of recognition, ideally in equal proportion to the amount of recognition given by the subject to the other in respect to their particular identity. The model thus effectively entails the exchange of distinct quanta of a social good called "recognition" between discrete (atomistic) agents, who, though they may in this way receive a psychological benefit (for example, "self-esteem"), remain otherwise fundamentally unaltered throughout the exchange. It thus preserves the atomistic ontology typical of liberalism all while ostensibly offering an alternative view.

Markell's discussion and critique of this model of recognition is rather puzzling. On the one hand, he offers a very compelling account of the problems it generates, and indeed, it is in part precisely because he understands recognition in this generally economic way that he thinks it must be abandoned in favor of his own alternative politics of "acknowledgment." He hints, at least, that he does not necessarily take the exchange model to be the best way of characterizing recognition theory, but he nevertheless appeals to that model throughout his text as he develops his critique.[5] He says of this economic or exchange paradigm that "insofar as it conceives of injustice as the unequal distribution of a good called 'recognition,' it obscures the relational character of acts and practices of recognition, treating recognition as a thing of which one has more or less, rather than as a social interaction that can go well or poorly in various ways" (2003, 18). This is a claim that I support wholeheartedly, and yet from this point on, Markell treats the exchange model as an ineluctable aspect of the politics of recognition, and offers his version of "acknowledgment" as an alternative to recognition that is superior, in large part, because it does not employ this economic model.

This approach to understanding recognition is quite common among its critics. Anyone who has read feminist, race, or decolonial theory will have encountered any number of offhand and cursory rejections of recognition theory (often focused on Hegel, but extended to include figures like Honneth and, to a lesser extent, Taylor) that characterize recognition on this model of exchange in the course of their dismissal of it. Beyond Markell, other critics engaged in a sustained and focused discussion of recognition take similar approaches. Kelly Oliver's critique of recognition draws in part from her view that it is "pathological," insofar as it necessarily maintains hierarchical relations of exchange (giver and receiver), such that "subjectivity is conferred by those in power on those they deem powerless and disempowered" (2001, 24). Given that the "logic of recognition" cannot escape the active/passive hierarchy inherent in the giver/recipient relationship, she concludes that it is inherently oppressive (29). Lois McNay, likewise, criticizes recognition theory because it requires a kind of "primal dyad," where "social relations of power are always a post hoc effect, distorting or otherwise, of some antecedent and primordial interpersonal dynamic" (2008, 9). This obscures, in her view, the role that social relations of domination and subordination (power) plays in shaping the very subjects that participate in these exchanges of recognition, and means that recognition theory cannot be effective in its efforts to account for truly transformative (liberatory) change. All of these critics share with Markell a general account of recognition in line with the economic model, and so in focusing on this aspect of Markell's critique, I trust that my observations will extend quite generally.

With this in mind, let us delve into Markell's critique of the economic approach to recognition. One initial observation to make is that it resonates quite clearly with Iris Young's critique of the "distributive paradigm" of justice endemic to liberal political theory (1990, 15–38), a fact he makes explicit in his text (Markell 2003, 179). Just as Young critiques liberalism for understanding concepts like "rights" and "self-respect" as quantifiable and external goods to be exchanged between discrete social atoms, so too Markell critiques the politics of recognition for offering an account of the exchange of recognition between discrete and, most significantly for his own purposes, "sovereign" individuals. Drawing upon the work of Hannah Arendt, Markell states that "sovereignty refers to the condition of being an independent, self-determining agent" (Markell 2003, 11). In short, the sovereign subject is the paradigmatic autonomous, independent subject that was the mainstay of European Enlightenment political thought. Markell goes on to argue, following in a long and well-established tradition of critique, that sovereignty is an ultimately incoherent account of the subject, and the aspiration toward sovereignty an untenable goal pursued through what are ultimately oppressive means. In other words, pretensions to sovereignty are only ever maintained at the expense of dependent/subordinate others, and thus require oppressive relations. Since, Markell argues, the politics of recognition inevitably, if at times only implicitly, endorses the sovereign subject, it must be rejected. As he puts the point early in his text: "One of the central arguments of this book is that the politics of recognition is characterized by certain important misrecognitions of its own—not misrecognitions of identity, but failures to acknowledge one's own basic ontological conditions—and that these arise from the fact that the pursuit of recognition expresses an aspiration to sovereignty" (2003, 10). Thus, the problem with the politics of recognition, according to Markell, is that it takes this sovereign subject as its normative ideal, and if we are truly to avoid the pitfalls of sovereignty, we must reject the politics of recognition.

As Markell points out, the appeal to sovereignty in recognition theory is more in keeping with Isaiah Berlin's account of "positive" liberty than it is with the more "negative" tradition of classical liberalism (11). Whereas the sovereignty of liberalism is principally a matter of others leaving one alone to choose one's own course, the sovereignty of recognition theory, according to Markell, is a matter of others openly and explicitly supporting (recognizing) one's *true* self. For example, Charles Taylor builds his account of recognition on the notion that each individual subject and social group has its own distinctive and particular identity, which must be given social recognition in order for those groups and the individuals who are their members to flourish (1994, 28–38). In this way, Markell describes Taylor as "casting sovereign agency now not as a matter of radically free choice, but as a matter of acting in accordance with who, by virtue of one's membership in a larger whole, one always already is" (Markell 2003, 57). This means that a major source of injustice and oppression, understood as *mis*recognition, becomes "the failure to accurately perceive and/or appropriately respect people as who they already really are" (59).

This points to the second common trend in discussions of recognition theory—the concern that it reifies or essentializes identities. If what is being recognized is not simply my universal personhood, or my standing as an abstract citizen, but rather my particular identity insofar as I am a member of one or more typically marginalized and denigrated groups (with respect to sex, gender, sexuality, race, ethnicity, immigrant status, ability, etc.), then there must be some positive content to the particular group identity(ies) being recognized. Yet any such positive content must, the concern goes, be necessarily essentialist. In other words, the argument is that, as an *object* of recognition, such group identities must have some positive content to be recognized—an essence that binds all members of such groups together as such. Furthermore, beyond its essentialist appeal, to demand recognition as a member of such groups is to capitulate to their reality in a way that legitimizes, albeit indirectly, their ongoing role in social domination. If groups emerge and are legitimated through ongoing relations of domination and subordination, then to "recognize" group membership and identity is to facilitate that relation.

This is a feature that Nancy Fraser sees as posing a profound danger to relying overmuch on recognition in our theorizing of justice. Indeed, it is what generates for her the deep tension between redistribution and recognition. While redistribution of social goods (broadly construed) would lead, in a Marxian fashion, to the elimination of dominant and subordinate groups as such (a classless society, most prominently), recognition poses a remedy to injustice wherein the aim "is to valorize the group's 'groupness' by recognizing its specificity," rather than aiming to bring about the conditions of its obsolescence (Fraser 1997, 19). What she has in mind here can be seen clearly in the relationship between class and race within a classical Marxist framework. Class division is a product of economic relations to the means of production. What the oppressed proletarian seeks is not "recognition as proletarian" but rather the elimination of the class *structure* altogether, precisely because there is nothing it means to be proletarian absent that ineluctably oppressive class structure. The eliminativist position with respect to race often runs an analogous argument. If there is nothing it means to be a particular race outside of a social structure that generates racial categories as a means of domination and exploitation, then calling for specifically *racial* recognition is lending credence to the false idea that there is something it means to be a member of a race beyond these relations of domination and subordination.[6] McNay, as well, points toward this concern regarding recognition when she critiques it for positing a concept of identity that in some way precedes social relations of power (2008, 164–65). Likewise, this also at the heart of Kwame Appiah's critique of Taylor's account of recognition (Appiah 1994), insofar as the "scripts" which he argues recognition compels us to follow, and that are at the center of his critique of Taylor, have to do with essentialized notions of authentic group identities. Thus, Markell's concern that recognition theory requires relatively fixed, stable, and essentialist identities echoes a long-standing and widespread trend in the literature on and related to recognition theory.

The task Markell sets for himself in response to these concerns with the economic model of recognition and its tendency toward reified or essentialized identities involves providing an account of intersubjectivity that avoids the affirmation of sovereignty, and thus the danger of essentialism. Along with Honneth, Fraser, and Taylor, Markell shares deep misgivings with liberalism, particularly in its account of the subject/agent, but sees recognition theory as offering up the same old "sovereign" subject, if in less austere garb. He grounds his alternative account, ironically, in Hegel's own treatment of recognition in the *Phenomenology of Spirit* (1997). In that work, Markell argues, Hegel takes up two different "voices" in relation to recognition: the "diagnostic" and the "reconciliatory." The former voice, which Markell draws out in a very stimulating reading of Hegel's discussion of *Antigone*, "echoes the tragic insight that action forever outruns the relations of recognition out of which it emerges, and that recognition is therefore inevitably belated" (Markell 2003, 94). Hegel's reconciliatory voice, on the other hand, which Markell finds in the preface to the phenomenology, but most especially in Hegel's later works (and the *Philosophy of Right* in particular), is "the voice that promises us that at the end of this journey there lies the prospect of a homecoming, of finally arriving at a state in which contradiction, division, suffering, and other manifestations of negativity have been not necessarily eliminated, but at least redeemed as moments of an intelligible, internally articulated, encompassing whole" (93).

In Markell's reading, Hegel's reconciliatory voice drowns out the diagnostic, such that the resulting account of recognition emphasizes the achievement of what is effectively a kind of universal sovereignty. This is a fatal flaw, according to Markell, because "Such pursuits are not only futile; in many instances, they are the very instruments by which we insulate ourselves from the weight of our finitude, displacing our aspiration to sovereign agency onto a larger whole with which we identify" (95). This points to a third general critique, which resonates with Lewis R. Gordon's diagnosis of the "theodicean" tendencies of European Modernity, and is "characterized by the rationalization of forms of life that are inherently justified versus those that could never be justified under the principles of the systems that form both" (2006b, 7). Just as medieval Christian thinkers sought to justify the appearance of evil in a world authored by a perfect God, modern intellectual projects often begin with the conviction that they are, at least in their ideal expression, perfect, and thus must explain away the appearance of failure or incompleteness.

In this broader, and often secular understanding, the underlying theodicy takes the form of a a kind of grammatical structure that engages itself well beyond strictly theological bounds. As Gordon points out, "so long as that grammar is there, there will always be something to fill the vacuum of a lost god even if that something is the system itself" (2006a, 40). The neoliberal economic order, for example, is not flawed, the appearance of failure in the form of rampant poverty is simply a result of the irrationality of some agents (typically understood as flawed in their rational faculties). Colonialism and white-supremacy, for example, often operate within these sorts of theodicean logics, insofar as they take the perfection of the European or white world-order for granted, and view any apparent problems or flaws not as problems with the system, but rather at best as problems with the implementation of that system, and more often as the result of the failures of "problem people" (Gordon 2000, 69). Such "problem people" are those who could never be justified *within* the system, and so must be contained, controlled, or eliminated altogether. This third general trend in critiques of (especially Hegelian) recognition thus holds that recognition theory undertakes a kind of theodicean project. It posits some as-yet-unrealized ideal, the appeal to which enables our evasion or disavowal of our inescapable finitude and vulnerability. Recognition, according to this reading, holds that we can achieve a final unity (the theodicean end-game), if only we would either try hard enough, or simply let the grand design fulfil its ultimate function.

Markell's text represents all three of these general trends in the larger critical literature on recognition. He (1) describes recognition as moments of "exchange," that (2) tend toward the essentializing of identity categories, and (3) rely on a larger theodicean framework in which all may be justified by appeal to a final satisfaction of our ultimate *telos*. His move in response to these concerns is to emphasize what he calls Hegel's "tragic insight" that our actions are produced by relations of recognition as much as they produce those relations, and place the "acknowledgment" of our own finitude, contingency, and dependence at the forefront of our model of intersubjectivity. Indeed, tragedy, beginning from his analysis of *Antigone*, is a recurring and very important theme throughout Markell's text. As he writes in his conclusion:

> The rhythm of the foregoing story about recognition, misrecognition, and acknowledgment is tragic. It is not a story of monstrous or ignorant people. It is a story of people who, understandably, respond to the experience of intersubjective vulnerability in overly ambitious ways—that is, in ways that do not acknowledge but instead try to overcome some of the basic conditions of human activity. (2003, 177)

Markell's argument, in short, is that the politics of recognition requires that individual agents recognize others as sovereign subjects, and in so doing, they assume and implicitly affirm their own sovereign subjectivity. I am the one who can give you recognition, and my granting of this social good (here again is that economic model) at the same time ostensibly affirms your independence while nevertheless reinforcing, through your position as recipient of my largess, your subordination to and dependence upon me. In this way I re-inscribe our relation of domination/subordination by preserving your dependence, and evade my own dependence and vulnerability by positing myself as sovereign.

In effect, though this is not the framework he uses, Markell describes recognition as saturated with Sartrean *bad faith*. For Sartre, the agent in bad faith pursues a project of flight or escape from a displeasing or threatening truth in favor of a pleasing and reassuring falsehood. It is a kind of self-deception (Sartre 1994, 48–50; cf. Gordon 1995a, 8–9). Of course, when one occupies simultaneously the position of deceiver and deceived, it becomes necessary to enlist the aid of others in one's self-deceptive project. Sartre describes several different moments or manifestations of bad faith, and for the sake of focus I will defer an extended account until chapter 6, but in the most basic sense they all take the form of either convincing oneself that one is the sole arbiter of one's existence (what Markell calls "sovereignty" and what Sartre calls "sadism") or convincing oneself that one is at the complete mercy of forces beyond one's control (which Sartre calls "masochism"). As Gordon has so aptly pointed out, both of these types of projects require the cooperation of others (1995a, 42; 1997a, 76). My efforts to deceive myself typically require that I get others to "play along" with my deception. Even if there can be some (though I think rather rare) instances where it is possible to engage in bad faith in solitude, maintaining such commitments over any significant amount of time requires quite a lot of help from others (which help can certainly be coercively obtained). This is amply clear in the psychosexual context from which Sartre draws his metaphoric (and sometimes literal) terminology: the sadist needs someone to dominate, and the masochist needs to be dominated by someone, neither can fulfill their project on their own.

As Markell understands recognition, the recognizer and the recognized play the roles of sadist and masochist respectively. The recognizer in effect uses the recognized to convince herself that she, as the one in a position to *grant* recognition, is an independent and sovereign ("full") subject, and in so using the recognized, effectively precludes the latter's potential for achieving the same end. Markell sees quite clearly that this is not a true achievement of sovereignty, but rather a kind of self-deception (bad faith). This is not only because, in Markell's view, such sovereignty is a forlorn hope in any event for what amount to metaphysical reasons (that is just not the sort of thing that we are or can be at an ontological level), but also because this view of oneself as independent crucially *depends* on these kinds of interactions with inevitably dependent others. This latter irony was not lost on Sartre, who points out that convincing oneself (in bad faith) that one is a self-sufficient perspective on the world turns out to require that one is *seen* as such. To use the visual metaphor that was Sartre's *lingua franca*, in order to hold the perspective of being the sole perspective that matters, I need to be regarded as such from some other perspective, which perspective thus matters a great deal even as I deny its significance. Likewise, to convince myself that I am just an object among other objects is to undertake a kind of project, and thus a kind of *action* (and therefore an expression of subjectivity) that necessarily belies its own goal. Recognition, according to Markell, can thus be understood as a kind of bad-faith project of sovereignty that, apart from being ontologically incoherent, requires the maintenance of a dependent and subordinate other for its enactment. For these reasons, it must be abandoned in favor of his own politics of "acknowledgment."

The acknowledgment in question is that of our tragic finitude, indeterminacy, and dependence. In Markell's own words:

> acknowledgment is in the first instance self—rather than other—directed; its object is not one's own identity but one's own basic ontological condition or circumstances, particularly one's own finitude; this finitude is to be understood

as a matter of one's practical limits in the face of an unpredictable and contingent future, not as a matter of the impossibility or injustice of knowing others; and, finally, acknowledgment involves coming to terms with, rather than vainly attempting to overcome, the risk of conflict, hostility, misunderstanding, opacity, and alienation that characterizes life among others. (2003, 38)

What distinguishes acknowledgment from recognition, in other words, is first and foremost the latter's outward direction (we are all seeking recognition from others) as opposed to the former's inward direction (we must acknowledge the tragic limitations of our own subjectivity). Recognition, ultimately, aspires to the ontological condition of the sovereign subject, while acknowledgment demands that we foreground the impossibility and ultimate incoherence of sovereignty, embracing our finitude, vulnerability, and dependence on others. This also significantly alters one's understanding of injustice. Whereas, within Markell's understanding of the politics of recognition, injustice is a matter of the maldistribution of recognition as a social good (the first general critique), such that justice demands the authentic identification of individuals and groups (the second general critique) so that in turn one may ultimately distribute to them the recognition they are due (the third general critique), the move to acknowledgment identifies injustice in the very insistence on clear and distinct identities in the first place (178–80). The demand for recognition, therefore, always involves the unjust privileging of the individual, group, or institution that is allegedly in the position to give recognition, while the act of seeking or demanding recognition of one's particular identity as fixed and given already entails the aspiration to sovereignty (and falls prey to essentialism and dependence on the dominant other). Acknowledgment, in contrast, sees injustice of this sort as a manifestation of privileged subject-positions, not maldistribution of social goods (181).

Markell's critique has much to recommend it. To the extent that he is accurately describing a particular and quite common view of our intersubjective life-world and the varieties of justice and injustice that inhere in it, his critique is powerful and compelling. Indeed, my contention in this chapter is that the target of his critique can be understood to be the politics of purity. That is, I will make the case that Markell's concerns about recognition theory (as he understands it) is its implicit commitment to the politics of purity, even if he is not articulating it in these terms himself. We can see this in each of the three general criticisms discussed so far, so again, what I say here I take to apply not only to Markell but also to a broader scope of critiques of recognition theory. However, after making this case, I will argue that part of the reason why Markell understands recognition theory in this way is not simply because this is the way its proponents understand it, but because he has an underlying commitment to purity himself, as evidenced in his

PURITY AND RECOGNITION

The general critique that focuses on recognition as essentializing offers the best point of embarkation for this discussion of the politics of purity. The essentializing critique has two interrelated aspects. On the one hand, there is a concern about appeals to a true or authentic individual identity, such that, if my demand to be recognized as a particular person is to be effective, it must be the case that my demand points toward some underlying yet hitherto unacknowledged aspect of my (real/true) identity. While there are certainly moments where Taylor's account of recognition seems to affirm something like this view, it can be recognized in any number of examples of political struggle among oppressed groups. Concerns about assimilation, cultural appropriation, and various accounts of "selling out" or "passing" can all be understood as making such appeals. The underlying claim is that there is something about what it takes to fully participate in the dominant social order that requires a degree of inauthenticity or alienation—a denial of the self—on the part of those dominated by that order. Resistance can thus take the form of the demand that one be allowed to be who one truly is without being made to suffer for it. This is certainly a reasonable and compelling claim on its face. We find a prominent example in the philosophical literature in Sartre's *Anti-Semite and Jew* (1948), when he points out that for the "democrat," his stand-in for the liberal humanist, there is a willingness to accept the Jew, provided that her Jewishness is constrained to the private sphere. Thus, to paraphrase Sartre, while the anti-Semite wishes to reduce her to her "Jewish-ness" and deny her humanity, the democrat will accept her as a human being, but deny her as a Jew.[7] Recognition, by some accounts, is precisely this call to be accepted for what one *is*, as distinct from what the dominant society would wish one to be. Insofar as this seems to require some antecedent identity that has been lurking unrecognized in the subject(s) of recognition all along, then it does seem to fall prey to a kind of essentialism. As Markell argues, recognition treats one's identity, including especially one's group identities, as a kind of *fait accompli*—as something that one can know and recognize in oneself and (potentially, at least) in others. It exists prior to our acts of recognition or misrecognition, and serves as a condition for the possibility of successful recognition (2003, 18). McNay, as well, laments that recognition theorists have a "tendency to understand social relations as extrapolations from a foundational dyad of recognition" that relies on some prior notion of identity and agency (2008, 164).

Of course, this appeal to authentic identities at the individual level is linked to the concern about essentialism at the larger-scale level of group identities. This is because, in order to be recognized in one's specificity vis-à-vis the dominant norm, one must demand recognition *qua* member of one or more subordinate or marginalized groups. That is, one must demand recognition as a particular over and against the allegedly universal norm. It is to affirm that one *is* such-and-such, that this is an intrinsic feature of one's identity, and that having that feature ignored or denigrated constitutes a significant psychological and often material harm. This constitutes a kind of pernicious essentialism insofar as that initial appeal to identity, the claim that one really is such-and-such, requires a fixed and stable account of the group such that one can positively affirm one's membership in it. There must be a clear definition of the group in order for one to know that one is a member of it. The essentialism of individual identity is in this way linked to essentialism with respect to group identities. Thus, my individual essence is predicated upon the group essences that serve as the building blocks of that individual essence. Insofar as the critics of recognition theory reject essentialism, and they understand recognition to be inherently essentialist in this way, then they reject recognition theory.

Essentialism of this sort, I contend, is itself a manifestation of the politics of purity. This is true for both the individual and the group versions of it that so vex the critics of recognition. At its root, an essence of this sort (I shall argue later that there is an alternative view of essence available to us) serves as a way of delineating clear and distinct boundaries—it gives us a way to determine what is inside and outside of the boundary of the group (us/other) or the individual (self/other). Such boundaries provide a way of sorting what is really or essentially "me" from what are merely contingent or accidental features, and fulfill the same function with respect to groups. Recognition, in this view, becomes fundamentally a project of purity. In seeking or demanding recognition, one is demanding that what is true or essential about one's identity be affirmed, so that one is not trapped or mired down by false accounts of who one is. It strips away what is false in order to reveal and affirm what is true and essential, so that one can be and act in a way that expresses that true self (which is another way of saying that one can be free). In other words, recognition amounts to the expelling or stripping away of what is false and *external* to the self, and the valorizing of what is internal to the self. Such an effort is clearly a kind of *purification* of the self. It aims toward a self that has been purified of "external" elements through being recognized for what it truly is, and this individual identity is predicated in part upon conceptions of group being that have likewise been purified of "outside" elements.

By way of example, consider a specific case in the context that is Taylor's focus in his essay—multicultural education. Suppose an African American high school student in Memphis begins organizing her peers to push for the addition of a course on African American history to be added to her school's curriculum. Recognition theory, according to these critiques, would understand this struggle in the following terms. The absence of such a course constitutes a kind of harm to the student insofar as, by ignoring or disavowing the history of African Americans, the school is denying recognition both to African Americans as a group, and to this specific student as a member of that group. Because realizing one's *self* is a process made possible through recognition, this denial of recognition retards the development of African American students. Note that this is independent from any argument based strictly on pedagogy—this argument from recognition holds that there is a kind of psychological and developmental harm to African Americans constituted by the absence of African American representation (recognition) in the curriculum, not that the education of the students in general is thereby impoverished (though such an argument can and should certainly be made).

The student's call to add the class, therefore, is a paradigmatic struggle for recognition, and illustrates two important features. First, it is a demand to be recognized in her particularity, not simply as a universal/generic "student." Thus, while the administration may regard their present curriculum as ideal training for its students as a whole, the point being made here is that *some* of the students can find themselves (in the form of people *like* them in the relevant ways) in the figures and events they study in their history classes, while our protagonist and students *like* her in the relevant sense do not (or rather, only find themselves as passive stage-setting in the background of the real historical actors). Second, her demand to be recognized by her school in her particularity is linked explicitly and inextricably to her shared group identity with other African American students. Her recognition is thus tied to the recognition of African Americans and their history in the context of the school's curriculum. Finding herself in the curriculum requires that the curriculum include people *like her* in the relevant ways.

As Markell and other critics of recognition read this situation, all of this is predicated upon at least implicit appeals to *essentialized* identities at both the individual and group levels, and in my view, such identities are wrapped up in the politics of purity. This is because our activist student, according to this account, understands the present curriculum to be treating her as something she is not. She is not a "generic" student (where, in the US context, "generic" really means "white") but, rather, though not exclusively, an African American student, and in ignoring this fact, her self-worth is being undermined. She must bring her true self into the open and have it recognized, and in so doing shed those imposed norms and standards that teach her to devalue herself. She must purify her *self* from these harmful external impositions. Likewise, a course on African American history, as a means of recognition, must maintain its own purity organized around that group essence. If the administration attempted to include within the course designated to meet the demands of the student elements of Native American and Latinx histories, this would, quite reasonably, be seen as a failure to properly meet the demand for recognition by lumping all of the "nonwhite" histories into a single class, which would communicate as much, if not more, about their disvalue as it would their value. Therefore, proper group recognition, according to this understanding of the concept, requires clear boundaries between relevant groups, which boundaries must be policed and maintained in ongoing projects of purification.

This aspect of purity with respect to essential identity categories in turn sets up a logic of purity in recognition's appeal to "exchange." These two general critiques of recognition are deeply linked to each other. This is because, in understanding recognition as a kind of exchange between two agents—a giver and a receiver—even when those agents might be understood to be collective or institutional, recognition theory imposes an understanding of the participants as distinct and ultimately only externally related. Recall, for example, Markell's critique that being the *giver* of recognition reinforces a dominant position, while being the recipient reinforces a subordinate position. This criticism clearly sees recognition theory as holding these two roles to be completely discrete—one cannot be *both* a giver and a recipient of recognition. Recognition theory, in this view, thus establishes, reifies, and legitimates these distinctions between and among individuals and groups. Such border-policing is clearly in keeping with the politics of purity. Furthermore, models of exchange always entail a clear distinction between the participants in the exchange and what is exchanged (in this way, the exchange is always of external goods). As McNay's criticism makes clear, the idea that agents as such are not merely participants in the exchange, but actually shaped *in their subjectivity* in and through the act of exchange, means that this view of recognition as a kind of strictly external "good" only serves to reinforce the (in her view, mistaken) idea that agents exist in a manner distinct both from other agents and from their interactions with such agents. In other words, such exchanges of recognition constitute a purification of the self not only because they reinforce the distinction between the giver and the recipient, but also because they deepen the sense that each agent is distinct from their relations (of recognition) with each other.

We can now see how purity bears on the third general critique, which holds that recognition relies on some larger theodicean framework predicated upon a grand and final *telos*. If it is indeed the case that recognition relies on a fundamental essentialism, wherein we "exchange" recognition of our underlying individual and group identities, all of which works within a logic of purity, then the end goal toward which it aims can be understood as a condition of purity. Acts of recognition, in other words, are rituals of purification directed toward a final state wherein all impurities have been cleansed and we are all perfectly recognized. In such a state, we would all be present to ourselves and each other as fully-realized agents. It would be a condition of pure presence and transparency arrived at through the efforts of those who have struggled to purify themselves and the social world of all that stands in the way of this final consummation of the long struggle. In this way (which is how Markell reads Hegel's account of recognition), our sovereignty and freedom as individuals is a matter of our realization of this purified state. Once achieved, any who stand outside of or opposed to this purity thereby demonstrate that they are outside of the scope of the genuinely political—they become impurities in the body politic. Of course, other versions of recognition theory might hold that this end state is only a kind of regulatory ideal beyond our grasp in practical terms—something toward which we aim even as we realize that we cannot ever achieve it fully or completely. This avoids the concern about placing some individuals, groups, or institutions outside of the realm of the political, since doing so requires that the genuinely political community has already been achieved, but it still falls prey to the critique in that it requires for its function some positive conception of the ideal toward which we are, even if imperfectly, aiming. In this way, though we may remain in some sense doomed (tragically, you might say) to an impure condition, it maintains an ideal standard of purity as that toward which we ought, albeit vainly, to strive, and in so doing maintains a logic of purity.

My claim here is that these three general critiques of recognition are drawing attention to ways in which recognition theory can, and often does, work within the politics of purity. It serves to draw ever more distinct boundaries between the self and the other, between those in a group and those outside of it, and between our present "fallen" state and some final glorious end toward which we must aim. Given that these critiques are leveled at an account of recognition which is indeed mired in the politics of purity in the ways I have described here, I share the general conviction that the politics of recognition as described by these critiques should be abandoned. In the next chapter, however, I will argue that these critiques, as again exemplified by Markell, do not on their own escape or evade the politics of purity, and so fail to offer a viable alternative account of intersubjectivity and liberation. In other words, Markell's critique of recognition, and his alternative account of "acknowledgment," are both bound up within the politics of purity. Fortunately, there is an alternative account of recognition that avoids these critiques. This alternative reading of recognition will be the focus of the next chapter.

Chapter 3

Recognition, Cognition, and Purity

In the previous chapter, I discussed three general trends of critique with respect to contemporary theories of recognition. I argued that each critique could be understood to demonstrate that recognition theories, or at least these dominant versions of them, fall prey to the politics of purity. In this chapter, I will argue that the politics of purity operates, if a bit more surreptitiously, in the framing of such criticisms of recognition themselves. That is, while the critiques demonstrate the commitments to purity in certain forms of recognition theory, the theoretical moves they make and the alternative accounts they offer remain themselves nevertheless mired in the politics of purity. Consequently, I will be offering an alternative account of recognition theory that avoids both the critiques discussed in the last chapter, and the lingering commitments to purity found in the critiques themselves.

PUTTING THE COGNITION IN RECOGNITION

As a way of initiating the interpretive move I am trying to make, I will begin with an epistemological point. One of the central recurring moments of contention in the current literature on recognition has to do with what, precisely, is being recognized. Is it my universality? Or my particularity? The former would focus on one's "humanity" or "personhood" in some universal sense (recognition as *a* person), while the latter emphasizes one's specific, often group-based, identities (recognition as *this* person). In addition, there is the crucial question of our epistemic relation to this "what" that is being recognized. That is, in properly recognizing the other, the assumption is that I must come to adequately and appropriately know that which I am specifically recognizing.[1] Likewise, if I am demanding to be recognized, I must know what it is toward which I am demanding that others direct their attention. In Taylor's version of recognition theory, for instance, what is being recognized is one's "true" identity, and so I must come to know the authentic identity of the object of my recognitive act when I give recognition (I see you for who you really are), and I must know my own authentic identity when I demand recognition from others (you are refusing to see me for who I really am). Markell, in particular, exploits this epistemic connection in his critique of the politics of recognition. As he states, "The ideal of recognition . . . anchors sovereignty in knowledge; that is, in the prospect of arriving at a clear understanding of who you are and of the nature of the larger groups and communities to which you belong" (2003, 12). Indeed, Markell's move to "acknowledgment" as an alternative to recognition is in part an emphasis on what he understands as the fundamental *un*knowability of oneself and others. It is, as I discussed in the previous chapter, precisely this limitation of our epistemic capacity, for Markell, that must be "acknowledged."

He sees this not only as a matter of our limited epistemic ability, however, but also as a matter of the ontology of the subject as such. Insofar as we are, he stresses, ongoing manifestations of becoming, as opposed to being, we are not the sort of things that can be properly known, even by a perfect knower, and consequently, we cannot be accurately or properly recognized (60). Therefore, any claim for or to recognition is effectively an appeal to a fundamentally false view of the ontology of the self, paired with an equally mistaken estimation of our epistemic abilities. Again, this is an approach with which I am largely sympathetic—certainly with respect to his rejection of a static/substance ontology of the subject. I will argue in this chapter, however, that his insistence that such an account of the subject is inconsistent with *recognition* is misguided. I will offer an alternative account of recognition that foregrounds a dynamic ontology of the subject, and makes clear the profound implications this has for our understanding of liberation and oppression. I will conclude by exploring the ways in which replacing the standard visual metaphors with sonic metaphors can facilitate a richer grasp of the shift to this dynamic ontology, a theme that will be carried forward through the remainder of this book.

My contention with Markell is best grasped by an initial focus on his treatment of the epistemic features of recognition, which assumes that the cognitive paradigm is fundamentally propositional, rather than practical. That is, in Markell's view, recognition follows the classical "S knows that p" model of cognition, such that proper recognition demands full and complete knowledge of the authentic identity of the recognized as a kind of static object to be "grasped" in a determinate and final way. The cognitive moment of recognition therefore assumes that the thing to be recognized, in this case the identity of a given subject, is a *fait accompli*—an object that can be fully and completely known through a discrete act of cognition. He argues, however, that since human subjects are in fact ongoing processes or moments of becoming (dynamic), as opposed to objects or manifestations of being, they are fundamentally unknowable, and thus recognition is a forlorn and misguided project predicated on a valorization of sovereignty (Markell 2003, 59–60). In short, we are always unfinished, incomplete, and developing processes, and as such cannot be properly known by ourselves, let alone by others. This, Markell tells us, and as we discussed in the previous chapter, is the essentially tragic nature of human existence that makes recognition an unwise and ultimately impossible pursuit (86).

There is thus an epistemological and metaphysical point at the heart of Markell's dismissal of recognition theory, and this is why he links struggles for recognition to a pursuit of sovereignty. The effort to fully and finally know oneself and others in this way (as Being or substance) is an effort to be fully realized or fully present, and distinct from or above the contingency and vulnerability that necessarily comes with being a kind of work in progress (Becoming or process). Markell is working within a largely Arendtian framework in his appeal to sovereignty, but we can easily see resonances here with the Sartrean account of the desire to be God, or Beauvoir's discussion of the "serious man" (Sartre 1994, 615; Beauvoir 1948, 35–43). In Sartre's view, this is the bad faith effort to be fully in-and-for-oneself, which requires, as Beauvoir emphasizes, a disavowal of the contingency that is at the core of our humanity as a consequence of our freedom. To aim at being sovereign, or being God, or being serious, are thus all variations on the same theme, where one seeks to *be*, fully and completely, what one *is* (allegedly), without any of the contingency or vulnerability or ambiguity that results from our being open-ended projects (Becoming) emerging from the unavoidable exercise of freedom.

For Markell, the cognitive moment of recognition is only coherent if we assume precisely this kind of sovereign self as an object of knowledge, and since this kind of self is a (self-)delusion, recognition must be abandoned as a way of theorizing the social world. Markell's argument here is a recapitulation of the three general trends in the critique of recognition that I identified in the previous chapter. His claim is that recognition demands a moment of *cognition* in which objects of knowledge are understood as static collections of quantifiable properties (units of *exchange*) waiting to be fully and completely grasped (in their *essence*) by a fully realized knowing subject (in a moment of *theodicean* reconciliation). As I have suggested, however, this critique assumes an essentially propositional model of cognition. Markell takes for granted that cognizing, and thus *re*cognizing someone, is at root no different from knowing that $2 + 2 = 4$, or that the cat is on the mat. If, on the other hand, we abandon this propositional model in favor of a more *practical* understanding of cognition, wherein the "objects" of knowledge are ongoing processes and activities that allow for differing degrees and qualities of knowing without ever admitting to full and complete mastery, then Markell's critique misses the mark, and his alternative of *acknowledgment* loses much of its force.

The first important observation to make is that just as "recognition" is a cognate of the verb "cognize" (as is, not coincidentally, "cognate"), the original German word *Anerkennung* is a cognate of the verb *kennen*, which is typically translated into English as "to know." However, the German *kennen* is differentiated from another word translated as "to know," *wissen*, in a way that is not always immediately apparent to the English-speaker. While both *kennen* and *wissen* mean "to know," the latter picks out the kind of propositional knowledge appropriate to the sciences (*Wissenschaften* in German), while the former points more toward a kind of *familiarity*. In English this is often captured in the distinction between "knowing how" and "knowing that," and can be best illustrated in English through examples. To know Memphis, for instance, is simply not the same thing as knowing that the sky is blue, or even that Memphis is in Tennessee, despite the fact that they both take the same English verb. To claim that I know Memphis is, for one thing, not clearly falsifiable. I have lived here for a few years, which means I am fit to give advice to visitors, recommend some favorite places, offer driving directions, and discuss typical weather patterns. In this way, it seems clear that my claim to know Memphis is true. Yet, compared to a native Memphian, I am no doubt profoundly ignorant, and they may well opine, quite sincerely, that I don't *really* know Memphis.[2] On the other hand, the claim to know that Memphis is in Tennessee is a very different, propositional, kind of knowledge. It is, in short, either true or false (if we are referring to Memphis, Indiana, or to the ancient Egyptian city, it is false), and I either know this truth or I do not. It is thus both clearly falsifiable and does not admit of degrees in the same way that my claim to know Memphis does. This is characteristic of all kinds of *practical*, as opposed to *propositional* knowledge.

Thus, rather than assuming propositional knowledge as the paradigm of the cognitive moment in recognition, theorists of recognition would be better served by taking up the model of practical knowledge. Knowing-how functions in a markedly different way from knowing that.[3] My knowing how to play guitar, or how to swim, for example, like my "knowing" Memphis, cannot be properly understood to function in the same way as propositional knowledge. Elsewhere, I have discussed a similar point using the example of the martial arts (Monahan 2007, 43–45). Suppose that I undertake the practice of a traditional martial art, and so begin to study, for example, an empty-hand form (*Hyung* in Korean, *Kata* in Japanese). After I have learned and memorized all the movements and practiced under the close supervision of my instructor for a month, it seems reasonable for me to claim, if asked, that I "know" the form. After all, how can I practice the form at home on my own if I do not know it? Of course, it is also true that I am only a beginner, and so senior students will know the form better than I do, and our instructors should know it better still. At the same time, mastering or perfecting the form is an impossibility—there is always room for improvement (my teachers, and their teachers, continue to practice and improve), and my knowledge, no matter how well developed, is never complete.[4] Anyone claiming to "know" the form in the sense of having completely mastered it, such that they no longer need to practice and strive for improvement, is thus gravely misunderstanding the proper epistemic relation to the practice of the martial arts (and the same would apply to music, or dance, or sport, etc.). While, in the propositional model, knowledge is in large part a matter of the collection of true propositions, and in this sense an appeal to static Being, practical knowledge manifests itself in and through the ongoing, and in principle never-complete, effort to improve one's understanding of a given process or activity, and is thus an appeal to dynamic Becoming very much in keeping with Markell's approach to the metaphysics of self (along with that of the existentialists, and, as I will discuss below, Hegel's as well).

(RE)COGNITION, PURITY, AND THE SUBJECT

Given Markell's own reference to Becoming in relation to identity (20003, 60), this shift from propositional to practical accounts of knowing would seem natural. And yet, his critique of recognition is predicated precisely upon his continued insistence that recognition theory is inescapably entrenched in the propositional understanding of the (re)cognitive moment. According to Markell, we must reject the politics of recognition because it demands of us that we come to know (in the propositional sense of complete mastery, or a kind of epistemic capture) the "true" identity of individuals and groups as static manifestations of Being in order to give them the recognition that is their due, while in fact such identities do not exist. They are as a consequence, "tragically," forever beyond our grasp. The knowing of an identity, in Markell's understanding of recognition, is treated as an all-or-nothing proposition, and since identities are not fixed and static objects to be grasped fully and completely (a point with which I agree), then they cannot be known at all (a point with which I disagree). Markell's critique, in other words, preserves a commitment to the politics of purity with respect to his epistemological framework, which insists on binary all-or-nothing, either/or frames of analysis.

If we accept, as I believe we should, Markell's basic point that identity should not be thought of as a *fait accompli*, as a simple and static object, it does not follow from this, as Markell mistakenly believes, that identities cannot be known. To be sure, they cannot be known in some final and complete act of cognition on the propositional model. And even if we turn to the understanding of knowing linked more closely to notions of familiarity, there remains a danger in reducing familiarity to the simple accumulation of true propositions regarding the object one "knows" in this way (though surely this is not the only way to understand familiarity, I point this out only as a danger). Rather, if we understand identity as an ongoing process (of dialogic articulation and contestation, as I have described it in my own work), then the knowing of an identity, whether one's own or that of another, is much more akin to knowing how something is done, rather than what something is. Practical knowledge, in other words, is the knowledge appropriate to becoming (and thus to questions of identity), while the propositional is suited best to being. And since I am accepting Markell's own positing of human agency and identity as a matter of dynamic becoming, practical knowledge is the more appropriate approach to the cognitive moment in recognition.

It becomes immediately apparent in making this shift to practical knowledge is that what matters most is not the simple yes or no of whether one knows a particular activity or process, but rather the *quality* of that knowledge. My neighbor and Eric Clapton, for example, both know how to play guitar, but there is a difference in the quality of their knowledge that becomes painfully obvious when my neighbor decides to perform in his backyard. It is a crucial point, however, to stress that the truth value of the claims "my neighbor knows the guitar" and "Eric Clapton knows the guitar" is *true* for both. The point here is that one characteristic of accounts of recognition that assume the propositional model is that they are utterly blind to *qualitative* differences in manifestations of recognition—one either recognizes (correctly) or one does not. In shifting to a model of practical knowledge, we avoid this problem.

The first consequence of this shift to practical knowledge thus has to do with the way in which it opens up qualitative distinctions between manifestations of recognition. We must focus not on "failures" or the "lack" of recognition but on the different ways and means whereby recognition is enacted. Thus, elsewhere I have argued for the crucial significance of the distinction that Hegel draws in both the *Phenomenology of Spirit* and the third volume of the *Encyclopaedia* between what he calls "pure" recognition (*Reine Annerkennung*), and more or less "corrupted" forms of recognition, like that described in the dialectic of Master and Servant (Monahan 2006). This is a matter of differences of degree, not an on/off switch. The second important consequence has to do with our understanding of pure recognition as itself not an end or ideal state, which would make it a static manifestation of being but, rather, as an ongoing process—a dynamic manifestation of becoming. Indeed, as I will argue later in this chapter, what Hegel thought of as "pure" recognition is in my view best understood (ironically, I must admit) as a kind of *creolizing* process. For now, we should acknowledge that, just as the perfection of musical performance, or athletic endeavor, is something that can never be achieved as an end state, but is a matter of ongoing practice, the purity of recognition, as a normative ideal, cannot be properly understood as some fixed and determined end state. In this way, the Hegelian ideal that Markell refers to as "reconciliation" need not be understood as committing one to the arrival at some static and utopian ideal state or condition but, rather, as demanding an ongoing commitment to deepening familiarity with oneself and the larger social world (to better-know in this practical sense).

The qualitative distinctions between manifestations of recognition are, it follows, not predicated upon proximity to some static ideal but, rather, made manifest in the ongoing commitment to the process itself, and the effort to open up new and richer ways of engaging in that process. Consider, by way of an athletic example, the good goalie in soccer. Anyone who says, "I have now learned all there is to know about goal-tending, I am the perfect goalie, and so I have no need to practice or learn more," has made clear that they are in fact not truly committed to knowing how to tend goal, for any such commitment would entail the effort at constant improvement. Likewise for the good guitarist, or sculptor, or martial artist, and so on. Indeed, the very best practitioners, those who *know* their instrument, sport, or art the best, are precisely those who never stop improving and even seeking out ways to challenge themselves. Thus, when we think of practical knowledge, there is something clearly misguided about the very idea that one can achieve a final state of perfect and complete knowledge, but it does not follow from this that knowledge is therefore impossible or illusory. Nor does the lack of such a final and perfect state or fixed ideal make it impossible to differentiate between better and worse practitioners, since such distinctions need not rely simply on proximity to this supposed ideal or end state.

This is a crucial, and often misunderstood, point. The claim here is not that "pure" recognition, or "truly knowing" an art, instrument, or person, functions as a kind of regulatory ideal where there is a goal that should be kept fixed in our minds even as we acknowledge that we can never attain it. It is the more radical claim that, as dynamic processes, "recognition," and "self" or "identity" as objects of knowledge or recognition, can never be properly conceptualized as a fixed and stable ideal of any sort, not even as unattainable regulatory ideals. To do so is to misconstrue them ontologically—as processes of becoming, they are not the sorts of things that can *be* ideals of this static sort at all. They cannot be properly conceived as perfect states that we can but asymptotically approach, for they are not and cannot be *states* at all. Of course, this raises a critical question: if there is no such final ideal against which to compare particular instantiations of a given practice, how is it possible to differentiate qualitatively amongst practitioners and performances? Accepting this basic account, what could possibly differentiate between better or worse instantiations of recognition, or between my neighbor and Eric Clapton, or any practice of the sort I have been using as examples, if there is no final ideal against which to compare them?

Again, the position I wish to take can perhaps be best approached through an examination of aesthetic practices, which reveal an important feature of this shift in our understanding of knowledge. Namely, the very highest levels of performance or practical knowledge all in one way or another shift our very understanding of the practice or activity in question and its limits. Think of the way our understanding of "good" basketball has evolved over the last seventy years—a contemporary professional game is very different from such games in the 1970s, and is barely recognizable as the same game at all when compared to the 1950s. What this illustrates is the fact that the greatest players do not approximate some static ideal but rather alter our very understanding of what is possible and challenge subsequent generations to push those boundaries even further. Or think of our understanding of good guitar playing before and after Sister Rosetta Tharpe, Jimi Hendrix, or Paco de Lucia. Think of jazz music before and after Charlie Parker, Billie Holiday, John Coltrane, or Nina Simone. If you think about the practices and activities dearest to you, you will doubtless come up with numerous examples of these sorts of paradigm-shifting practitioners, for such revolutionary figures abound in painting, sculpture, dance, literature, and on and on.

What these exemplars all illustrate is that the very idea of a static and final "ideal" that good practitioners are meant to approach is nonsense from the start. And it is nonsense not because it is epistemically inaccessible to us (as a sort of tragic flaw in our epistemic abilities), but because the "ideal" is an ever-evolving process, rather than a fixed target. These paradigm-shifting figures expand our conception of the practice itself precisely because they do not constrain themselves to what was considered "the ideal" at the time. The truly revolutionary practitioners, historically, have typically been indifferent to the ideals and standards of their day, rather than assiduously applying themselves to realizing the standards of their contemporaries. Their excellence is expressed precisely through their transcendence of the limits of what could even be conceived of as "great" prior to their re-shaping of the very landscape of the practice. Thus, any attempt to describe what the perfect basketball player, or guitarist, or martial artist should be able to do will fail because the greatest exemplars of these activities always push the very boundaries of what we even take good performance to be. What once before seemed to approximate an ideal eventually comes to appear staid, unimaginative, and limited. Normative differentiation between better and worse performances of a dynamic activity is thus rooted in this fundamental feature—the best practitioners alter our very sense of what the activity could possibly become.

Of course, not all of us can or will rise to this level of performance, but there still remain ways of making qualitative judgements without appeal to a static ideal. There is, on the one hand, the simple matter of ability and technique—who can perform the tasks and operations with the greatest facility and ease. Returning to a recurring example, my neighbor and Clapton may play the exact same series of notes on the exact same instrument, but Clapton will do it with more precision, economy of motion, and clarity of expression. As it happens, good technique, achieved through intense practice (as a clear way of *knowing* one's activity/instrument), facilitates the kind of performance that is paradigm-shifting in the ideal way described above (which is no static ideal). Another feature of good practitioners as opposed to mediocre ones is that they seek an ever-deeper familiarity with their practice—they seek the unfamiliar and challenging in their efforts to explore the possibilities of their practice. Excellent performers/practitioners will seek out ways to leave their comfort zones precisely as a means to enhance the depth of their knowledge of their practice (this is another example of the link between the strange and the familiar explored in the introduction). Finally, the best practitioners are able to improve the performance of others with whom they are interacting (think of a sports team, or a musical ensemble, or a sparring partner here). Good players improve the performance of those playing with them, or in the case of competitive practices, even *against* them. There is, as it happens, a kind of reciprocity here, for by enhancing the performance of those with whom one is playing, one's own performance will likely, if perhaps not necessarily, improve. Once again, this interest in and ability to enhance the performance of others is conducive to cultivating the kind of performers and performances that stretch the boundaries of what is even conceivable as "good." In this way, there is what I call a *telos without a terminus*—a general directionality that does not point to some fixed and determinate end state or goal, but nevertheless makes possible the differentiation between positive growth or development, on the one hand, and decadence, foreclosure, or ossification, on the other. We thus have ways of making qualitative judgements about these sorts of dynamic and open-ended processes even without recourse to some static ideal toward which we take such activities to aim and against which we measure them.

All of this, it should be apparent, has significant implications for our thinking about recognition. We must think of it not as a thing that we achieve or accomplish (let alone as a "good" to be "exchanged"), but as an ongoing practice with which we are constantly (though not always consciously) engaged. And just as it is misguided to think that one has mastered the guitar, and thus need not study or practice it any more, it is equally misguided to believe that one has achieved perfect or "pure" recognition, and thus need not work on improving it any more. Hegel's own example of love is very instructive here (1977, §772; 1971, §436z: 1991b, §7z). If we think about genuine loving relationships we have with others (in the broadest sense of "love," not only erotic/romantic), there is no point at which we say that we have achieved love now, and so we no longer need to nurture or develop this relationship. Indeed, if something like this were to be said, we would be more likely to understand it as an example of taking someone for granted, and thus as a breakdown of the relationship, rather than as a sincere declaration. For the best or most true love is a relationship that is changing, growing, and developing, insofar as love is itself a dynamic process of growth and development—of nurturing, as bell hooks has described it (2000, 4). Likewise, since recognition is better understood as something that I am constantly doing, the important questions are not *whether* or how *much* I am recognizing (as in the "exchange" model) but rather how *well* am I recognizing (or even better: how well we are recognizing each other).

It is thus apparent that, as with the examples of great musicians, the quality of recognition is a matter not of arriving at or achieving some end state, but rather best thought of as opening-up further avenues for recognition going forward. In particular, and this is why the epistemic focus can be so productive, recognition goes well when it facilitates a deeper knowledge (in the sense of familiarity) of oneself and those with whom one is interacting. Lest it appear I am just kicking the normative can here by appealing to epistemic "depth," I must stress that what makes this sort of knowledge better or worse (deeper or shallower) is the way in which it opens up new possibilities of growth and development (again, a telos without a terminus) for the very process/activity I am coming to better know (including, of course, the *self* as process). Corrupted recognition, therefore, will foreclose or impede the ongoing dynamic growth of one or more of the selves involved and one's coming to know them, while relatively more "pure" recognition will foster that development and growth and enhance one's familiarity with those ongoing processes *in their movement*. Indeed, at its very best, it will foster those paradigm-shifting instantiations that alter our very conception of what is possible.

HEGEL AND THE LOGIC OF RECOGNITION

The roots of this response to Markell's critique, I have already hinted, can in fact be found in Hegel. The first question we must ask is what exactly is it that recognition is supposed to be doing or accomplishing? In the *Phenomenology*, Hegel's discussion of pure recognition helps to answer this crucial question.

In these paragraphs (§178–85), Hegel credits recognition with being a necessary and crucial moment in the development of self-consciousness. While this basic point will already be familiar to those with even a passing acquaintance with Hegelian recognition (and certainly is maintained in the late twentieth-century re-articulations of recognition), all too often the inattention to pure recognition leads to exactly the sort of misreadings of Hegel that Markell, and so many others, exhibit. Through pure recognition, the interdependence of our negating, abstract, and allegedly independent consciousness (the for-itself) with our concrete, positive, and dependent aspect (the in-itself) is made manifest to us. For those less steeped in Hegel's terminology, the main idea he is trying to get at here is that we all, as conscious human beings, experience ourselves as at once physically/materially as well as culturally/spiritually located and limited on the one hand (this would be the "in-itself"), and qua conscious beings, able to move beyond (to *negate*) these present conditions in a variety of ways both physically and mentally (the "for-itself"). This basic experience goes a long way toward explaining the broad appeal of Cartesian dualism in its myriad forms (as was discussed briefly in chapter 1). As part of our development, according to Hegel, we are inclined to identify almost exclusively with this "for-itself" aspect to such an extent that we see any limitation or dependency as a threat to our independence that requires overcoming, annihilation, circumvention, or consumption. This is what Hegel calls the moment of "Desire" (*Begierde*) (1977, §174–76), but we can see in it echoes of Markell's sense of "sovereignty." Indeed, the more well-known dialectic of Master and Servant emerges when two subjects equally committed to their own independence and self-sufficiency encounter one another as threats to that independence, struggle, but then arrive at a temporary truce involving domination and subordination.

Before he discusses this dialectic of struggle and subjugation, however, there are several crucial passages on "pure" recognition, which describe what relationships of mutual and reciprocal recognition ought to look like. Under conditions of pure recognition, each participant freely recognizes the other not simply as either "for-itself" or "in-itself," but as both simultaneously. The implications here are perhaps best described through a protracted example. Imagine that Karen and Ken participate in a moment of pure recognition. Karen is engaging her subjectivity (for-itself) in the act of recognizing that Ken is *both* a subject (for-himself) and an object (in-himself). In this way, she is not reducing him to a mere object in the form of an obstacle, threat, or tool to be overcome or exploited, but nor is she merely acknowledging some abstract status that treats his specific objective qualities as irrelevant. Rather, she is recognizing that Ken is like her, not because he is *identical* to her but, rather, in that he is a unique subject with a unique objective status. Of course, their shared uniqueness entails that they are also different and distinct—that is, they are also "the same" by virtue of their each being unique (more on the implications of this apparent contradiction below). Now, when Ken is reciprocating this moment by likewise recognizing that Karen is both a subject and an object like (and simultaneously unlike) Ken, then the real work of recognition can occur. What is actually happening is that Karen is recognizing Ken who is himself in the act of recognizing her as both subject and object, and in this moment of Karen recognizing Ken as recognizing her, the unity of her self-consciousness is, in Hegel's words, "given" back to her through the act of reciprocal (pure) recognition (1977, §181). That is, because Ken is affirming Karen's shared status and she has recognized his own status, she can encounter herself as both subject and object *simultaneously* through Ken's recognition of her in a way that would not be available to her on her own. Pure recognition thus enables a kind of unification or even reconciliation of the self (as both in- and for-itself) that is simply impossible in the absence of reciprocal recognition. Clearly, this is a cursory account of what is a very complicated and nuanced set of concepts, but hopefully any exegetical inadequacies can be forgiven in the interests of brevity.[5]

The upshot of all this is that Markell simply cannot be talking about Hegelian recognition when he states, "On my reading, the crucial connection between the pursuit of recognition and social subordination lies in the fact that the pursuit of recognition involves a failure of acknowledgment of one of the basic circumstances of human action—the fact that action is always, ultimately, interaction, and that this interaction introduces an ineliminable contingency into life among others" (119). This is *prima facie* implausible as a reading of Hegelian recognition. As it is described not only in the *Phenomenology*, but throughout Hegel's corpus, recognition places human interaction in the foreground of our activity from the earliest moments of what Hegel understands to be genuine self-consciousness.

Nevertheless, Markell is, as I have already affirmed, offering a very valuable critique of a certain quite common (mis)understanding of recognition, but his account of "acknowledgment" and his rejection of "reconciliation" in favor of the "tragic" insights of Hegel's "diagnostic" moment misses something very crucial. In order to better illustrate what this is, I will turn to a key passage from Markell's text.

Subjectivity's trouble arises from the contradiction between its commitment to epistemic and practical sovereignty on the one hand, and its experience of vulnerability in action on the other. This, I suggest, is the deepest sense in which the *Phenomenology* might be said to be "tragic"—not, as is usually assumed, because it contains moments of ethical conflict between opposed but equally valid powers (though that is also sometimes true), but because, at least in its diagnostic voice, it shares with tragedy a keen appreciation of the contingency of human interaction and the dangers involved in our efforts to deny or suppress that contingency (102–3).

What Markell misses here is, first, the way in which a "commitment to epistemic and practical sovereignty" is always a *corruption* of recognition in the first place. If one demands or seeks recognition *as sovereign*, that is, as already fully realized or wholly independent, then one is already committed to a corruption of recognition. In its relatively "pure" moments, recognition emphasizes precisely the ways in which both the recognizer and the recognized are *not* wholly self-sufficient and sovereign subjects, but neither are they utterly dependent. In the dialectic of Master and Servant, of course, there is such a commitment to this the ideal of sovereignty, insofar as the Lord seeks absolute independence and relates to the Servant in a way defined or constrained to their dependence. Part of the brilliance of Hegel's account, however, is the way in which he demonstrates that this commitment to sovereignty is a kind of self-deception (presaging Sartre's later account of bad faith) doomed to a final failure or collapse. In other words, it is far from normative, contra the vast literature that seems to take the dialectic of Master and Servant as somehow *prescriptive* for Hegel in a way that is, as I read him, utterly mistaken (cf. Monahan 2006).

Pure recognition, therefore, is not an effort to grasp as a complete whole some static category of identity as the "ground" of my (or your) action, any more than it is an assertion of mastery or absolute independence/sovereignty. Nor is pure recognition a final state toward which we ought to aim as some static ideal, let alone set as a feasible goal. Once one understands the object of recognition (both of the self and of the other) as not an "object" at all but rather as a process or activity, then what is demanded cannot be the self's *expression* in action, as if self and expression were separate and distinct. Nor should recognition be understood as aiming toward the accurate cognition of some fixed and determinate self (in the manner of propositional knowledge). Recognition, in other words, is not the acknowledgment of sovereignty, mastery, independence, or one's "true self" as some static description or sovereign substance, but rather it is the ongoing activity of enacting our identity, understood as both subject and object, such that, rather than seeing identity and action/expression as distinct, we conceive of identity or the self *as* expression/action. This prioritization of activity over substance necessarily entails interaction with others not as limitations, or sites of vulnerability, contingency, and dependency (though they can certainly be all of these things) but rather as the foundational condition for finding our subjectivity given back concretely to us in a meaningful and ultimately, if the interaction is genuinely reciprocal, empowering way.[6] In other words, acting in an ineluctably social world will predominantly (though not exclusively) take the form of interaction, and the character of that interaction will inevitably condition who we are (as a self-in-action).

Ultimately, the result of this moment of pure recognition—as having our selfhood (quo *process*) given back to us by the other—is not that we then have it simply as an object of the other's gaze, nor merely as an abstract and independent kind of mastery (as if it were property to be exchanged) but, rather, that the gift of reciprocal recognition enables (this is what I mean by "empowering") and conditions yet further enactment of subjectivity (though in an always altered and developing way) and future manifestations of recognition. What is given, in other words, is not a discrete object or quanta, nor in a significant sense, is it the same "self" as was originally offered. Rather, the giving here is itself a new enactment—a process of articulation and manifestation of the self in relation to some other(s).

Again, a musical example might prove helpful. Imagine a long-established ensemble of accomplished musicians playing together—a group whose ensemble playing is, in musician's terms, exceptionally "tight." Each musician is bringing a unique contribution to the whole not only in terms of her specific instrument but also because of what musicians will often refer to as her distinct "voice," which contributes to the whole in a way that only she can. This is, in effect, her *giving* of herself to the ensemble for the sake of helping it realize its potential (and, at the best moments, going beyond prior conceptions of that potential). The other musicians will respond to and build upon that "gift," which in effect means that what she was doing is now given back to her, not as a *fait accompli* or as a discrete moment of expression, but rather as a continuation of her original *praxis*, and as an invitation to expand on that contribution in new directions. Her "voice" is thus given back to her in a way that often enhances her own understanding of what she was up to originally, and makes possible further and deeper articulations of that voice. In other words, her self-understanding is enhanced, along with her ability to make positive contributions to the ensemble in the future. Pure recognition operates in this general way.

This process of self-expression and development is ultimately what I take Hegel to mean by *freedom*, and will be a crucial aspect of my development of that concept later in this text. Corruptions of recognition, therefore, can be understood in part as efforts to arrest this ongoing process—to fix or solidify our own identity and that of others. That is, one way that corruptions of recognition work is by taking dynamic processes of becoming and offering them, to oneself and others, as if they were static aspects of being. To participate in misrecognition will thus take the form of attempting to fix and define one's own or the other's identity/self, when pure or proper recognition affirms the open-endedness of the participating selves as ongoing practices/processes in a mutually constitutive relation.

Markell's account of "acknowledgment" asserts only that we are unknowable both to ourselves and to others, and that we are better off if we keep that "tragic limitation" in mind. Of course, the idea that we are "unknowable" is plausible in Markell's account only to the extent that one takes up a strictly propositional account of knowledge. To be sure, we cannot be "known" in the same way that one can know that it is raining outside my window right now, or that tomorrow is Friday, or any other proposition of this sort. And this is true not only because of our limited epistemic abilities, but because, as always incomplete and ongoing processes of becoming, there is no closed and complete set of facts or data to be "known" in this way at all. Acknowledgment, according to Markell, invites us to come to grips with this tragic limitation, and, in effect, foreground this fundamental unknowability. My point in drawing this distinction between propositional and practical types of knowing is that none of this applies when we switch paradigms from the propositional to the practical. Of course, I can know myself and others, even as ongoing and incomplete processes, but only in the same way that I know Memphis, or that I know the guitar. One's knowledge in this sense can always be deepened and improved, but it does not follow from this that we are tragically unknowable to ourselves or others. To treat it as an all-or-nothing proposition in this way—either we can fully and completely "grasp" the object of knowledge or it is "unknowable"—is a profound misunderstanding of the dynamics of this sort of epistemic relation, and, at root, a manifestation of the politics of purity.[7]

One key aspect of Hegelian recognition that needs to be emphasized at this point is the way in which this process of coming to know oneself and others better requires social interactions that facilitate this deepening knowledge. This is obvious when we consider coming to know others, but what Hegel's account of pure recognition makes clear is the way in which my own grasp of myself cannot be deepened through mere introspection (indeed, this seems like a reliable formula for self-deception), but rather one comes to know oneself in and through interactions with others. As Hegel put the point so aptly, we are given back to ourselves in moments of recognition in ways that enrich our sense of who we are. In the end, therefore, what a more properly Hegelian account of recognition brings to the foreground is the way in which the distinction between self and other, like that between thought and action, is far less clear and distinct than we tend to think. It is not that I need recognition from the other in order to achieve some distinct end, it is rather that I am who I am (again, understood as an ongoing process of becoming, rather than as a fixed substance) only in and through "the other."

Importantly, this other is not "the Other" in any radical or total sense, but is always also importantly similar. Again, to treat the self-other relation as either a totalizing drive to unity or as rooted in a foundational alterity is to impose an either/or dichotomy inappropriate to dynamic processes of becoming (yet very much in keeping with the politics of purity). Let me stress here, furthermore, that I do not take my appeal to recognition to be the only, or even necessarily the best, approach to this way of thinking the relation between self and other. Indeed, this is an insight quite common in Africana philosophical traditions, especially those clustered under the umbrella term of "Ubuntu." In her own writing on the concept, South African philosopher Mpho Tshivhase draws on TshiVenda expressions to offer the following account of Ubuntu: "one's personhood is recognizable or becomes evident through one's interconnectedness with others" (2018, 198). I point this out not to say that Ubuntu "just is" Hegelian recognition (a move that should be emphatically rejected), but to point to the possibility of multiple paths to this same insight regarding human social life. There is, I am suggesting here, at least a sympathy or harmony (or better, as I shall argue below, a *resonance*), therefore, between recognition as I am describing it and alternative traditions and approaches that point toward the same general way of thinking, even if they do not use the same terminology or arise from the same traditions.

THE DYNAMISM OF RECOGNITION AND THE CRITIQUE OF PURITY

The key takeaway from the discussion in this chapter so far is that there is an underlying unity of self and other (which is not a featureless wholistic amalgam or relation of *identity*), made manifest through the ongoing activity that I have described in terms of recognition. As processes and activities, we can be "known" to greater or lesser degrees, but the truth and depth of our knowledge claims lies not simply in their correspondence to underlying facts about the objects of our knowledge but rather in the ongoing commitment to improving that knowledge. I therefore "know" you to the extent that I am engaged in the ongoing process of better *coming to know* you. And since you are essentially an ongoing and dynamic process, this does not mean that I am collecting static facts about you but rather that I am nurturing that development and providing you, as best as I am able, with the resources you need to flourish (where, again, flourishing is not a state to be achieved, but an ongoing process to be made manifest). When, at the same time, you are recognizing me, it means that I am also coming to know myself through the ongoing activity of coming to know you, and vice versa. That is what "pure" recognition means, and how it serves to make real my own subjectivity to me, and to make clear the lack of any absolute distinction between self and other.

Perhaps most importantly, unlike the frequently-evoked economic model of recognition, the account I am offering here is one in which the participants in the interaction are, to varying degrees, fundamentally altered through the course of that interaction. That is, the accounts of recognition as *exchanging* quanta of some external good (esteem, status, etc.) leave the participants unchanged throughout the exchange. The idea is that the participants are in effect constants throughout the interaction, and indeed, the models that emphasize recognition of one's "true" self necessarily assume that such a self is waiting there already in order to be recognized. My argument is that recognition properly understood, through its emphasis on the dialogic constitution or formulation of the (dynamic) subject, insists on an ontology in which the subjects engaging in manifestations of recognition (of whatever quality) are, for better or worse and to a greater or lesser extent, altering who they are in and through the interaction.[8] Such an essentially dynamic ontology resists hard and fast distinctions between the self and the other—who one is as a process cannot be easily or neatly distinguished from how one interacts with others, and vice versa. If one is genuinely recognizing another, therefore, one is recognizing exactly that dynamic aspect, that process-in-development. Furthermore, since that process in development has a particular history and a specific set of conditions and influences, recognition is not simply the affirmation of some abstract and featureless "subject," but entails necessarily the recognition of that history and its influence on that ongoing process (a point very relevant to questions of identity, intersectionality, and oppression, for instance). Finally, because that history includes at least one encounter with me, I am, in recognizing another, also recognizing myself as part of that larger conditioning milieu, which self has in turn been conditioned in and through the present encounter, and a long history of prior interactions. We are social, in other words, to our roots, and this dialogic account of the subject is the essential core of recognition theory in Hegel.

Crucially, accounts of recognition that remain entrenched in the model of economic exchange, where essentially distinct subjects exchange packets of social esteem and recognition as fundamentally external social goods (like a kind of private property), omit this point entirely. Likewise, accounts that emphasize dependence, vulnerability, or "tragic" finitude, like Markell's "acknowledgment" (which serves the same explanatory function, even though he does not call it "recognition"), do not make this radical shift to a truly dialogic account of the subject but rather maintain a basically monological social ontology. Markell, in other words, may emphasize that subjects must, of necessity, interact with other subjects, which makes their actions contingent upon the decisions of others, their plans vulnerable to that contingency, and their lives overall dependent upon recurring interactions with myriad others, but he does not make the more radical shift that I am attempting to describe in Hegelian recognition. This shift posits a social ontology in which subjects are not merely dependent upon or vulnerable to others (though they surely are) but are, rather, constituted by and through their interactions with other subjects, groups, and institutions. It is not just that my expression of my "self" or identity is contingent upon the actions of others but, rather, that my "self" or identity only ever *is* (as a dynamic mode of becoming) in and through interactions with others. This is the sense in which my concern with recognition is actually metaphysical in a way that many contemporary theorists of recognition (like Honneth) disavow.

Markell's theory stands as an admonition not only to "acknowledge," but to ultimately affirm our own contingency and vulnerability, and to forego the temptation to posit a fixed and stable identity which, in order to be maintained (always in bad faith), requires the subordination of others, who come to serve as stand-ins for the contingency, dependence, and vulnerability that has been denied in oneself. This is surely an important and all-too-often necessary reminder. However, in his complete dismissal of Hegel's "reconciliatory" moment, Markell is missing something crucial, and we can see this most clearly in his insistence on characterizing the insights of Hegel's "diagnostic" moment as "tragic." Why is the impossibility of complete (propositional) knowledge of our own or others' identities tragic? Why is our contingency and vulnerability tragic? Contingency, fallibility, vulnerability, and dynamic change are only "tragic" to the extent that they fail to attain some greater or preferable ideal. The implication is that our condition must be understood as tragic because, of course, sovereignty would be best (ideal), but achieving that goal is impossible. Sadly, we must resign ourselves to our miserable lot, and not delude ourselves into thinking that sovereignty is possible. We must, in the end, *acknowledge* this lamentable tragedy and suffer through life as best as we can. Markell's reference to the impossibility of knowing ourselves or others as "tragic" therefore continues to hold up as an ideal (albeit a forlorn one), the notion of sovereignty that he so ably critiques. To "acknowledge" the impossibility of an ideal as a "tragic" feature of the human condition is to nonetheless maintain that ideal *as* an ideal, even while denying that we can realize it.

The truly radical response to the critique of sovereignty, therefore, is not simply to affirm or acknowledge its tragic impossibility but, rather, to reject it as a norm or standard altogether, and this, I submit, is what Hegel is in fact attempting to articulate in the "reconciliatory" moment that Markell dismisses. If the "diagnostic" moment reveals the interdependence, contingency, and vulnerability that characterizes human life, the response need not be to describe this simply as the tragic insight that human action will always fail to live up to its ideals. One could, rather, commit to leaving behind those ideals altogether.

In making this more radical move away from the ideal of sovereignty (even as a tragic impossibility), the shift to practical knowledge is once again crucial. Hegel's system is fundamentally one of movement and activity. The truth always comes to light, not through the process of taking things apart and reducing them to their constitutive elements, but rather by setting them in motion, by seeing how they interact not only with other objects but also with the very consciousness attempting to understand them. This is indeed what makes reason itself dialectic (as opposed to analytic) for Hegel (1969, 833–34 and 837; 1991a, §81, §215, §227z). And if truth and reason are a matter of movement and interaction, then they cannot be properly understood as static states to be achieved, even in the ideal. This is a point often misunderstood in Hegel. "Absolute Knowledge," for example, is not a final end state in which perfection has been achieved as a *fait accompli* but rather is a manner in which reason (*Vernunft*) is performing in top form. Again, "top form" here should be understood on the model of "mastery" in music or sport—as a mode of (necessarily social) practice fostering open-ended improvement of that very practice, not as some final and static end point. Furthermore, if we should stop trying to perform ever-better and thus to understand ourselves and the world more and more, then reason will have *failed*, not reached some ideal end goal. If reason is above all a dynamic activity, then a static endpoint is not the realization, but rather the *cessation*, of reason. Thus, for a given subject, the choice is not simply between the false comforts of sovereignty or the tragic acknowledgment of the impossibility of sovereignty. The project of pure recognition, the project of "reconciliation," is above all the commitment to move beyond the all-or-nothing standards presented by this dichotomy. It is, to put things differently, a rejection of the politics of purity.[9]

At this point we can begin to see how Markell's critique of recognition, which I argued in chapter 2 is consistent with certain key elements of the critique of purity, nevertheless retains at its core an ideal of purity, and thus remains bound up in the politics of purity. The ideal of sovereignty understood as an independent and distinct subject "sovereign" over all that is external to it, is clearly an ideal of purity. To achieve and maintain one's sovereignty in this sense involves a process of purification—a purging of external influences that generate the dependencies and vulnerabilities that threaten one's alleged sovereignty. Of course, as Markell recognizes, such sovereignty is only ever illusory, and the viability of that illusion is only plausible to the extent that one positions oneself in relations of domination over others. My apparent invulnerability, in other words, comes at the cost of enhanced vulnerability for others, and my alleged independence requires the chronic dependence of others. Even under ideal conditions, however, such apparent sovereignty is dependent upon maintaining those relations of domination, and vulnerable to collapse should those relations begin to weaken. All of this is evident in Markell's critique of recognition, even if he does not himself appeal to notions of purity in the same way. In this way, he is offering a critique of a certain version of recognition theory as committed to politics of purity.

What emerges from the discussion so far in this chapter, however, is that the politics of purity informs Markell's critique itself, and not just the target of that critique. As I have argued, in demonstrating that this version of recognition valorizes sovereignty (purity), showing that it is impossible, and treating this as a tragic insight, he maintains sovereignty as an (unrealizable) ideal. We are *tragically* impure, and we are best served by acknowledging this. His epistemic argument, furthermore, maintains a static/propositional account of knowledge all while (rightly) advancing a dynamic account of the political subject—his theory of knowledge, and thus of human beings as "unknowable," in this way presumes the kind of all-or-nothing epistemic relations that characterize the politics of purity. Against this account, I have argued first that a properly dynamic approach to epistemology that tolerates incompleteness and ambiguity (that is, one that does not valorize purity) reveals that we are far from unknowable. I have further argued that there are resources in Hegelian recognition, especially his account of "pure" recognition (I confess that I rather wish he had chosen a different terminology, given my own critique of purity), that open a path for a genuinely dynamic account of human existence, and especially human social existence (though, part of what this shows is how this latter phrase is redundant—human existence is necessarily social existence). What this enables is a way to see dependence, vulnerability, and ambiguity not as tragic flaws or failures to realize a pure/sovereign ideal but as positive features of our existence. That is, rather than taking the concept of the self or subject to be *threatened* by these features, we can recognize them as the very conditions for the possibility of a self or subject at all (though emphatically *not* a static or sovereign self/subject).

To be sure, appeals to a dynamic account of the subject, and a suspicion of all-or-nothing or dualistic thinking, is hardly new, and is indeed a common or recurring theme in Western philosophy both in American pragmatism and in the "continental" tradition at least from Nietzsche on. Yet there remains, as with Markell, a tendency to reject the actuality of sovereignty, or autonomy, or a coherent self, while preserving such notions as (unrealizable) ideals. The roots of the politics of purity run deep, and even its apparent critics find it hard to escape them. There is a tendency to assert, for example, that the sovereign subject is an impossibility, and that therefore the subject is a suspect idea, precisely because a "real" subject can only be understood as sovereign. Such a critique of the sovereign subject preserves the ideal even as it rejects the existence of that ideal in the actual world. We see this over and over in the history of Western philosophy. The prioritization of the universal, as for example, with European Enlightenment humanism, is oppressive or colonial, and therefore we must prioritize difference or the particular. The idea of a coherent and unitary self or will cannot be supported, and therefore the existence of a "self" must be altogether rejected. We see this basic pattern repeated again and again.

At root, this pattern recurs because there tends to remain a threshold beyond which the rejection of dualistic thinking dares not go. Namely, it tends to collapse into variations on an ultimately dualistic formulation: ~(dualism). But to simply negate dualism in an all-or-nothing fashion is to recapitulate a dualistic logic. As I have argued, any truly radical response to the problematic features of dualism cannot take this form of outright rejection. A truly adequate response to the politics of purity, in other words, cannot simply be ~(purity), for this merely sets up the further dichotomy between the pure and the impure (as the historical example of the generation of "mixed" racial categories across linguistic and cultural traditions I discussed in the first chapter illustrates), which in turn tends to collapse into a pure universality where all are equal in their status as impure, or a pure particularity where all are equal in their absolute and insurmountable otherness (radical alterity). What I am calling for in this text, and what I find lacking in the various critiques of sovereignty, static forms of being, and dualism that populate the history of Western philosophy, is a response to the critique of purity that does not itself implicitly recapitulate the politics of purity. As I will argue below, this necessitates a move beyond "Western" philosophy as it is typically understood.

My discussion of recognition so far has been intended first and foremost as an exemplar of a general trend in approaches to the theorization of freedom and liberation. Recognition theories, as an account of freedom, have been subject to the politics of purity, I have argued, yet this need not be the case. Even the critiques of recognition, furthermore, exhibit an implicit appeal to purity, in that they maintain "pure" ideals even as they dismiss the possibility of attaining them. This diagnosis of the operations of purity within the debates around recognition opens a space for articulating an account of freedom that is *creolizing*, and this will be the focus of the next chapter.

Chapter 4

Toward a Creolizing Freedom

The core of my argument so far is that any account of freedom that aims to resist a collapse into the politics of purity must be a *creolizing* theory of freedom in two senses. First, it must seek out moments of difference and contrast, never ossifying into a final and static repose *as a theory*. Second, it must see the practice of freedom as an ongoing effort to creolize—to draw together moments and elements of difference into an ever-changing and developing, yet never complete and final, whole. It must resist ideals of purity both within itself as a theory and in its expression as a practice of freedom. This means there can be no fixed, permanent, and distinct boundaries between self and other, between individual and state, or between what is "internal" and "external" to the self. Key here is my reference to "fixed," "permanent," and "distinct" boundaries. Boundaries in-themselves are not only permissible, they are necessary, because processes of creolizing cannot continue in the absence of difference. Such boundaries may even be relatively stable (a point to which I will return below), but properly understood and constituted, they must be plastic, temporary, porous, and ambiguous. Finally, a creolizing theory of freedom must see the absence of such distinct and permanent boundaries and stable categories not as some flaw that renders any hope of freedom forlorn or misguided ("tragically"). In this chapter, I will offer an introductory sketch of freedom as creolizing. Once this first glimpse has been offered, I will turn, in the remaining chapters, to taking up the task of creolizing that theory of freedom itself by placing it into conversation (what I will call *productive friction*) with a variety of different interlocutors that are in various ways outside of or marginal to the Western canon.

REASON, CONTRADICTION, AND MOVEMENT

My appeal so far to Hegelian recognition, its later twentieth-century proponents, and their subsequent critics, has been motivated by the conviction that this is a theoretical tradition of taking on questions of identity, freedom, and liberation that offers a clear way to illustrate what I mean by the politics of purity and the idea of creolizing freedom. It is *a* way of advancing my project, but I do not pretend that it is the *only* way to do so. The interpretations of Hegelian recognition that Taylor and Honneth exemplify are, as I discussed in chapter 2, modes of addressing political liberalism and its corresponding accounts of freedom and the political subject. Favoring a "dialogical" account of the subject where the encounter with "the other" is a necessary moment in the development of a flourishing self, these interpretations endorse, in different ways, an account of political life in which the social world, rather than being an obstacle to be negotiated around or controlled/dominated, is a positive element of our psychological wellbeing. As later critics such as Patchen Markell have argued, however, there remained in these accounts an implicit commitment to binary logics of self/other, to a view of the subject as closed and sovereign, and to a teleological account of liberation that aims toward some final state of unity and reconciliation that favors identity over difference. My own response to this critique has been to argue that there remains a commitment to purity as an ideal in these critiques, and that the seeds, so to speak, of a viable alternative are to be found in what I take to be a more promising reading of Hegelian recognition. Because my ultimate project here is not to offer a sustained interpretive work on Hegel but, rather, to use some Hegelian insights as a jumping-off point for the development of a theory of freedom, I will keep my remarks on the interpretation of Hegel here relatively brief.[1]

The key to my approach to Hegelian recognition is found not in the *Phenomenology of Spirit* but rather in Hegel's major works on logic (the *Science of Logic* and volume 1 of the *Encyclopaedia of the Philosophical Sciences*). This is because he offers in his works on logic an account of reason and truth as fundamentally dynamic. The insistence that truth can be captured in static propositions and that reason is the effort to define, pin-down, or capture those propositions is characteristic of what Hegel refers to as "the Understanding" (*Verstand*), rather than what he thinks of as reason proper, which he calls "Speculative Reason" (*Vernunft*). The Understanding operates precisely by drawing boundaries and distinctions—attempting to *fix* its objects.[2] In Hegel's words, the Understanding "stops short at the fixed determinacy and its distinctness vis-á-vis other determinacies; such a restricted abstraction counts for the understanding as one that subsists on its own account, and [simply] is" (1991a, §80). He describes the Understanding as either-or thinking (§80) in which the fixed determinations it generates "persist both in their antithesis to each other, and (even more) in their antithesis to the Absolute" (1991a, §25). What Hegel means by "Absolute" is quite complicated, but for present purposes we can gloss the term as "the larger whole," which means that he is pointing out how each determination is discrete from each other, and from the larger whole of which they are a part. One can readily see, as I have argued in more detail elsewhere (Monahan 2017), that the Understanding is an expression of the politics of purity.

In keeping with the politics of purity, the Understanding views any ambiguity or contradiction as a sign of failure or incompleteness. If we arrive at an unclear or ambiguous determination, or worse yet, a contradictory determination, then that demonstrates a clear moment of failure. Angelica Nuzzo makes the point as follows:

> The logic of the understanding engages in the analysis or dissection of what lies in front of it and proceeds by isolating the moments thereby obtained in the attempt to separate truth from falsity, the positive from the negative. To such logic, however, movement and change—the transition that lies between the terms of its dichotomies and blurs its classifications—are in principle unintelligible. For its chief assumption is that truth and falsity (as well as good and evil) must be kept separated, that their contradiction must simply be avoided and left aside. Contradiction, which is the very root of movement, is precisely that from which the fixed order of the understanding takes flight as the worst enemy of an alleged unmovable and unmoved truth. (2006, 94)

Nuzzo's appeal to movement here is significant. If an object, for example, is in motion, then there can be no final and unambiguous account of where it is *qua* object *in motion*. One could, in principle, take a sort of time-slice, and ascertain that it is at some determinate position at that determinate "slice" of time. But of course, to take a time-slice in this way is to freeze time, and thus movement, at some fixed and determinate moment. In order to preserve the motion, we must preserve the flow of time, which means that objects in motion have, by virtue of their motion, an ambiguous location. Once we are looking at more than a mere "slice" of time (an abstraction akin to the mathematical "point" in Euclidean geometry), we can speak of the area or range through which the object in motion has moved, is moving, or will move, but a defined, discrete location is impossible precisely because it calls for a *static* object. The classical paradoxes of motion, Hegel suggests, arise when one attempts to account for it within the determinations of the understanding (1991a, §89). Zeno's paradoxes, for instance, operate by appeal to static slices of time of gradually decreasing magnitude (asymptotically approaching zero), yet despite these paradoxes, Hegel observes, motion clearly exists. What they reveal, as he puts the point, is that "motion is *existent* contradiction itself" (1969, 440). To be in motion is to be *both* "here" *and* "there," which is another way of saying both "here" and "not-here" (or if you prefer, both "there" and "not-there"). For Hegel, it demonstrates not that motion is itself a paradox but rather that motion and contradiction are intimately linked. The Understanding cannot account for motion because, needing static, either/or distinctions, it cannot tolerate contradiction and ambiguity.

Fortunately for Hegel, there exists an alternative mode of thought to the Understanding in the form of "speculative" reason. Dynamism, ambiguity, and contradiction are, it turns out, characteristic of this form of reason, which he takes to be reason *proper*. The Understanding, in generating these either/or distinctions and attempting to fix them in place (for movement yields contradiction and ambiguity, which cannot be tolerated), inevitably leads, according to Hegel, to deep contradictions and paradoxes, like those of motion already mentioned, or like Kant's antinomies of reason. As with Kant's antinomies, one common response is to view this as a limitation of reason. Hegel, however, holds that this "commits the mistake of thinking that it is reason which is in contradiction with itself; it does not recognize that the contradiction is precisely *the rising of reason* above the limitations of the understanding and the resolving of them" (1969, 46, emphasis mine). Speculative reason, in other words, emerges out of these contradictions, not by simply negating them, but rather by putting them in motion and relation. As Hegel puts the point, "The struggle of reason consists precisely in overcoming what the understanding has made rigid" (1991, §32).

One way to approach this aspect of reason is by taking up the way in which *truth* functions within speculative reason. Again, Nuzzo offers a helpful summary: "The logical process *is* (identical with) the movement of truth. Truth is not a concluded, fixed object, event or proposition *of which* a concept should be provided; truth is a complex movement of transformation that must be caught and expressed *in fieri* as it were, in its transforming quality and development. This movement *is* the concept of truth" (2006, 95).

The determinations of the Understanding may be "correct," Hegel tells us, but "truth" is altogether different from correctness (1991, §172), and is to be "expressed only as a becoming, as a process, a repulsion and attraction—not as being, which in a proposition [*Satze*] has the character of a stable unity" (1969, 172). Reason (and the truth it manifests) is thus a movement and relation of determinations that, if posited as discrete and static or fixed, would yield contradiction and paradox. As such, the truth is only manifest *in the movement* of the apparently contradictory elements.

One rather direct way that this abstract discussion of reason and truth bears on the approach to recognition is via the account of the subject that emerges from it. Consider the subject in a moment of recognition, the "I" that recognizes some other "I." As Hegel points out, when we say "I" we mean something quite particular—this I who is uttering this phrase or writing this sentence or perhaps recognizing *you*. Nevertheless, the term itself has no particular content, and applies equally (without modification) to any and every other subject. It is thus at once completely particular and totally universal (Hegel 1991, §24). Put in a more quotidian way, I am an absolutely unique individual with a unique subjectivity, and in this regard, I am identical to everyone else. Here is exactly the sort of contradiction ("we are identical insofar as we are unique") Hegel has in mind as giving rise to speculative reason. What could it possibly mean to know the truth of myself as at once a unique individual that is in this regard identical to everyone else, given this clear contradiction?

The key to approaching this task is to realize the way in which the subject as such must be comprehended as a *process*. The "I" that is universal in this sense is, in Hegel's terminology, pure "negation." It is negation in the sense that it distinguishes itself from its object or content, including even itself as an object. The I that is thinking or acting is differentiated from what it is thinking about or acting on, even when it is thinking about or acting on *itself*. Nevertheless, as Rocío Zambrana makes clear, negation in this sense "is never mere negativity, sheer destruction (which Hegel calls 'abstract negativity'). It is an exclusion that sets or posits alternative boundaries and hence a relation of something and its now established other" (2015, 17). Negation is, in other words, a negation *of* something specific, which, even in the act of differentiating itself from that something, stands in a constitutive relation to its content. The *form* of the "I" is negation, and is in this way universal (just like every other "I"). However, insofar as this negative moment is never simply abstract negation, but always a particular negation *of* some particular *content*, then each "I" is also perfectly unique. Given this form/content relation in the idea of a subject, Zambrana further points out that "it follows from the negativity of form that any content is never fully stable or fixed, that is it is never fully authorized" (2010, 121). Put differently, *I*, as active negation of some positive content (including even myself as positive content) am always more than the sum of my parts. I am in this way not only an active and ongoing process, but a process involving a complex series of *relations* between constitutive conditions and objects, including, significantly, other subjects. It is in this way that we can follow Terry Pinkard's reading of Hegel in claiming that "Self-reflection on essential self-identity is necessarily *social reflection*, on the positioning of oneself in 'social space' and on the possibilities of self-conception that are both opened and foreclosed by that 'social space'" (1994, 265, emphasis mine).

We can now come to terms with the implications of Hegel's work on logic for our thinking about recognition. To posit participants as discrete and self-contained individuals capable (in principle, if not in practice) of being fully and completely "grasped" by themselves or by others is to operate within the either/or thinking of the Understanding that demands clear boundaries and distinctions between fundamentally static objects and concepts. To see recognition as something that can (again, in principle, if not in practice) be completed or fully realized likewise exhibits the model of the Understanding in that it seeks a final resolution into a static *end*. None of this is consistent with Hegel's account of speculative reason. Truth, as we have seen, is ultimately itself a kind of movement and relation between differentiated (and even contradictory) terms or determinations. Hegel is often critiqued for claiming that such differentiation and contradiction can be resolved or reconciled, as we have seen in our discussion of Markell's critique of Hegel's "reconciliatory voice," but for Hegel, this "reconciliation" is itself never final or static. As he puts the point, what emerges from the reconciliation of contradictory terms is not some "quiescent third" but rather a "self-mediating movement and activity" (Hegel 1969, 837). Furthermore, as a movement and relation *of parts*, the reconciliation (*Aufhebung*) Hegel proposes does not do away with or entirely dissolve the distinctions or contradictions between the elements. What emerges is thus neither static ("quiescent") nor unitary and distinct from its parts (a "third").

In this way, moments of reconciliation, including even the way Hegel understands "absolute spirit" or the "absolute Idea," are thus first and foremost *moments*. A moment, as a temporal concept, picks out what is *in process*. Grammatically, "moment" may function as a singular noun, but it is a (category) mistake to approach it as a static object. These moments of reconciliation pick out a *way* things happen and relate, rather than a static and final relation or state of being. According to Robert Bruce Ware, "Hegel's doctrine of the Absolute Idea requires that the dialectic should culminate not in the termination of its dialectical development but in the self-conscious recognition of the *method* by which the dialectic necessarily continues" (1999, 73, emphasis mine). This is because, if the very metaphysics of (speculative) reason, or the subject, or even freedom, for example, is dynamic, then the moment it arrives at some static and final reconciliation, then the movement stops, and it ceases to *exist*. So long as it exists, it is in motion, and absent that motion, it cannot exist. Likewise, recognition, because what is being recognized (and what is doing the recognizing) are ontologically dynamic and open-ended processes of becoming, cannot reach or attain some final and static end point (in the same way that, as we have seen, practical knowing cannot arrive at some final terminus). Recognition, therefore, is only ever *manifest*, it is never simply given, received, exchanged, or even denied (more on this below). Furthermore, this inability to achieve some final satisfaction does not mean that we are tragically incapable of fully or truly recognizing each other. To draw this conclusion would be to remain at the level of the Understanding, or in my terms, to capitulate to the politics of purity.

THE PRACTICE OF RECOGNITION
AND THE POLITICS OF PURITY

What, then, does all of this mean for our understanding of recognition? There are several key implications.

1. The cognitive moment of recognition should be modeled on knowing *how* rather than knowing *that*.
2. As a *relational* process, recognition is always deeply social.
3. As a relational *process*, recognition is not a binary on/off condition.
4. Corrupted recognition or *mis*recognition often takes the form of disavowing this fundamental dynamism and sociality/relationality.

These implications are interrelated and mutually reinforcing. So, while I will offer more detail about them each in turn, their power, and their implications for our thinking about freedom, will more fully emerge only once all of the proverbial cards are on the table.

First, as I have discussed at some length already, we must think of the cognitive moment of recognition on the model practical knowledge (knowing *how*) rather than propositional knowledge (knowing *that*). To recognize another is not to know a thing but to familiarize oneself with an ongoing activity. Recognition is thus never truly a *fait accompli*, it can be interrupted or allowed to languish, but it can never be finished. Again, the comparison to music is apt. Learning an instrument is necessarily an ongoing process that never admits of completion—true masters always remain, in significant ways, students. One's learning can be interrupted, or even halt altogether (I may lose interest, or lose the physical ability to play), but it can never be *finished* in the sense of arrival at a point of completion. Likewise, manifestations of recognition must be thought of not as discrete events (exchanges) but as moments in an ongoing process involving the emerging relationships between elements that are themselves ongoing processes in part *constituted* by those very relationships and interactions. One can only commit to improving one's familiarity with these processes, not to completing or fully realizing some final ideal state (of knowing), and yet it does not follow that one does *not* know, nor does it make it impossible to qualitatively differentiate knowledge between different agents. Here again we see a kind of contradiction driving or informing this process. Recognition involves a moment of knowing as familiarity: I know my friend Bob, but part of what it means to really know Bob is to know that he is a work in progress, and in this way I do not yet (fully) know Bob, and can ultimately never "know" Bob in some compete and final way. Or rather, perhaps one should say that I know Bob best when I know he is not reducible to what I know *about* and *of* him.

This emphasis on dynamism also helps to illustrate another key contradiction that often vexes critics of recognition theory. Namely, the distinction between the particular and the universal within and between different subjects. For Hegel, part of what speculative reason reveals is the way in which the contradictory determinations of the Understanding reveal themselves to be in fact interrelated, such that each term is only intelligible *in relation* to the other, and in this way the truth, as a dynamic relation, emerges only through this interplay between ostensive opposites. Universal and particular are clear examples of this, for each only emerges in relation to the other—a Universal is a universal to the extent that it binds together distinct elements (otherwise, it is simply a monistic "one"), and the particular stands as such because it is part of some larger whole (to even say "everything is particular" is to appeal to a universal in the form of "everything").

Earlier, this tension between the universal and particular emerged in the question of whether what is being recognized is one's universal status as an agent/subject, or one's particularity as a member of a specific community, or even just as a unique individual. Notice here that at the point where we appeal to recognizing that one is a unique individual, we are illustrating precisely Hegel's point about this relationality between apparently contradictory terms, since being a unique individual is a universal feature of human beings. The concern among critics of recognition, however, is that these are mutually exclusive and contradictory projects, where success at one necessarily entails the failure or erasure of the other. What I am, qua subject, is a simultaneously unique (particular) yet universal process of becoming, insofar as the negating "I" shared by all (universal) is uniquely situated (particular). Thus, when I recognize someone else as a subject like me, I am recognizing that they share with me these apparently contradictory features. They are a unique process of becoming, just like me, and just like everyone else, but part of what it means to be a process of becoming just like everyone else is precisely that we are each unique. The apparent tension between the universal and the particular, therefore, is a product of locating recognition within the either/or logic of the Understanding—it capitulates to the politics of purity. Instead, the dynamic nature of both recognition and of human beings qua processes of becoming means that what we all share is precisely our open-endedness as ongoing processes, but because the *opening* of this process must always be *from* some specific location/situation, this universal aspect in fact *requires* the particular in order to manifest itself. Consequently, to properly (I will say something about improper recognition below) recognize another *as another subject* necessarily entails familiarizing oneself with their universality *and* their particularity in a way that maintains not only the necessary interdependence of the universal and the particular, but also between the recognizer and the recognized (and, significantly, their broader social and material *milieu*).

Furthermore, moving to the model of practical knowledge means that recognition need not be subject to the critiques that it is essentializing or offers only empty abstractions. To be recognized as a member of a particular race, for example, only appears as essentializing if one assumes that there must be some fixed and stable content to racial membership (it functions as a substantive essence, in other words), which is then "recognized" according to precisely the kind of "grasping" cognition appropriate to propositional knowledge (and the Understanding). This critique of recognition thus presumes the kind of static ontology characteristic of the politics of purity. Understood as dynamic processes, these features of our particularity that lend content to our agency/subjectivity do not admit of fixed, substantive essences, and thus cannot be known or "recognized" in the propositional sense, but can certainly be known or recognized in the practical sense. These features of our particularity that inform our manifestations of recognition, like race, function as what Lewis Gordon, following in the phenomenological tradition, refers to as an "essence without essentialism," where what makes something the sort of thing it is—its essence—is not something fixed and "internal" to the thing, but rather emerges through its relational and dynamic interaction with other things (Gordon 2012, 9; see also Monahan 2011, 192–93). In this way, recognizing someone *as Black*, for instance, does not mean to know in the propositional sense that they belong to a fixed and stable category with clearly defined boundaries and a substantive essence (as critics of essentialism rightly point out, this is deeply problematic), but rather that they are active participants in the ongoing negotiation of the socially-constituted meaning of that category as a dynamic and relational process (this point will receive further elaboration in the next chapter). In addition, recognizing someone as a person, or as *human*, is neither an empty abstraction (formalism) nor necessarily a surreptitious appeal to some implicit particular, where "human" implicitly means something like "white, male, bourgeois" (I will have much more to say about this in chapter 6). Rather, this is a recognition of a universal feature, but it is a universal that is constitutively bound up with particularity—it is a universal form that always needs and is expressed through particular content.

In this way, the emphasis on dynamism and practical knowledge enables an account of recognition that avoids what Sonia Kruks refers to as the "epistemology of provenance" (2001, 85). According to the epistemology of provenance, because individuals and their experiences are always unique and particular, knowing an individual and understanding their experiences, especially across different particularities (across races, or genders, etc.), is impossible. The initial impetus for this move is the important goal to resist what might be thought of as a kind of epistemic colonization, where privileged epistemic agents presume that the world around them, including the "worlds" of other people, are transparent to them.[3] In other words, it is the presumption that there can be an isomorphic correspondence between one's own way of understanding the world and everyone else's. This is precisely the sort of pernicious universalism that is the target of many critiques both of recognition theory and of Eurocentric humanism. The problem, however, and this is clearly a problem symptomatic of the politics of purity that emerges when one takes this laudable critique of pernicious universal*ism* to the opposite extreme, where the mere presence of particularity makes knowledge or understanding across difference impossible. The idea that you couldn't possibly understand *my* experience because it is different from yours (that is, *particular* to me) both preserves the hard dichotomy between particular and universal characteristic of the politics of purity and appeals to the propositional model of knowledge. Furthermore, as Kruks notes, "Although important in enabling previously marginalized and silenced groups to speak, an epistemology of provenance can also be problematic for it threatens to undercut notions of shared (or even communicable) experience to such an extent that possibilities for a broadly based emancipatory politics are de facto subverted" (2001, 85). Within the model of practical knowledge, however, the goal of "understanding" or "knowing" another does not admit of some final and complete realization, but neither is it impossible. Recognizing, for instance, that your experience is uniquely your own, and conditioned by the particularities of your history, *just like mine*, actually makes possible a kind of understanding that would be impossible if one were to cling to the all-or-nothing epistemology proper to the politics of purity. In this way, the cognitive moment of recognition, understood as an ongoing relation of familiarity with an open-ended process, allows for there to be knowledge of that process that is only ever incomplete to various degrees, and this incompleteness is not a failure or a fatal flaw but, rather, a key feature of what it means to *really know* in this practical sense.[4]

Let me turn now to the second implication for this emphasis on dynamism and practical knowledge for our understanding of recognition. Given that the cognitive moment of recognition involves a deepening familiarity with an ongoing activity, rather than a propositional "grasping" of some fixed and stable truth, and that a significant aspect of the object of our growing familiarity is its particularity, which particularity emerges out of a deep and active relationality with other particularities, then what we are coming to (re) cognize just is a relational and profoundly social *process*. Our particularity is something that emerges from Pinkard's "social space," where the contours of that space are something that we are actively shaping even as it shapes and conditions us and our capacities for acting (1994, 265). Who I am, in other words, as an ongoing process, necessarily involves the participation of others, who give meaning and salience to the kinds of content that shape my agency and in turn are shaped by me. It is the establishing of various positions and relations, each of which, by virtue of being part of a dynamic and interactive system, is a transient and ambiguous process made possible only through the ways in which others take on these positions and relations in different manners both similar and distinct.

This level of profound relationality in turn undermines the self/other and individual/social dichotomies, both of which, it turns out, depend upon the static ontology of the politics of purity for their coherence. Once we allow that everything is in motion and shift to the practical epistemic model, then we see that our individuality is contingent upon the kinds of relations we inhabit and that inhabit us, such that "the other" is in a very real way a part of me, and vice-versa. That being said, this mutual imbrication in no way eliminates "otherness" altogether—the result here is not some final unity or identity. Again, "relation" as a concept entails difference—in order for there to be relation at all, different relata need to exist—so the claim here is not that difference gives way to identity via recognition (which would preserve the either/or of the politics of purity), but rather that recognition always involves both identity and difference (both universal and particular). Furthermore, an adequate knowing of oneself or another (as dynamic processes) is never truly limited to the I/thou dyad, since we each stand in constitutive relation to numerous others. Elaborations of recognition that focus exclusively on such a dyad are heuristic devices at best, and gross misrepresentations at worst. Again, it does not follow from all of this that the individual is illusory, only that who I am is more a *function* than a *matter*, and it is a function of the ways in which various relations and processes are cohering, but never in a final and fixed way, because, as we have already discussed, a key feature of anyone's agency is their incompleteness (negativity).

The third implication builds upon the first two, and serves to repudiate the tendency to discuss recognition in a binary or dualistic manner, such that one is either recognized or not, or gives recognition or denies it. This is a common way of speaking of recognition among both the proponents and critics of recognition theory, but it is particularly prominent within what I have been calling the "exchange" model. Recall that what characterizes the exchange model is the treatment of recognition as a discrete and quantifiable good capable of being, in effect, traded. One may give it, receive it, withhold it, or be denied it, and it can be quantified, but one rarely encounters a way of speaking of recognition as qualitatively differentiated. Yet understanding recognition as a social/relational process means that, just as the binary between self/other must be called into question, so too must the tendency to treat recognition itself as a binary. Rather than understanding recognition as either present or absent, given or received, it is necessary to think of it as admitting of myriad different qualitative forms, many of which can certainly involve relations of domination and oppression. Recognition *as* subordinate or inferior, for instance, is still a relation of recognition, it is just that is a *corrupted* form of recognition that strives to constrain or *fix* the participants. Moments in which a given individual or group is utterly left without recognition may in principle be possible, but they are incredibly rare. It would require not merely that one "objectify" or "dehumanize" another individual or group, but rather that one be naively unaware that such an individual or group *could* be recognized at all. The implication here is that what is often referred to as "withholding" or "denying" recognition is in reality a manifestation of (profoundly corrupted) recognition. This is because actively *denying* or *withholding* recognition requires that the one doing the denying necessarily take a particular kind of relation to the one being denied as potentially *recognizable*. It is an active determination of a kind of relation to another individual or group. Corrupted forms of recognition are thus nevertheless forms of recognition, and part of the harm they generate stems from the fact that they communicate the implicit message that we could do better.

Another way to articulate this point is by appeal to the notion of "dehumanizing." It is common to refer to oppression as dehumanizing or as denying the humanity of its victims (this point will be developed in more detail in chapter 6). Yet one never undertakes the project of dehumanizing or oppressing literal objects. I don't exert myself to deny the humanity and freedom of the desk at which I sit, or the house in which I live. The very act of trying to convince oneself and one's victim that they are not free or not truly human is only ever undertaken as an implicit recognition of that freedom and humanity (one can see this as analogous to the difference between being naively unaware of something, and of *ignoring* it). This is a feature of the profound bad faith of dehumanization as a project. Furthermore, such a project can only ever be truly complete, as Hegel well recognized (1977, §188, §432), upon the death of the victim, at which point it is not a successful moment of oppression or dehumanization at all, precisely because part of what the oppressor seeks is status as dominant *over another person*, not over a corpse. None of this is to deny that oppression can have profoundly disempowering and even deadly effects on the oppressed, or that many oppressors hold sincere and explicit belief in the lack of humanity of their victims.

Consider, for example, the paradigmatic case of enslavement in the antebellum United States. Certainly many whites, whether they personally owned other people or not, held explicit beliefs about the constitutional suitability of the enslaved to their condition—that Black people were divinely or naturally ordained for servitude, that they were better off, and even "happy" with their lot, and so forth. Yet at the same time, whites were terrified of uprisings of the enslaved, and actively participated in or were complicit with a systematic regime of brutality and terror directed at preventing "another Haiti." The enslaved were at various times forbidden to learn to read, to form large groups or gatherings, to carry weapons, or to otherwise give the slightest appearance of equality with whites. In other words, there is a very clear contradiction between those beliefs about the "natural" servility or less-than-human status of Black people and the actual state of affairs, which would be readily apparent if one weren't already committed to (actively) *disavowing* them. If it were true that Black people were naturally subordinate, then many of the measures described would have been unnecessary. At the same time, one can readily recognize on the part of the enslaved, in the face of such overwhelming brutality and degradation, that choosing either revolt or capitulation are in fact very *human* responses. Oppression, even at this extreme, is thus a project undertaken in bad faith—it is an attempt on the part of the oppressors to convince themselves of a "truth" belied by their very need to make the effort to convince themselves (and others) in the first place—that can never in fact completely dehumanize or objectify those it targets as its victims. It may certainly result in individual death, but the dead cannot be oppressed (though of course, acts of killing within an oppressive context can certainly fulfill an oppressive function for those who remain alive).

What, then, does it mean to say that recognition has been "corrupted"? The approach to recognition I am advocating is one in which human freedom is necessarily linked to recognition, but freedom is manifest only through the right sorts of recognition, and can be actively thwarted by corruptions of it. Allowing for precisely this qualitative distinction between kinds of recognition is the fourth key implication of grounding recognition in a radically dynamic ontology, and it is intimately connected to the other three. What Hegel called "pure" recognition involves the affirmation of the other, whether individual or collective, as an ongoing and open-ended process that is at once embodied, situated, historical, and particular, yet, as a process, radically undefined and incomplete (a *negation*), and in this way universal. Furthermore, the other, by likewise affirming oneself *as other*, in effect *gives* our agency or identity back to us in exactly this same dynamic sense. In this way we come to *know* the other and ourselves in the mode of practical knowledge or familiarity, which knowledge can only be sustained and deepened through further such manifestations of recognition. We must, like the musician, keep practicing recognition, even (perhaps especially) with those whom we know best. This ideal expression of recognition can be thwarted or corrupted in several ways. Insisting on final, defined, or closed conceptions of identity, for example, denies dynamism. Holding oneself or another (again, individual or collective) as either fully known or radically unknowable in the sense of propositional knowledge again denies our dynamism, if only implicitly. Positing oneself, one's group(s), or another as wholly independent or in some sense distinct from the larger social whole denies our *relational* or social aspects, while positing oneself or others as utterly dependent on or determined by others denies our dynamic open-endedness. Taking one's status, or one's relation to others, as a given, or as a *fait accompli*, likewise denies our dynamism and ongoing relationality. In sum, we can say that corrupted recognition takes the form of disavowing or evading the fundamental dynamism and sociality in ourselves and others. It seeks to arrest, to define, to conclude, and to *grasp* in ways consistent with the politics of purity.

Since recognition is linked to freedom understood as self-development and self-expression, the corruption of recognition inhibits freedom, and may thus be understood as oppressive. This is precisely because the "self" at the heart of any account of freedom is only properly understood as dynamic and relational/social, which means knowing the self in order to develop and express it must be understood as a kind of practical knowledge enabled and developed only through ongoing interactions (encounters with difference) characterized by the kind of recognition that avoids exactly the disavowals or evasions of that dynamism and relationality which mark the corruption of recognition. One clear consequence of this approach is that freedom, like recognition, can never be properly understood as a static thing, as an end state, or as a *fait accompli*. Like recognition, freedom can be manifest in more or less rich and profound ways, but it cannot be fully realized, attained, or seized in any final way. As with any kind of practice or process, one can always improve upon it, and some improvements can even enable the revelation of previously unrecognized flaws or weaknesses, in the same way that certain levels of proficiency with an instrument make it possible to perceive new avenues for failure and for improvement that were previously beyond one's ability to even recognize. Ultimately, freedom is manifest only ever as an activity that is bound up directly with recognition, and as such requires ongoing exercise or practice in relation with others.

FREEDOM, FRICTION, AND THE SONIC

There is much more to be said here, but a full development can, I will argue, only unfold over the course of the later chapters in this text. Before moving on, however, there are two crucial points to make, the first of which helps to explain why such a full development will need to wait. Namely, this is because both the practice and the understanding of freedom must be *creolizing*. In my account of the ways in which corrupted recognition manifests above, one can observe a recurring theme of purity. It is expressed, for instance, in the collapse of identity into the either/or of universal and particular, identity and difference. Or, by way of another example, in the insistence on clear and fixed boundaries between self and other—in a closed and bounded (pure) identity. Even the tendency to see relations of recognition in all-or-nothing binary terms exhibits the politics of purity. This, in turn, is expressed in the related accounts of freedom as requiring purified internal/external distinctions, as I have already discussed in the first chapter. We must, therefore, think of freedom not only as an ongoing process, but because of its inherent relationality, as an ongoing process that does not merely tolerate but *requires* difference and distinction. This requirement should be understood not as a reifying process that simply collapses into complete particularity (for, as we have already seen, even to claim that everything is particular is to necessarily appeal to the universal) but, rather, in a way that maintains a differentiation (as itself an ongoing process) within a dynamic whole (which is more than the sum of its parts). However, just as it is mistaken to reduce all to difference, one should not make too much out of this appeal to the universal or whole, for likewise, to claim that all is universal is to necessarily appeal to the particular as that which comprises that whole.

Again, the emphasis on dynamism is crucial here, for the tendency to miss this point about identity and difference or universal and particular emerges out of the (sometimes only implicit) appeal to a static ontology. Thus, freedom must be thought of as creolizing insofar as it is the ongoing and dynamic relationship between diverse elements that shape and re-shape each other through this interaction, generating new particulars in the process. Interrupt that dynamism or collapse those relationships and you have the degradation or inhibition of freedom—that is, *oppression*. One way to see the significance of this endeavor is that it is a way to generate productive moments of what José Medina calls "epistemic friction." Epistemic friction occurs when our settled epistemic framework comes into contact with forms of resistance that disrupt or unsettle it, and when we respond appropriately to these moments of friction, it can help reveal the incompleteness or weaknesses in that framework, resulting in what Medina calls "meta-lucidity" (2013, 192). The cognitive moment of recognition, and consequently our capacity to manifest freedom, can thus be understood to be dependent on the generation of different sorts of epistemic friction in order to function well. The continual introduction of contrasting moments of difference that introduce a sort of productive friction or tension, in other words, makes possible the uncovering of the gaps in our knowledge (of the practical sort) about ourselves and our relations to others (think of the discussion of travel in the introduction). Coming to *recognize* these gaps is an essential part of the cultivation of new ways of developing and expressing freedom. Without this kind of productive friction, therefore, freedom is inhibited.

This, in turn, points toward the evasion or disavowal of these moments of friction generated by difference as one key aspect of oppression. This need for friction is a feature not only of the *praxis* of freedom, but also of the theorization of freedom itself (that is, the project of this text). Just as the practice of freedom requires productive friction arising from the encounter with difference, our *thinking about* freedom needs to undergo a continual and deliberate process of the cultivation of friction, which I frame in terms of "creolization." This cultivation will take the form of placing my unfolding articulation of the concept of freedom in dialog with different contexts and traditions in order to produce moments of friction that can draw out underdeveloped or misguided aspects. This is why it will be crucial in the coming chapters to take the initial articulation laid out so far and "travel" with it.

This means, additionally, that the Hegelian roots I have been cultivating so far are neither necessary nor sufficient for providing an adequate account of freedom. While I believe, to carry on this botanical metaphor, that they provide fertile conceptual ground for making some key moves in the development of the project, I take these Hegelian roots to be incomplete on their own, and I in no way take them to be the only way to make these key moves. As a result, it is necessary to not only to lay out a theory of freedom *as* a creolizing practice, but also to understand the very process of articulating that theory as itself a creolizing one. I must offer, in other words, a creolizing theory of freedom as creolizing. In the following chapters, I will explore the implications and limitations of the theory in dialog with figures from profoundly different contexts and traditions. The goal will be to generate precisely the sort of friction that Medina described, and to produce out of that friction a richer and more sophisticated theory of freedom. It will be a theory of freedom as itself necessarily creolizing that is at the same time produced through and as an ongoing creolizing process.

Lastly, before moving on to take up this project, I will emphasize that Medina's appeal to friction points toward a crucial way to begin this creolizing development of the theorization of freedom. Namely, it suggests a shift in the perceptual metaphors we employ in describing and theorizing dynamic processes like identity, recognition, and freedom. As Linda Alcoff, among others, has pointed out, the traditional appeal to visual metaphors has imposed significant limits on philosophy historically and in the present (2006, 188–92). While it is, it so happens, predicated upon a deep misunderstanding of how vision actually works, the metaphor nevertheless tends to impose a strict subject/object divide and treat objects of perception as at least in principle "captured" or "grasped" in static terms (like a still photograph, or a series of connected still photographs, as in film). That is, the viewer/observer is understood to be unconnected to the object of vision, which object can be accounted for as a static collection of visual data (properties). Again, any adequate understanding of how vision works will recognize that this is misleading, but it nevertheless exerts a powerful impact in the function of the visual *metaphor*. In a review of Medina's book (Monahan 2014), I argued that his appeal to *friction* already distinguishes his account from the visual metaphor in a significant way (though his appeal to "meta-*blindness*" remains quite traditional). This is because, as a physical phenomenon, friction is necessarily dynamic, taking place only over time, and it requires the interaction of the objects that generate it. It is thus dynamic and relational. Without change over time and the interaction of elements, there can be no friction.

What friction suggests, in fact, is the shift from vision to *sound* as a principle (though certainly not exclusive) metaphor, since one product of friction is the generation of sound. Unlike the standard appeal to vision (erroneous though it often is), sound is necessarily dynamic and relational. This is not only true, as I have already pointed out, of the moment of the generation of sound out of friction, but this dynamism and relationality is in fact a feature of every aspect of sound as a phenomenon. First, the result of the friction, whether the percussive slap of a drum head, or the lingering vibration of a bow on a cello string, even fingernails on a chalkboard, is a sound wave. Waves are physical phenomena that are again necessarily dynamic. We can represent a wave through a static image (a graph), but any actual wave must manifest itself over time, and even the graph, which represents *frequency*, includes time as a function of the ratio it represents. Sound exists as a dynamic *shifting* in the medium through which it travels, whether that medium is the Pacific Ocean or the air between your voice box and my eardrums. But even this appeal to the traveling of the wave is misleading, for the sound wave in fact exists only as this movement *of* the medium, there is no wave absent that movement. These dynamic processes of movement can, for example in a standing wave or a long and steady musical note, be more or less *stable*, but they remain nevertheless dynamic. This is a crucial appeal for the sonic metaphor, since we can more readily recognize the way in which sonic phenomena are, as "objects" of perception or knowledge, incapable of being "grasped" or "captured" in any static way. A sound is always a phenomenon in motion, and to halt that motion is to destroy it *as sound*. However, because it can admit of stability, as in a standing wave, it allows for a way to account for something like *identity* that does not simply collapse into an indistinct and constantly shifting blur. Identities, whether individual or collective, can thus be best captured by this sonic metaphor—they can be more or less stable and coherent, but they are always dynamic and ambiguous, and always in a constitutive relation (friction) with other sources and media around them and through which they exist as such.[5]

Furthermore, insofar as sound always involves a medium through which the wave, as a process, "travels," there is connection between the source of the sound, the medium, and the observer of the sound. It is, in other words, necessarily relational at a fundamental level. Features of the medium, such as its density, or its own dynamic behavior, alter the character of the sound waves, and thus of the phenomenon of sound. Likewise, the movement or even orientation of the source or the recipient of the sound wave alters its character (as with the Doppler effect, for instance). The overall phenomenon, therefore, can only be properly understood when all of these interactions or relations are taken into account, and even then, since all of these elements are dynamic, any account is necessarily provisional and incomplete. There is, therefore, a clear connection, mediated though it may be, between the observer and the observed in sound that is less apparent within the traditionally-understood visual metaphor. When I hear your voice, or a drum, there is a way in which, through the mediation of the medium of air, the source of the sound is literally touching me. We are thus connected in a way typically obscured when we focus on vision (though, again, this is predicated upon a standard misunderstanding of vision).

Finally, another advantage of sound is the way in which different waves can interact. A wave from source #1 and a wave from source #2, if they intersect, will affect each other, building upon each other ("constructive interference"), undermining each other, or even cancelling each other out ("destructive interference"). The related terms "resonance" and "dissonance," which refer to the ways in which different sounds "fit" together, appeal to a musical context, in which a combination of sounds "enhance" each other resonance, or "clash" and sound "harsh" in the case of dissonance. They are thus embedded in a normative framework (what "sounds good") that is always relative to a given musical tradition, and so are not strictly speaking the same thing as "constructive" or "destructive interference," which deal more directly with the physical properties of intersecting waves. In the case of freedom and recognition, however, the appeal to the concepts of resonance and dissonance can be useful, since, like musical expression, our social interactions take place in a larger normative framework that is often not explicitly acknowledged. It may thus come to pass that a given interaction may be thought of (metaphorically) as "dissonant" yet "constructive," where the larger framework *normalizes* destructive interference (and thus makes it appear as "resonant"). We might think of racist/colonial contexts as operating in exactly this way—where the undermining and destruction of the expressive capacities of others "sounds good," challenging that status quo will appear "dissonant" precisely because it is constructive. I will refer to such a context explicitly in this text as a manifestation of a kind of "white noise."

This notion of resonance and dissonance, construction and destruction, is conditioned further by the interaction of waves with different media, as well, which one can observe by the way in which certain notes can resonate with objects around them, causing sympathetic vibrations, for instance (as when a bass note is felt in one's chest, or rattles the windows of one's house). The sonic metaphor, in sum, offers a variety of resources whereby we can better represent the ways and means of dynamic processes than does the more traditional visual metaphor. To wit, the distinction between liberatory versus oppressive manifestations of recognition can be expressed through the distinction between resonance and dissonance. The kind of recognition that is conducive to freedom results in or expresses constructive interference, where different waves interact in a manner that is mutually enhancing (I shall describe it in the sixth chapter as "empowerment"). Corrupted recognition, therefore, is akin to destructive interference, where the waves interact in a way that diminishes them both. Bearing in mind that resonance/dissonance and constructive/destructive are not necessarily the same phenomenon, it is possible to describe moments of dissonance as not always problematic. Consider the moment in a song where a dissonant note is introduced, but then gradually resolved into an intricate harmony (a frequent move in a capella vocal music). The experience of that harmonious moment is made all the more powerful by virtue of its dissonant beginning. This can be a critical metaphor for creolizing processes and epistemic friction. Moments of dissonance can, and sometimes should, be actively sought out or generated, in order, through their gradual integration and the establishment of *resonant* relations, to bring about a more complex and expressive overall sound. In addition, since what is resonant or dissonant will depend on the normative context in which the interactions take place, what is in fact constructive may appear dissonant in a given context, just as what is destructive appear resonant. In a context that normalizes certain kinds of destructive interference as "resonant," it may be quite necessary to introduce "dissonance" as a way, ultimately, to alter that context. Thus, this sonic metaphor may accurately capture oppressive contexts as precisely ones where destructive interference is normed as resonant, revealing how dissonant expressions are often *necessary* for effective liberatory practice. The appeal to dissonance throughout the remainder of this text will elaborate this aspect of the sonic metaphor in the context of the theorization of freedom.

I can now draw this appeal to the sonic metaphor together to help illuminate the emerging account of freedom as creolizing. In order to resist the politics of purity, I am arguing, freedom must be *creolizing* in two senses. First, it must be understood to emerge out of and be expressed or made manifest through moments of what I am calling a kind of *productive friction*. It is a kind of movement, and above all, one that requires difference and distinction with which to interact in the ways that are conducive to and productive of that movement. That is, rather than a property one possesses or lacks, or a quiescent state one may achieve (or aim toward as an ideal), a creolizing freedom is found only in the ongoing processes of articulating, contesting, and re-articulating an agency or subjectivity that is characterized first and foremost by its dynamism and relationality. This is why the sonic metaphor and the appeal to friction is so crucial. Friction, and thus sound, is necessarily dynamic and relational—it requires the moving interaction of different elements over time. This in turn means that freedom is always ineluctably social. It is only ever manifest *with* others, because others are an essential element in the generation of this sort of friction. Finally, as a dynamic process, freedom can be manifest or expressed more or less deeply, but never completely realized or "achieved" in any final sense. Freedom is thus a creolizing process in the sense that it emerges through the bringing together of disparate elements in ways that are more than the sum of their parts, and that create the conditions for yet further moments of creolization.[6] The second sense in which freedom is creolizing involves the commitment to a proper theorization as emerging through, and even demanding, a creolizing *methodology*. That is, any adequate effort to account for freedom cannot mire itself in a single figure, tradition, or method, but must seek, through the productive encounter with different traditions and methods (productive friction that challenges the larger normative framework in which resonance and dissonance appear), to develop and change *as an account of freedom*. This is because the theorization of an ongoing and dynamic process of productive friction must, if it is to be remotely adequate to its subject, be itself an ongoing and dynamic process of productive friction.

These two senses of creolizing are, of course, interdependent and interrelated. On the one hand, how we are able to manifest and express freedom will be shaped and conditioned by the accounts and theories of freedom with which we operate. The practice of freedom will in this way be conditioned by our theories of freedom. Yet, on the other hand, the kinds of theories we are able to develop will be conditioned by the practices of freedom in which we engage. Our theories of freedom will be shaped by our practices. But this is not simply a kind of hermeneutic circle. For, given this interrelation, and given that freedom is an ongoing and dynamic process, then as freedom changes, so too must our theories, and deeper theories of this process will in turn foster a more robust process of change. No theory of freedom, therefore, can ever be complete, since the content of theorization must necessarily be involved in an ongoing process of becoming. To the extent that my efforts in this book are successful, therefore, it will stand only as a new beginning, not a final statement.

In the succeeding chapters, I will take on the challenge of further exploring and developing a creolizing theory of freedom in both of these senses, with a particular emphasis on the sonic metaphor for freedom. This will emerge by means precisely of placing the practice of freedom in different "media" and in relation or interaction with what may at first manifest as "dissonant" competing accounts. The aim here is not simply to "test" my theory, nor to demonstrate its universal applicability, but rather to develop and nurture a complex interactive process by seeking out moments of dissonance and working to bring them into a constructive relation that can appear as resonant. This process, I will stress, is not a matter of taking fixed and stable elements and simply revealing their compatibility (as is the standard approach in "comparative" philosophy), but it will involve a flexible and dynamic development on the part of the elements themselves in order to manifest these moments of resonance. It is, in other words, a creolizing process, the "result" of which is simply another process ready for further encounters with and development out of dissonance. This metaphor, along with the larger account of freedom, will thus emerge more fully only as I place it in productive friction.

Chapter 5

The (We-)Subject of Liberation

Freedom, I have argued so far, is an activity or process that emerges through the interaction of diverse elements in a larger (social/relational) medium. The ontology here is dynamic in every aspect—agents are processes interacting with other processes in ineluctably co-constitutive ways conditioned by an always both enabling and limiting set of larger contexts that are themselves ongoing processes constituted by and constitutive of the agents acting within and through them. I have appealed to a sonic metaphor to attempt to describe this complex interactive series of processes as forms of friction and sound. When the processes are empowering and enhancing, there is a kind of constructive or productive friction, and when they are disempowering and inhibiting, there is destructive friction. Freedom as creolizing actively seeks moments of productive friction that do not strive for the dissolution of difference (for that would eliminate the moment of friction) but rather pursue moments of "constructive interference" that appear, in a liberatory context, as instances of "resonance." Sometimes, importantly, the ultimate goal of resonance must begin by a cultivation of dissonance—a disruption of staid norms of interaction that generates a moment dissonance at first, but opens up the possibility of a new manifestation of resonance. This is because what appears to a given "ear" as "resonant" or "dissonant" is always a matter of the norms that condition our aural perception. When those norms of aural perception are oppressive, what are actually instances of destructive interference can "sound" resonant while upsurges of constructive interference appear dissonant. Liberatory praxis will therefore often generate dissonance in the act of introducing productive friction, but as that productive friction gets "uptake," it will begin to appear resonant precisely because it has altered the normative context of its perception as such.

Furthermore, I have argued that freedom in the theoretical register must itself unfold through a creolizing methodology. The attempt to account for (theorize) freedom demands productive friction every bit as much as (and because of) the dynamic processes it is striving to render intelligible. Shifting theoretical registers can produce moments of resonance in our collective understanding of freedom as such. Nevertheless, once again this collective understanding does not express, or even aim at, a single grand unified account or definition of freedom, but is rather oriented toward an ongoing process of articulating what are themselves ongoing processes. Consequently, our theories of freedom must seek different modes of expression (theorization) that yield moments of productive friction—they must in this way be processes of creolization.

The aim of this chapter is to advance this creolizing project (in both of the senses described above) by engaging with the work of Steve Biko and Gloria Anzaldúa. In particular, I want to focus on the way in which each of these thinkers and activists, in their unique contexts, is working to articulate a collective subject (we-subject) of liberation. This is an aspect that is largely left only implicit in recognition theory, but as Biko and Anzaldúa demonstrate, it is a necessary feature of the practice of freedom. In other words, Biko and Anzaldúa are each working to spell out a *we*-subject of their particular liberatory struggles, generating an important and, I will argue, productive contrast with the account of freedom emerging from my discussion of recognition theory so far. What they draw out are the ethnic, racial, gendered, and sexual obstacles to and avenues for the emergence of this we-subject. Because so much of the force of these features of social life are bound up in Euromodern practices of colonialism and enslavement, it should come as no surprise that European theorizations of freedom have either actively supported and legitimated oppressive relations, or at best expressed a studied disinterest in them. Hegel is certainly a paradigmatic exemplar of this, and so by bringing theories of Hegelian recognition into contact (friction) with Biko and Anzaldúa, the aim is to build upon and develop further this creolizing account of freedom and liberation. This is, therefore, a crucial moment of the creolization of freedom in both of my senses of the term. By engaging with the work of Biko and Anzaldúa, putting them into dialog (productive friction) with both the western tradition and with each other, I hope to further elaborate the creolizing theory of freedom that is the subject of this text. I will begin, however, with a brief turn to the work of Frantz Fanon, whose work serves as a productive way to introduce the problematic of the collective subject of liberation in a context shaped by coloniality.

FANON AND DECOLONIAL LIBERATION

Freedom is actional—it at once expresses and enacts a self-in-progress. Liberation, as the effort and struggle to better and more fully enact freedom, is likewise always a process of the liberation of *someone*. Thus, as I have argued throughout this text so far, in the effort to articulate a creolizing account of freedom we confront immediately the question of the *subject* of freedom and liberation. This is the reason why theorizations of freedom and liberation cannot avoid questions of ontology. Given that the account offered here has emphasized freedom as a kind of dynamic movement (becoming), then we can think of oppression as the effort to confine, control, or even halt altogether that *movement* of selves-in-progress. If freedom is motion, then oppression seeks stasis. Thus, liberation is not simply a matter of bringing a pre-given subject into a new condition or state, but involves rather the effort to create (or recreate) the subject of liberation in the very struggle for liberation itself. Furthermore, this subject, whether individual or collective, is always ineluctably social—it is always relational. This is so not only because the view I am articulating is one in which all subjectivity is necessarily social and relational (a metaphysical claim), but also because both the operation of oppression and any corresponding movements for liberation from oppression are never simply individual projects. One is not oppressed *qua* individual (Young 1990, 40) nor does one's liberatory struggle seek only to liberate oneself (though this can be an important aspect or moment). Instead, *we* are oppressed qua member of our group membership(s), and must struggle for *our* liberation. This in turn means that this sense in which liberation involves the (re)generation of the subject (individual and collective) in the act of resistance and struggle is the *constitution* of both the individual and collective subject of liberation (recognizing that the individual/collective distinction is often blurry, at best). In sum, we do not take a prior subject and liberate them but rather create the subject of liberation as we engage in the activity of resisting our collective oppression.

This is why a creolizing theory of liberation must emphasize the need for the oppressed to take an active role in their liberation. Fanon makes this point quite clearly in his discussion of Hegel in *Black Skin, White Masks* (2008). To receive "liberation" from someone else (from the "outside") is to remain in a passive relation to oneself and one's world, and thus to remain in a significant way subordinate to and dependent upon the beneficent donor of one's so-called freedom. Above all, it is clear that such a receipt of freedom as a kind of largesse on the part of one's oppressors involves no *movement* in the relevant sense. Because liberation, as I have been emphasizing, involves the constitution of a liberatory subject-in-progress, any genuine liberation therefore demands that one assume responsibility for oneself precisely as this open-ended and ongoing process, which in turn requires active participation in the struggle to resist those forces that seek to constrain and curb that process. Liberation is in effect the creation of ourselves anew. This is what Fanon means when he points out that, if one doesn't participate in one's own liberation, one may well shift "from one way of life to another, but not from one life to another" (2008, 195). The move "from one life to another" is precisely the move from a colonized/oppressed subjectivity to a liberatory one, while the shift in "way of life" preserves the initial oppressed subjectivity while merely altering the conditions of its ongoing impoverishment.

Of course, this moment in Fanon's text occurs in his discussion of Hegelian recognition, and it is worth dwelling on this relation both to better grasp Fanon's point, and to further illuminate aspects of my prior discussion of recognition and freedom. The focus in Fanon's brief discussion of recognition and Hegel, it should be noted, is on *reciprocity*. Unlike so many of the interpretations of Hegel that I criticized earlier, Fanon makes it clear that recognition is not about a donor and a recipient, but rather a mutual and reciprocal encounter. "There is at the basis of Hegelian dialectic an absolute reciprocity that must be highlighted," Fanon writes early in this section of his text (2008, 191). To be sure, he is offering a critique of Hegel's dialectic insofar as it is Eurocentric (though ostensibly universal and race-blind), as when he points out that unlike in Hegel's *Phenomenology* account, the colonial masters seek not recognition but *work* from their slaves (195n). Yet in foregrounding reciprocity, Fanon's reading of recognition is very much in keeping with the account I have been advocating in this book.

In particular, Fanon is emphasizing the way in which, by truly recognizing another *as an agent*, one is recognizing precisely the open-ended and dynamic process of becoming that defies being pinned-down and defined. Consider the following passage, where Fanon is interpreting the significance of the "struggle to the death" in Hegel's account: "I ask that I be taken into consideration on the basis of my desire. I am not only here-now, locked in thinghood [*enfermé dans la choséité*]. I desire somewhere else and something else. I demand that an account be taken [*qu'on tienne compte*] of my contradictory activity [*activité négatrice*] insofar as I pursue something other than life, insofar as I am fighting for the birth of a human world, in other words, a world of reciprocal recognitions" (193).

What Fanon is emphasizing here is precisely the account of subject-as-process that I have argued is key to a proper reading of Hegelian recognition. Recognition does not seek to "enclose" (*enfermé*) the self. One is not struggling to have a fixed and stable definition or identity properly cognized or "grasped" by the other. Rather, eschewing the model of propositional knowledge, Fanon asks that we "take into account" (*qu'on tienne compte*) or take seriously not who or what I *am*, but instead my "negating activity" (*activité négatrice*), which we can see from my earlier discussion is an explicitly Hegelian concept. In other words, Fanon is emphasizing the subject as an ongoing and open-ended dynamic process of becoming-in-relation with others. The reciprocity that Fanon draws out is a relation between "negating activities," and his claim is that colonialism and racism obscure, disavow, and "enclose" this activity—and what is "enclosure" but a restriction of *movement*. This notion of movement and enclosure, I would suggest, is at the heart of Fanon's appeals to *alienation* and *disalienation* throughout his corpus.

Alienation, in my reading of Fanon's work, is not to be understood as the estrangement from some primordial or authentic self or identity on the model of a fixed and static substance (thinghood). Nor is disalienation the return to or revelation of such a self or identity. What we see throughout Fanon's corpus, from *Black Skin, White Masks*, to his writings on clinical practice, and all of his writings on the revolution in Algeria up to and including *Wretched of the Earth*, is a call for the generation of the conditions for a genuine reciprocity in precisely the dynamic sense characteristic of freedom as creolizing. A "world of reciprocal recognitions" requires the generation of *relations* between agents understood as open-ended processes of individual and collective self-generation. This foregrounds, in other words, what I have described as a central theme of recognition—that our individual agency comes to being (as a dynamic process) only in and through our relations with others. When any of us, either as self or as other, seeks "enclosure" in ready-made, fixed, and stable identities, that is a kind of alienation in the form of "thingification" and oppression.

At the same time, however, Fanon's demand that his "negating activity" be "taken into account" is not an appeal to a pure and abstract negativity. As so much of his work makes clear, the proper response to colonial alienation is not the stripping away all history, context and content. Fanon's consistent focus on context and lived experience, on the ways and means whereby we are able to exercise our "negating activity" helps to illustrate a central sense in which his work contributes to a creolizing account of freedom. While this negating activity is clearly significant and must be taken into account, understanding freedom or the self in terms of *pure* negativity is likewise a form of alienation very much akin to the understanding of sovereignty at the heart of Markell's critique of Hegel (and, as we shall see in the next chapter, an aspect of Sartrean *bad faith*). We see illustrated in this diagnosis the dangers of a commitment to purity. Pure content absent negation leads to enclosure or thingification, while pure negativity results in forms of sovereignty. The question that emerges at this point is thus how best to understand the kind of content that is consistent with Fanonian *disalienation*. Or, put differently, how do we articulate an account of the proper *subject* of a creolizing freedom, especially when we take into account the kind of collective struggle for liberation appropriate to the colonial context?

Steve Biko, likewise, saw this problematic clearly, and has much to contribute to the creolization of freedom. Like Fanon, Biko stresses the need for the oppressed to take an active role in their liberation, and to articulate an identity through that active struggle that does not collapse into a static and substantive enclosure of the self. For the Fanon of *Wretched of the Earth*, this took the form of an emergent "national consciousness" (1963 197–205),[1] while for Biko, the cultivation of a we-subject of liberation was a matter of Black consciousness. As Biko describes it, Black consciousness makes explicit the need to re-invent the liberatory subject as an integral part of the struggle itself. Insofar as oppression targets individuals *qua* members of oppressed groups, the emergent subject of liberation must likewise be a collective or social subject. Black consciousness is thus directed toward the cultivation of an actional collective *Black* subjectivity out of the passive and alienated *thinghood* imposed (though never completely successfully) by the antiblack racism of apartheid South Africa. In an effort to better understand the subject of liberation within a creolizing context, let us therefore turn to a more in-depth analysis of Biko's project.

BIKO AND THE PITFALLS OF IDENTITY

Steve Biko first rose to prominence as an anti-apartheid activist while a medical student at the University of Natal. In 1967, Biko was an active member of the National Union of South African Students (NUSAS), a white-dominated student organization dedicated to nonviolent resistance to apartheid in the mode of the US struggle for civil rights. That year a national NUSAS conference was held at Rhodes University in what was then called Grahamstown (now Makhanda), and Biko attended as a delegate. Apartheid norms required all nonwhites, including Biko and the (relatively few) other nonwhite delegates, to sleep outside of Grahamstown proper. Biko and his fellow nonwhite delegates were unsuccessful in their efforts to persuade their white colleagues to join them in their dormitory outside of Grahamstown in solidarity. In response to this act of cowardice, the Black delegates staged a walkout that ultimately led to the formation of the South African Students' Organization (SASO) a year later (Mangcu 2012, 17). SASO, of which Biko was a founding member and key theorist, emerged as a powerful alternative to the white-dominated NUSAS, and Biko was elected its first president.

In a 1969 SASO presidential address Biko delivered at the institution then known as the University of Natal (now part of the University of KwaZulu-Natal), he enumerated six aims of SASO under his leadership. The third, fourth, and sixth goals pertain directly to the subject of collective identity and liberation that is the focus of this chapter, and so I will quote them here in their entirety.

3. To heighten the degree of contact not only amongst the nonwhite students but also amongst these and the rest of the South African student population, to make the non-white students accepted on their own terms as an integral part of the South African student community.
4. To establish a solid identity amongst the non-white students and to ensure that these students are always treated with the dignity and respect they deserve.
6. To boost up the morale of the non-white students, to heighten their own confidence in themselves and to contribute largely to the direction of thought taken by the various institutions on social, political and other current topics. (Biko 2012, 4–5)

Evident in these three goals is a focus on and attention to the cultivation of a collective sense of identity and purpose among nonwhite students involved in the decades-long struggle against apartheid. There is an overarching goal of forming a "solid" identity amongst nonwhite students as a distinct collective entitled to dignity and respect and able to carry themselves with confidence in their shared struggle. This overarching goal came to be called "Black Consciousness." Ultimately, Black Consciousness, as a theory and a movement, became the primary vehicle through which SASO pursued its goals.

To be sure, Biko's emphasis on taking an active role in the struggle against racist oppression was in part pragmatic. He writes:

> We must learn to accept that no group, however, benevolent, can ever hand power to the vanquished on a plate.... As long as we go to Whitey begging cap in hand for our own emancipation, we are giving him further sanction to continue with his racist and oppressive system. We must realize that our situation is not a mistake on the part of whites but a deliberate act, and that no amount of moral lecturing will persuade the white man to "correct" the situation.... This is where the SASO message and cry "Black man, you are on your own!" becomes relevant. (2012, 100)

For Biko, the need for active struggle is in part an echo of Frederick Douglass's recognition that "power concedes nothing without a demand" (1857). Patience and moral suasion are unlikely to yield results absent real struggle. It is equally, however, linked to Biko's observation that "the most potent weapon in the hands of the oppressor is the mind of the oppressed" (Biko 2012, 101–2). Setting aside questions of political pragmatics, in other words, Biko is further saying that without taking an active role in one's liberation, and thus taking responsibility for the ongoing articulation and generation of a liberatory *subject*, one's consciousness remains a weapon in the hands of one's oppressors. This kind of "mental colonization" is in a sense what Anibal Quijano referred to as *coloniality*, and is at the heart of the ongoing discourse of "decolonial" thought (2007). We can also see it as an echo of Fanon's emphasis on the need for the colonized to play an active role in their liberation (2008, 194–95). Biko's larger project of Black Consciousness can, as a result, be read as an effort to engage in precisely this sort of decolonization of the mind of the oppressed, and is articulated as the formation and expression of a liberatory subject.

It follows that, for Biko, there is a clear dialectical relationship between the pragmatic or concrete aspects of these goals on the one hand, and the more abstract or theoretical aspects on the other. The attempt to understand lived reality in order to better confront and improve it, especially when that reality is one that consistently undermines and devalues one's agency, necessitates the shaping of new conceptual tools (theories and concepts) for the purpose not only of altering that world, but of altering the very *self* confronting that world. In other words, one must generate the tools that enable one to open up the cracks in a crumbling and decadent lived reality, creating spaces and fissures where new possibilities, new life, and ultimately a new world can begin to emerge. These new tools, of course, are seldom, if ever, generated *ex nihilo*, but rather one must take up whatever resources are at hand in order to repurpose and reshape them. In Biko's case, both the concepts "Black" and "Consciousness" emerge as precisely such reshaped and repurposed tools, wrenched from the hands of the masters and turned not simply toward destruction or dismantling, but to the "building [of one's] own houses of thought" (Gordon and Gordon 2006, ix).

The development and exercise of Black Consciousness, therefore, must be understood as precisely the sort of effort to generate a collective liberatory self that is the focus of this chapter. In the words of Mabogo Percy More, Black Consciousness means "to choose to be Black in the face of antiblack racism" (More 2008, 62), and More's formulation is particularly evocative, appealing as it does to *choice*, and centering antiblack racism. But a clear question emerges at this point. If part of the aim is to resist the static categories of Being imposed by racist oppression and to thereby generate a dynamic and active subjectivity, then what does it even mean to "*be* Black" in this sense at all, let alone as a choice? Surely Blackness is a product of antiblack racism, and has at its center the effort to define and constrain the subjects it purports to describe in a fixed and given sub-human status. Wouldn't, therefore, the alleged choice to "be Black" necessarily contradict the effort to emphasize dynamism? Wouldn't Black Consciousness, in other words, remain oppressive in some sense despite its stated liberatory aims?

These questions demand a dialectical response on Biko's part. As an action, the choice to cultivate and express Black consciousness must emerge from a particular set of conditions and circumstances. For SASO, those circumstances were the apartheid regime. As Biko wrote for a SASO leadership training course, "We have in our policy manifesto defined Blacks as those who are by law or tradition politically, economically and socially discriminated against as a group in the South African society and identifying themselves as a unit in the struggle toward the realization of their aspirations" (Biko 2012, 52). Blackness is here described as a kind of position or condition within the apartheid milieu, but even here, Biko is positing an account that diverges from the mere passive acceptance of one's position within an oppressive regime. First, he is in fact casting a wider net than the standard account of blackness within the South Africa of his day would allow. Above all, SASO was keen to offer a means to draw together the disparate nonwhite elements of South African society under apartheid—the "Black," certainly, but also the "Coloured" and the "Indian."[2] As is typical with settler-colonial racist regimes, especially while, as in South Africa, the dominant group is in the numerical minority, "divide and rule" was very much the order of the day. Slight material and juridical advantages were afforded the Coloured and Indian groups over and against the Black, while at the same time the division of the Black population into various ethnic homelands or "bantustans" provided a way to further divide and place into imposed competition (and political as well as geographical isolation) the vast majority of the populace (Welsh 2000, 449–50).[3] By offering an account here in which Blackness entails those "discriminated against in South African society," Biko is already implicitly counting *as Black* the Coloured and the Indian, though not, as we shall see below, in a straightforward way.

Secondly, Biko's reference to "identifying themselves as a unit in the struggle" already points toward the actional, and his appeal to "their aspirations" is a gesture toward collective and shared agency.[4] This second point becomes the principle focus of his training course. He goes on to claim that "being Black is not a matter of pigmentation—being Black is a reflection of a mental attitude" (Biko 2012, 52), and in this way a fissure is opened in the apartheid Lifeworld through which the possibility of unity across the differences and divisions it imposes can emerge. Thus, at a very immediate and practical level, Black Consciousness is a response not only to the "divide and rule" tactics of apartheid South Africa, but also a call to affirm the struggle against apartheid and cultivate a collective agency built around shared aspirations and goals. Black Consciousness offers a way to articulate a shared (collective) identity as *Black*, but this identity is linked not simply to an imposed category of oppression that one passively receives but, rather, to a "mental attitude" that one actively cultivates.

In order to begin to grasp what Biko means by this "mental attitude," it is important to explore the distinction he draws between the *Black* and the *nonwhite*. "If one's aspiration is *whiteness*," Biko tells us in that same training course, "but his pigmentation makes attainment of this impossible, then that person is a nonwhite" (2012, 52). To be nonwhite (as opposed to or distinct from *Black*), therefore, meant to be barred from full personhood by the white-supremacist regime, yet continuing to work within and abide by the strictures of that regime. Blackness, alternatively, came to indicate a deliberate (i.e., conscious) identification with that which white supremacy holds in the deepest contempt—*the Black*—precisely as a way of resisting that regime. Significantly for Biko, this resistance was both external or concrete—expressed through acts of political protest and activism directed toward undermining and ultimately destroying the apartheid regime, and it was also internal or mental/spiritual—directed toward freeing the *mind* of the oppressed, which as we know Biko understood to be a powerful weapon when in the metaphorical hands of the oppressor. Nonwhites were thus those who remained either passively quiescent or actively aligned with the apartheid regime (and thus with *whiteness*). In the analysis of Black Consciousness, the "aspiration" or *telos* of the nonwhite remains, to a greater or lesser extent, *whiteness*. The models of success, of power, of "civilization," of culture, and of religious salvation, in other words, all remained profoundly white, and the "nonwhite" subject strives in vain toward this impossible ideal. As Biko put the point in 1976 while testifying in the trial of SASO leaders, "you tend to begin to feel that there is something incomplete in your humanity, and that completeness goes with whiteness" (Biko 2012, 111). This is what More meant in his reference to an "antiblack world," and it is this fundamentally white *telos* that Black Consciousness ultimately aims to disrupt both in its specific "mental attitude," and it is political praxis directed toward dismantling apartheid. Black consciousness, a consciousness *intending* (in the phenomenological sense) and enacting Blackness, disrupts the "proper" functioning of the antiblack world, a world which mandates a collective orientation *away* from Blackness.

The identification as and with *Black* is thus understood by Biko to be a profound disruption of the governing normative telos of white supremacy generally, and apartheid in particular. In this way, Black Consciousness emerges as a deliberate evocation of *dissonance* meant to disrupt a regime in which the disempowerment (destructive interference) of nonwhites "appears" (oppressively) as resonance. Lewis Gordon captures this aspect of Black Consciousness as follows:

> Coloured, Asian, and brown function as degrees of whiteness and blackness. The slipperiness of these categories means a system of unceasing conflict the subtext of which is a teleological whiteness. Biko's notion of Black Consciousness demands shifting such a telos. (Gordon 2008a, 85)

By actively and explicitly avowing and affirming Blackness, one is organizing and articulating a collective sense of self as that against which the apartheid world is primarily organized (what I will refer to below as "white noise"), and in this way striking directly at its normative core. Whiteness posits itself as the *pure* realization of the human, denying that there is any perspective outside of whiteness capable of offering, following Fanon, any "ontological resistance" to the white point of view (Fanon 2008, 90). Thus, Black Consciousness, as an assertion of a mode of *consciousness* that affirms Blackness, explodes that purity (as a moment of dissonance) precisely by offering a Black *perspective* on the world. In the existential phenomenological framework that both Fanon and Biko inhabit, a Black perspective *on whiteness* is inherently threatening to the white *telos*, since such a perspective posits a kind of reciprocity (the power of which Fanon saw clearly, as we have already noted) between Black and white that the bad faith structure of whiteness cannot abide. A *Black perspective*, especially a Black perspective on whiteness, is thus always understood within a white *telos* to be an illicit appearance (cf. Gordon 2022, 28–30).

What this means ultimately is that Black Consciousness aims at shifting whiteness from its position as the *pure* human, and its corresponding false universal (as *the* human), by generating the conditions in which reciprocity, and thus a more genuine universal, becomes possible.[5] In an anti-Black world, because whiteness functions as the pure form of the human and the *telos* of human consciousness, nonwhite people (in the general sense, not in Biko's more technical sense) come to occupy what Fanon referred to as the "zone of nonbeing" (Fanon 2008, xii), beneath the level of reciprocal self/other relations reserved for genuinely human (that is, *white*) relations. Functioning as neither-self-nor-other, the Black subject's presence *as a subject* is disavowed (in bad faith) by white subjectivity (and the antiblack world it constitutes), and thus the enactment of Black Consciousness comes to function as a radical disruption of this anti-Black order of things. It is, as Gordon puts the point, "an effort to achieve Otherness," and "enter the realm, in other words, where ethical [i.e., reciprocal] relations are forged" (Gordon 2000, 85). Again, this operates both at the level of disrupting the *internalized* valorization of whiteness, and by virtue of its practical enactment, through challenging the institutional and symbolic mechanisms that legitimize and reinforce this larger white *telos* at the center of the antiblack *world*.

Understood in this way, Black Consciousness is a call for the identification with and of Blackness as a profound disruption of what I have been describing as the white *telos* as it operates both in one's own sense of self and in one's world (each of which, recall, conditions and is conditioned by the other). It is a call for the constitution of a collective sense of agency and identity, and a fervent call to action and larger responsibility. As Biko wrote:

> The first step therefore is to make the black man come to himself; to pump back life into his empty shell; to infuse him with pride and dignity, to remind him of his complicity in the crime of allowing himself to be misused and therefore letting evil reign supreme in the country of his birth. This is what we mean by an inward-looking process. This is the definition of "Black Consciousness." (Biko 2012, 31)

What is striking about this passage is the way in which Biko links pride, dignity, and "coming to oneself" with a confrontation with complicity in one's own oppression. Coming to oneself and taking responsibility for oneself, are therefore clearly linked in the concept of Black Consciousness as Biko understands it, and this is at the core of its synthesis of the internal and the external, of theory and praxis. For Biko, affirming Blackness as a reclamation of one's humanity in the face of dehumanizing anti-Black oppression means the constitution and articulation of a collective sense of self, which in turn entails the affirmation of one's agency and responsibility both by engaging in the struggle against that oppression, and in acknowledging one's responsibility for past (and ongoing) complicity. The "inward-looking process" is thus necessarily in a dialectical unfolding with what is "outward," insofar as one's sense of self is bound up constitutively with one's intersubjective lifeworld, and the genuine affirmation of one's *Black* agency in the face of an anti-Black world must, if it is to indeed be genuine, actively (and necessarily *externally*) oppose its disavowal and erasure in that lifeworld. It must, in short, actively participate in the *social* reconstitution of the anti-Black world into a more genuinely reciprocal, and thus, more truly universal and human, lifeworld.

One immediate feature of this understanding of Black Consciousness is that it is a kind of orientation first and foremost, rather than a factor purely of ancestry or pigmentation. The appeal to "orientation" here is, again, indebted to the work of Sara Ahmed, and meant to emphasize the sense in which Black Consciousness is a kind of turning *toward* Blackness as a means of turning *away* from whiteness as the ultimate *telos*. To reject this white telos and its false universality and orient one's consciousness toward Blackness is at the heart of Black Consciousness, and so having dark skin not a sufficient condition. "According to the Black Consciousness philosophy," as M. J. Oshadi Mangena puts the point, "skin pigmentation was neither the primary nor the decisive factor in the definition of blackness" (2008, 253–54). Consciousness is, first and foremost, an activity, and the Blackness of *Black* Consciousness is not a property or feature, but an orientation or mode—it is a *way* of consciousness, not a *kind* of consciousness. It is, as More asserts, "black solidarity in the face of subjugation and domination" (2008, 56). As a mode of Freirian *conscientization* (More 2017, 264–68; Magaziner 2010, 125), which can be understood as a kind of "consciousness-raising" or "coming-to-consciousness," it is a bringing-into-existence of a collective Black agency (a we-subject) out of those conditions of subjugation and domination that characterize the apartheid milieu, and the anti-Black world in general. The anti-Black world posits the existence of the Black as always already illicit, and Black Consciousness, in affirming the legitimacy of Black collective agency oriented toward liberation, ultimately functions in a way that "undermines the legitimacy of whiteness" (Gordon 2008a, 85).

Put differently, if the anti-Black world creates conditions in which, as Fanon puts the point, "there is one destiny. . . . And it is white" (Fanon 2012, xiv), Black Consciousness is the rejection of this *telos* and the valorization of Black existence. Existing Blackly, however, is different from *being* Black, which is at the heart of Biko's distinction between *Black* and *nonwhite* referenced above. The nonwhite preserves the white *telos* of the anti-Black world by occupying their Blackness as a mode of being defined by its distance from, or essential lack of, whiteness as the defining feature of the (pure) human. However, to *exist* in the relevant sense is to act or be in motion—it is a mode of dynamic becoming as opposed to the stasis of being. Black Consciousness, therefore, is the name given to a shared or intersubjective intention, against the white imperative of the apartheid milieu, to bring into existence a collective Black identity as precisely this mode of dynamic existence in the face the ongoing disavowal of that existence understood in this dynamic sense. It evokes the idea of the "standing wave" discussed in chapter 4—it is relatively stable, yet still a kind of motion and relation of moving parts.

For whites, the situation is, as one would expect, quite different. While dark skin is, as Mangena pointed out, not the "decisive factor" in the emerging Black identity, it is not simply reducible to a mindset, either. Recall that Biko linked the "first step" of Black Consciousness to and awareness of "complicity in the crime of allowing himself to be misused" (2012, 31). For the white South African (or indeed the white visitor to South Africa) there is no such misuse. For the white South African, the "subjugation and domination" in the face of which "Black solidarity" can be organized is not present (More 2008, 56). It is thus a necessary condition for Black Consciousness that one be positioned as a fundamental *lack* with respect to the "teleological whiteness" of the apartheid context. This is a condition shared by, in that context, "Black," "Coloured," and "Indian" people, but not by whites. Of course, Biko's account of the "nonwhite" as contrasted with (conscious) Blackness makes clear that dark skin is certainly not sufficient for Black Consciousness, but it is necessary. Whites, Biko wrote in 1971, are not "allowed to enjoy privilege only when they declare their solidarity with the ruling party" (2012, 71). Even the most sincerely committed and well-meaning white must therefore face "the fundamental fact that total identification with an oppressed group in a system that *forces* one group to enjoy privilege and to live on the sweat of another, is impossible" (71, emphasis mine). According to Biko, these sincere whites, rather than seeking to participate in the collective liberatory identity that is Black Consciousness, "must realize that they themselves are oppressed, and that they must fight for their own freedom and not that of the nebulous 'they' with whom they can hardly claim identification" (72).

Biko is here making clear that white supremacy harms and oppresses even its beneficiaries, but the path to liberation for the beneficiaries and the victims is simply not the same. Echoing a recurring Fanonian theme, Biko points out that Black and white subjects in an anti-Black world are psychically marked by inferiority and superiority complexes respectively, and the strategies for overcoming those complexes must be different (70). There is, in effect, a default "white consciousness," and Black Consciousness is at once a response to it and a product of it, in true dialectic fashion (More 2008, 56). It is a response in that, as a moment of *conscientization*, Black Consciousness is the expression and affirmation of Black agency at the individual and collective levels (stressing the necessary connection of the individual and social). It is a product in that the denial of such agency in the first place is a condition for the possibility of that process of conscientization (but not that, the possibility of the moment of conscientization makes clear that the "denial" of agency was only ever a doxastic commitment, not an accomplished fact). Drawing deeply on the phenomenological tradition, More emphasizes that this is a function of grappling with *embodied* consciousness, where Blackness is a contingent feature that enables the original context of oppression (and the resulting inferiority complex), and thus must serve as the situation or "facticity" from and through which the liberatory consciousness must develop and express itself (More 2017, 55). Whites, too, are positioned by their embodiment, but rather as the dominant *norm* within the anti-Black world ("forced" to enjoy privilege, as Biko put the point), and the resulting superiority complex renders any total "identification" with the oppressed impossible. What this means for whites is not the focus of this work, so I will set the question aside for now. It is worth noting, however, that Biko's long-term aim remains, like Fanon's, deeply *humanistic*. Evoking dialectical thinking, Biko points toward an *aufhebung* of the thesis of white supremacy and the antithesis of Black Consciousness as "a true humanity where power politics will have no place" (2012, 99).

The implications and perils of this humanistic turn will be the focus of the next chapter. At this point, I want to continue the investigation into the collective subject of liberation by turning to the work of Gloria Anzaldúa, before concluding with an analysis of the outcome of the "productive friction" brought about via the engagement with and between these two thinkers.

IDENTITY AND AGENCY IN ANZALDÚA

Gloria Anzaldúa's writing, throughout her works, and regardless of whether she was producing fiction, or poetry, or theoretical essays, almost always engages in some form or fashion with questions of identity. These questions are often profoundly personal, for, as AnaLouise Keating notes in her introduction to *The Gloria Anzaldúa Reader*, Anzaldúa's work "performs radical acts of self-excavation" in which she consistently works "to put herself 'on the line' and strive for an extreme degree of 'nakedness'" (Keating 2009, 1). Yet Anzaldúa is never self-absorbed or solipsistic. She describes herself as a "feminist visionary spiritual activist poet-philosopher fiction writer" (quoted in Keating 2009, 3), and as an *activist*, her explorations of identity are also always concerned with questions of solidarity and coalition, of recognition, and, I will argue here, of liberation.[6] This is in large part because, as Andrea Pitts has observed, Anzaldúa articulates a "relational ontology" that "relies on the continuously transforming relationships that give rise to conceptions of stability and fixity," in contrast to the kind of substance ontology that has been a focus on criticism in this book, and which "considers the qualities of matter to inhere within a pregiven substrate" (Pitts 2021, 19). This leads Pitts to argue persuasively that Anzaldúa "rejected models of agency that relied on *insularity*, *isolationism*, *individualism*, and *imperialism*, and opted instead for an agential model of shared interaction, distribution, interdependency, and coalition" (29). In other words, Anzaldúa's various reflections on identity throughout her writings touch upon the very questions of collective identity that are the focus of this chapter. After a brief account of her earlier work, I will focus on some of the key concepts that emerge in Anzaldúa's later writings, as I believe they shed the most productive light on the account of liberation that is the focus of this book.

Anzaldúa opens her monumental *Borderlands/La Frontera* with an account of the titular "borderlands" of the Rio Grande Valley in Texas, and of her own place (and lack thereof) in it. "The US—Mexican border," she tells us, "*es una herida abierta* [an open wound] where the Third World grates against the first and bleeds" (2007, 25). And even as the borderlands do not "fit" into either the US or into Mexico easily, Anzaldúa herself does not fit comfortably into her natal community. In the autobiographical (*autohistoria*) essay *La Prieta*, written before the publication of *Borderlands/La Frontera*, she offers a candid glimpse of, in María Lugones' words, "the self in between, . . . a self that is intimately terrorized by two different worlds of sense, the Anglo world and the traditional Mexican world" (Lugones 2003, 113). Living on the margins of a marginalized community, Anzaldúa places herself among the *atravesados*, "the squint-eyed, the perverse, the queer, the troublesome, the mongrel, the mulato, the half-breed, the half dead; in short, those who cross over, pass over, or go through the confines of the 'normal'" (Anzaldúa 2007, 25).[7] As one who crosses over the confines of the normal in a community that itself already exists as an open wound, Anzaldúa struggles to generate an identity that draws together disparate elements and tensions. She refers to this effort as an act of "kneading" (*amasamiento*) and a kind of "spiritual *mestizaje*" (103). As Lugones puts the point: "She resists intimate terrorism by taking stock of the limits of these two worlds and inhabiting the in-between world squarely: in germination toward becoming the new mestiza" (2003, 113–14). Anzaldúa's move here in terms of the question of identity is thus to affirm this status as a crosser of boundaries, as one who transgresses the norms of (the politics of) purity, articulating this ever-emerging in-between identity as the "new *mestiza*."

The final chapter of *Borderlands/La Frontera*, like all the chapters in the book, has a bilingual chapter title: *La conciencia de la mestiza*/Towards a New Consciousness. In that final chapter, Anzaldúa appeals to the concept of *nepantla*, which is a Nahuatl word meaning "in the middle," and can be understood to connote both a kind of violent collision, and a kind of "abundant reciprocity" where this middle generates a both/and rather than a zero-sum either/or (Pitts 2021, 42).[8] Out of a condition of "mental nepantlism," Anzaldúa writes, "*la mestiza* is a product of the transfer of the cultural and spiritual values of one group to another" (2007, 100). Because the cultures we inhabit shape our perception of reality, when there is this friction (an open wound) between conflicting cultures, the result is a "cultural collision" (*un choque*) and an "inner war" brought about by "the coming together of two self-consistent but habitually incompatible frames of reference" (100). This often-brutal *choque* sets the conditions that shape the development *la mestiza* as, in effect, conditions of "attack" and "threat" that demand a response (100). Anzaldua is clear, however, that a simple negation or "counterstance," is not a sufficient response, since it "locks one into a duel of oppressor and oppressed," where "both are reduced to a common denominator of violence" (100). Such a "counterstance" is at best a "step towards liberation," but it is not sufficient on its own (100). The division or border between oppressor and oppressed must either be "healed so that we are on both shores at once," or one must "disengage from the dominant culture, write it off altogether as a lost cause, and cross the border into a wholly new and separate territory" (100–101). Anzaldúa's point here is that this condition of *nepantla* generates real and varied forms of trauma (material/physiological and spiritual/psychological), and while a strong *reaction* may be a significant first step, true liberation demands a commitment to *action*, which in turn requires a new critical *consciousness* in the form of *la conciencia de la mestiza*.

La mestiza thus emerges in the first instance as a product of the collision of cultures or worlds, and Anzaldúa's call for a *mestiza* consciousness emphasizes a turn toward action as opposed to reaction, a toleration of ambiguity and contradiction, and ultimately a "continual creative *motion* that keeps breaking down the unitary aspect of each new paradigm (Anzaldúa 2007, 102, emphasis mine). It is important to note that, though she does appeal to José Vasconcelos's discussion of *mestizaje* at the opening of the chapter on *mestiza* consciousness, Anzaldua's understanding is at once more particular and more expansive than the accounts of *mestizaje* dominant in much of Latin American history. Her account is, as Mariana Ortega has observed, "anchored in her lived experience as a Chicana living on the US—Mexico border" (Ortega 2016, 25). It is in this way an account of a specific border, and a specific embodied history of cultural collision (a specific and unique *choque*). At the same time, the call for a toleration of ambiguity and contradiction, for resisting and challenging dualisms, and to act in a way that is *healing*, all speaks to widely-shared experiences and goals. The borders, divisions, and collisions, in other words, are at once quite specific accounts of particular experiences, and broadly applicable ideas capable of theoretically illuminating a wide array of disparate phenomena and experiences. There are important criticisms to be raised here, and Pitts, for example, offers an exemplary and sensitive engagement with some of them, especially as regards Anzaldúa's relation to indigeneity, in particular the utility of *mestiza* consciousness for decolonial thought and indigenous sovereignty (2021, 130–60). I will return to this latter critique (the tension between celebrations of ambiguity and "mixture" and crises of indigenous sovereignty) toward the end of this chapter. At this point, there is much more to be said about Anzaldúa's account of *mestiza* consciousness and her developments of this idea in her later work.

As an act or mode of consciousness, *mestiza* consciousness is, as Natalie Cisneros has observed, "characterized by a unique awareness of the functions of power that construct this form of subjectivity" (2020, 50). It thus has a significant epistemic function. Just as Black Consciousness entails a moment of "conscientization" for Biko, *mestiza* consciousness involves a coming to awareness and a "taking inventory" that involves "a conscious rupture with all oppressive traditions of all cultures and religions" (Anzaldúa 2007, 104). Her epistemology, however, is quite complicated, and though there are clear resonances between *mestiza* consciousness and Black Consciousness, there are also, of course, important differences.

Significantly, while there is this element of "conscious rupture" for both figures, for Biko this process is largely a deliberate one, while Anzaldúa is clear in her early writings that much of the work of conscientization "takes place underground—subconsciously" (101). This underground process is clearly linked to her articulation of *la facultad*, which in turn is linked to her deep-seated spiritualism and is a kind of "work that the soul performs" (101). *La facultad* is a key feature of Anzaldúa's conscientization process, and she clarifies the concept as follows:

> *La facultad* is the capacity to see in the surface phenomena the meaning of deeper realities, to see the deep structure below the surface. It is an instant "sensing," a quick perception arrived at without conscious reasoning. It is an acute awareness mediated by the part of the psyche that does not speak, that communicates in images and symbols which are the faces of feelings, that is, behind which feelings reside/hide. (60)

She makes clear that *los atravesados*—the outcast and marginalized who have crossed over cultural norms one way or the other—are those most prone to developing *la facultad*. This unconscious "sensing," as Cynthia Paccacerqua notes, is a capacity that, "is clearly evidenced in peoples subjected to violent cycles of shifting hierarchies of power and symbolic orders" (2016, 344; cf. Vizcaíno 2021, 84). Anzaldúa's commitment to the spirit world must in part be understood as emerging from the toleration for ambiguity and contradiction at the heart of *mestiza* consciousness. The division between "analytical reasoning that tends to use rationality to move toward a single goal (a Western mode)" and "divergent thinking" is yet another border which must be negotiated by *mestiza* consciousness (Anzaldúa 2007, 101). Anzaldúa understands this call for a "spiritual activism" as an effort to uproot this rational/spiritual dualism expressed not only in her frequent appeal to myth and spiritual traditions in her writings but also in her use of poetry and fiction, which far from being separate or distinct modes of expression for her, are inextricably integrated into her texts—her way of writing, in other words, is itself an expression of *mestiza* consciousness (cf. Schutte 2020, 130).

The power of *la facultad* and Anzaldúa's evocation of spiritual traditions and practices lies in her understanding of the role of myth and culture. "Like all people," Anzaldúa writes, "we [*las mestizas*] perceive the version of reality that our culture communicates" (2007, 100). As I read her, Anzaldúa's point here is akin to the way in which Sylvia Wynter describes human beings as necessarily utilizing interpretive schemas by which they mediate their relation to the world and their understandings of themselves, a point crucial to the discussion of Wynter and humanism in the next chapter (Wynter 1984, 24; 2001, 53–54; 2006, 116–17). Furthermore, as other contemporary commentators have noted, Anzaldúa's position here is also resonant with phenomenology (Martinez 2000, 4–6; Ortega 2016, 51–58; Pitts 2021, 13–17; Ruiz 2020, 221–22), in that she is gesturing toward what Husserl described as our intersubjective *constitution* of the world as meaningful (the *Life*world)

(Husserl 1970, 168; cf. Natanson 1973, 93–94, and Moran 2005, 52–58). At root the idea is that our perception of reality, and of ourselves in that reality, is always mediated by the larger intersubjective contexts ("cultures") through which any meaning-making is possible in the first place. Note that the claim here is not just about our *interpretation* of reality but our *perception* of it. Our intersubjective contexts condition, in other words, the way the world is *given* to us in the act of perception (*intention*), and the moment of conscientization is in part an effort to make this process itself an object of conscious reflection. It's goal, however, is not to arrive at some final "unconditioned" perception of the world ("God's-eye view" or "view from nowhere"), but rather to open a space for *taking responsibility* for this process—for attending to and working with and through it in (hopefully) liberatory ways.

Thus, the situation of the *mestiza*, and of *los atravesados*, is one in which multiple cultures with incommensurable or at least conflicting versions of reality are vying for dominance in the same place and person. This tension creates a wounded world and self, and the response, as we have already seen, is not simply to concede to one or the other reality, nor is it to deny the cultural/mythical altogether. Anzaldúa is clear that we do not simply passively accept our cultural inheritances, for we have the capacity, at least, to reinterpret and reshape them (this is the moment I linked to responsibility above). This is, indeed, at the heart of Anzaldúa's "spiritual *activism*." According to Rafael Vizcaíno, *la facultad* "is an invitation to understand the imbrication of materiality and consciousness, which Anzaldúa describes as a process of spiritual transformation," and which in turn is "why Anzaldúa's work in general cannot be understood in strict secularist terms that a priori dissect the spiritual away from examination" (2021, 84). This process of spiritual transformation involves "creating a new mythos—that is, a change in the way we perceive reality, the way we see ourselves, and the ways we behave—*la mestiza* creates a new consciousness" (Anzaldúa 2007, 102).[9]

This creation of a "new mythos" is thus at the same time an effort to change the world, and to change oneself (where the changing of one dialectically entails the changing of the other). One section of Anzaldúa's final chapter in *Borderlands/La Frontera* is titled *"La encrucijada/*The Crossroads," and it opens with a brief poem referencing Èṣù, the Òrìṣà (mediating entity between the human and the divine) associated with chance and unpredictability (indeterminacy) in the Yorùbá tradition. Èṣù commonly appears, though by different names, in many of the syncretic religions of the Americas, and often manifests at or is associated with crossroads, which symbolize the moment-of-choice in which chance and indeterminacy exert themselves. The poem is thus rich with symbolism despite its brevity, and describes the sacrifice of a chicken to bless the beginning of a journey. Anzaldúa is in this way evoking a blood sacrifice to inaugurate the undertaking that is the creation of a new consciousness. In this act, she tells us, "La mestiza has gone from being the sacrificial goat to becoming the officiating priestess at the crossroads" (Anzaldúa 2007, 102). She goes on to describe herself as an "*amasamiento*," as "an act of kneading, of uniting and joining that not only has produced both a creature of darkness and a creature of light, but also a creature that questions the definition of light and dark and gives them new meanings" (103). The poem closing this section of the chapter describes the process of grinding corn in a mortar and pestle (*molcajete*), and Anzaldúa writes that "we" (*las mestizas*) are each element and action in the process of producing tortillas—the "squatting on the ground," the "coarse rock" of the molcajete, "the grinding motion," and even the "hungry mouth" (103–4). The "we" that emerges here is thus both product and process of the creative act of generating new selves and new worlds out of the disparate elements (material and spiritual) from which "we" are constituted in the first place. Here again at this point in her early work, we see a resonance with Biko on the theme of the we-subject.

As Anzaldúa continued to think through questions of identity, her ideas developed in ways that offer important contributions and challenges to the project of this book. She moved away from the terminology of *mestiza* consciousness, in part as a response to misunderstandings and critiques generated by the complicated history of the concept of *mestizaje*. The themes already established in *Borderlands/La Frontera* were thus refined, and new terminology emerged. Concepts such as *las nepantleras*, the path of *conociemiento*, "new tribalism," and *nos/otras* all play key roles in Anzaldúa's later work, though they remain very much in the spirit of *el camino de la mestiza*. I will take each of them up in turn.

Nepantla is a term that Anzaldúa reworks in the shift from her earlier to later writings. As discussed above, in *Borderlands/La Frontera nepantla* is understood principally as a condition or position—one of being-in-between or being-in-the-middle of two (or more) "worlds." In her later works, Anzaldúa emphasizes the way in which *nepantla* is a kind of unconscious space or condition. It is, as Pitts notes, "a term that she adapts to refer to potential spaces for movement between differing hermeneutical and normative sites, or a movement *entre mundos* ('between worlds') that are not driven by an individual will or desire" (2021, 40–41). This is certainly in keeping with her use of *nepantla* in her earlier work. The real innovation comes with the development of *nepanlteras*. Again, Pitts offers an illuminating summary: "In contrast [to *nepantla* as the unconscious position/condition], 'nepantleras' may be interpreted as those forms of agential positioning across and between these differing sites of meaning and normativity" (41). The concept of *Nepantleras* is thus a way of capturing the agential/active aspect of *mestiza* consciousness, but avoids the pitfalls of *mestizaje* as a material condition and as a long-standing racialized concept.

In a 2002 essay titled "(Un)natural bridges, (Un)safe spaces," Anzaldúa takes up the theme of bridges that span a middle-ground or space-between as an elaboration of both *nepantla* the condition and the emergence of *las nepantleras* as a praxis or commitment (2009, 243–48). This appeal to the bridging metaphor is hardly new at this stage in her writing. Indeed, in the opening poem of *Borderlands/La Frontera* she refers to herself as a bridge—"*yo soy un Puente tendido del mundo gabacho al del mojado*" (Anzaldúa 2007, 25), and her profoundly influential edited anthology *This Bridge Called My Back* (Anzaldúa and Moraga 2002 [first published in 1981]) clearly invokes this same sense of one's embodied self as a bridge. This later "(Un)natural bridges" essay, which was the introduction to the anthology *this bridge we call home: radical visions for transformation* (Anzaldúa and Keating 2002), substantially develops the metaphor, however. In it, she writes: "For nepantleras to bridge is an act of will, an act of love, an attempt toward compassion and reconciliation, and a promise to be present with the pain of others without losing themselves to it" (Anzaldúa 2009, 246). Nepantleras thus both *are* a bridge, and they enact *bridging* as an effort, she tells us in this same essay, to engender community and to open oneself to intimacy and its concomitant risk of being wounded (246). In one of her final published essays (in 2003), she expands on this relationship between the condition of *nepantla* and the commitment to enact as a *nepantlera*. It is worth quoting at length:

> Este choque [collision of worlds] shifts us to nepantla, a psychological, liminal space between the way things had been and an unknown future. Nepantla is the space in-between, the locus and sign of transition. . . . In nepantla we undergo the anguish of changing our perspectives and crossing a series of cruz calles [crossroads], junctures, and thresholds, some leading to a different way of relating to people and surroundings and others to the creation of a new world. Nepantleras such as artistas/activistas help us mediate these transitions, help us make the crossings, and guide us through the transformation process—a process I call conocimiento. (2009, 310)

The role of the *nepantlera* is thus as a guide or aid, yet clearly also an active participant, in negotiating the anguish of change and conflict/collision, and echoes the evocation of the priestess and her sacrifice at the crossroads in the earlier poem discussed above.

Anzaldúa's term for this overall process, *conocimiento*, is the substantive form of the Spanish verb *conocer*, which means "to know," but specifically the kind of knowing proper to knowing a person or a city, what I have referred to in this book as a kind of *practical* knowledge. It is thus akin to a kind of familiarity or intimacy, and not the kind of knowing that one would associate with, for example, predication or propositional knowledge, and is thus resonant with the account I have been offering so far. Let us now delve more deeply into *conocimiento*.

Linked as it is to the concept of familiarity, *conocimiento* involves processes of connection and openness. It does not erase distinctions or boundaries altogether, but it seeks to *bridge* that which those boundaries and distinctions divide. "Self-righteousness creates the abyss," Anzaldúa tells us, while "conocimiento builds bridges across it" (2009, 312; cf. Ruíz 2020, 220). It has an epistemic aspect, to be sure, but as an embodied and relational process, *conocimiento* must be understood as the ongoing deepening of familiarity in a dynamic process, rather than the accumulation of final and static claims/propositions/facts. At its root, it is the process or "path" (Anzaldúa 2009, 311) whereby one confronts the harmful and damaging conditions and relations that characterize oppression in order to find productive ways to (re)construct new relations. It is a complex "transformation process" in which the traumas and wounds that emerge from *el choque* are confronted, and new relations to the past, to others, and to oneself are generated (cf. Ruíz 2020). As Paccacerqua summarizes the concept:

> Briefly, I understand *conocimiento* as knowing to act so as to provoke shifts within a shared material world, creating conditions for restructuring our otherwise alienated intersubjective and inter/intra-collective relationships among one another and nature, to foster the flourishing of life. *La nepantlera* is *conocimiento*'s agent, the person who nurtures abilities to become affected by what lies beyond our singular sense of self and to extend ties into the world. (Paccacerqua 2016, 335)

Conocimiento is thus linked to *la facultad*, in that most of the critical insights emerge unconsciously out of moments of rupture and fragmentation that thrust one into what Anzaldúa calls a "Coyalxāuhqui state" (2009, 311).[10] She takes up the symbolism of the dismembered goddess Coyalxāuhqui to represent the fragmentation and alienation one experiences as a result of moments of woundedness and rupture, and more broadly as "the necessary process of dismemberment and fragmentation, of seeing that self or the situations you're embroiled in differently" (312). The path of *conocimiento* involves not only the confrontation of this Coyalxāuhqui state, but a commitment "to heal and achieve integration," which Anzaldúa calls the "Coyalxāuhqui imperative" (312; cf. Anzaldúa 2015, 95–116). The Coyalxāuhqui imperative, the "ongoing process of making and unmaking," thus drives the practice of *conocimiento*, which culminates not in some final realization of unity, but in a "process of healing" in which "the healing of our wounds results in transformation, and transformation results in the healing of our wounds" (2009, 311).

The next key concept from Anzaldúa's later work relevant to our thinking with respect to the subject of liberation is "new tribalism." It emerges as a response to a critique from David Reiff (1991) that charges Anzaldúa with misappropriating indigenous symbols, and so she adopts the term "new tribalism," as a way "to formulate other takes on identity, particularly a more expanded and inclusive identity" (Anzaldúa 2015, 232n6). She begins by grounding her approach in embodied experience. "Struggling with a 'story' (a concept or theory), embracing personal and social identity," she writes, "is a *bodily* activity" (2015, 66). To develop her theory of new tribalism, she turns to the story of *El árbol de la vida* (the tree of life), which is a recurring image throughout her text *Light in the Dark/Luz en lo Oscuro*. Immediately before linking the tree of life to the new tribalism, she offers a passage from one of her earlier writings ("El Paisano Is a Bird of Good Omen") discussing a mesquite tree in her family's yard (66). The passage emphasizes the depth and complexity of the root system, and how it connects to surrounding organisms up to and including herself and all the earth's creatures, and she points out that it "symbolizes my 'story' of the new tribalism" (67). She thus adopts an ecological account of identity, in which individuals are constitutively connected to larger systems through diffuse relations. Key to the new tribalism is thus the idea that, while one seeks out and needs "roots," these roots need not be connect to fixed and substantive notions of ethnicity or race (68). Invoking Deleuze and Gautarri's rhizomatic metaphor, Anzaldúa emphasizes that our rootedness becomes a source of strength, even as we recognize that the strength of a root system is dependent in part upon the health and strength of all to which it is (inter)connected. As a result, the new tribalism as a *process* of identity emphasizes inclusion over exclusion (Anzaldúa 2009, 245), establishing an approach that is "relational" and "multilayered" (Anzaldúa 2015, 69).

Once we assemble these diverse concepts and metaphors, we can see that she turns to the new tribalism as an effort to theorize identity in a way that is profoundly embodied, historical, and relational, yet at the same time something that we take up and (re)shape through acts of (*mestiza*) consciousness (73–75). This does not mean that one may simply disavow or excise one's past or one's embodiment, including even race or ethnicity. As the process of *conocimento* progresses, and one adopts the approach of the new tribalism, "you begin to see race as an experience of reality from a particular perspective and a specific time and place (history), not as a *fixed* feature of personality or identity" (127, emphasis mine). Thus, she tells us, "the point may not be to move beyond a nationalistic search for indigenous roots but rather to undertake transformative work that processes and facilitates evolving as a social group, becoming an extended tribe, and developing new tribalism" (75). The new tribalism is ultimately about negotiating and contesting the sense of self and other (including self-as-other), and their interrelation in a way that is consistent with what Pitts has identified as Anzaldúa's "relational ontology." In other words, if both the self and the other are ongoing and unfolding processes shaped by and shaping their mutual and co-constitutive relations (their interconnection in *el árbol de la vida*), then appeals to identity, including collective identity—"us" and "them"—must abandon "rigid borders" that "hinder communication and prevent us from extending *beyond* ourselves" (75). Note that the claim here is not a world without borders altogether (a form of monism), but rather a refusal of the kinds of borders proper to the politics of purity. This call to avoid the pitfalls of the politics of purity becomes even more explicit as her discussion of collective identity turns finally to her account of *nos/otras*.

In the "Geographies of Selves—Reimagining Identity" chapter that is a key resource for Anzaldúa's later theory of identity, and on which I have been relying heavily so far (Anzaldúa 2015, 65–94), the introduction of "new tribalism" is followed by a discussion and lamentation of the ways in which differences among the oppressed (*atravesadxs, nepantlerxs*) come to generate points of conflict and friction. "Wounded," she writes, "we let our anger stomp on others as if they're ants . . . we disregard the fact that we live in intricate relationship with others, that our very existence depends on our intimate interactions with all life forms" (76). She refers to these conflicts as "civil wars" as one "we" struggles to assert itself among other "we's" even as those in power draw them all into the "remolinos [eddies/whirlpools] of their ideologies" (77). This is, she tells us, the existential condition of *"nos/otras."* The term plays with the first-person plural feminine pronoun in Spanish— *nosotras* (*nosotros* is the masculine form). By placing a slash (*rajadura*) where she has, Anzaldúa draws out *"nos,"* which is the first-person plural reflexive pronoun (us), and *"otras"* (this is the feminine form of the term) which would translate to "others" in English. Thus, *"nos/otras"* evokes all at once "we" (*nosotras*), "us" (*nos*), and "others" (*otras*) as part of her "identity narrative" (79). Her elaboration of this concept deserves quoting at length:

> La rajadura [the slash between nos and otras] gives us a third point of view, a perspective from the cracks and a way to reconfigure ourselves as subjects outside binary oppositions . . . An identity born of negotiating the cracks between worlds, nos/otras accommodates contradictory identities and social positions, creating a hybrid consciousness that transcends the us versus them mentality of irreconcilable positions, blurring the boundary between us and others. We are both subject and object, self and other, haves and have-nots, conqueror and conquered, oppressor and oppressed. Proximity and intimacy can close the gap between us and them. (79)

We see here a clear repudiation of the politics of purity. Anzaldúa is advocating a toleration and even affirmation of contradiction, of hybridity, and the "blurring" of the distinction between self and other. The call in the final sentence for proximity and intimacy, furthermore, is a clear appeal to *conocimiento* (a coming-to-know in the practical sense of deepening familiarity), which must be understood in intimate relation with *nepantleras* (those who guide and participate in acts of "bridging"), the new tribalism, and *nos/otras* as essential moments of her liberatory project, understood as "spiritual activism."

Let us now take a step back and draw together all the different strands of Anzaldúa's account of identity in her later work. I noted in her earlier work that her account of reality bears a certain similarity with phenomenology, in that she sees intersubjectivity (understood loosely as *culture*) as unavoidably conditioning the ways in which we encounter reality ("worlds"). This remains the case in her later writing. We unavoidably encounter a world already constituted by the cultures in which we participate (willingly or reluctantly) and which have shaped us. We consequently participate, consciously and unconsciously, in the (re)shaping of the world(s), but there is no escaping the fundamental cultural mediation between self and world(s) (Anzaldúa 2015, 42–43). This means that, "because your reconstructions are always in progress, the world, society, and culture are always in compositional/decompositional states" (43). Those who are in between worlds—*las mestizas, las nepantleras*, those in a Coyalxāuhqui state—experience *el choque,* the collision between worlds that is generated by and generates spiritual and material wounds (wounds of the psyche, wounds of the flesh, wounds of the community, and wounds of the ecosystem). Confronting oneself in this condition, one may walk the path of *conocimiento*, seeking to understand and heal the wound(s), or one may walk the path of *desconocimiento. Desconocimiento* (ignorance or un-knowing) is "the ignorance we cultivate to keep ourselves from knowledge so that we can remain unaccountable" (2), and when one travels this path one "succumbs to righteous judgement and withdraws into separation and domination, pushing most of us into retaliatory acts of further rampage which beget more violence" (Anzaldúa 2009, 311–12).[11] The path of *desconocimiento*, in other words, is the path of purity—it seeks security, enclosure, clear and rigid distinctions that establish a fixed and immutable sense of self, place, and belonging. Note also that Anzaldúa's reference to *desconocimiento* as an effort to "remain unaccountable" points to the link between *conocimiento* and responsibility. If *conocimiento* "builds bridges" and fosters accountability/responsibility in relation with others (think of the *árbol de la vida* metaphor), then *desconocimiento* builds walls evades responsibility to and for oneself, others, and the world. *Las nepantleras*, those who take up the commitment to the path of *concimiento*, work to refashion the world(s) in which they find themselves in a way that renders permeable the boundaries between self and other, us and them. This involves the articulation of a "new tribalism," where collective identities are multiplicitous, fluid, and open, directed toward the ongoing processes of transforming self and world in coalition with others (*nos/otras* becoming *nosotras*).

THE WE-SUBJECT OF LIBERATION: LESSONS FROM BIKO AND ANZALDÚA

Both Steve Biko and Gloria Anzaldúa are struggling to theorize, articulate, and enact a collective subject of liberation—a *we* who are remaking ourselves and our world(s) in a way more expressive of our collective humanity. The contexts of their struggle are of course quite distinct, and they draw upon different intellectual, spiritual, and material resources for their works. Yet each writes from a place outside a prescribed norm. Biko wrote as a Black person in the overtly white-supremacist regime of mid-twentieth-century apartheid South Africa, and Anzaldúa describes herself as occupying the "cracks" of dominant norms in terms of her health, her complexion, her gender, her sexuality, and her use of language. Both dedicate themselves to an account of identity that is authentic to their experience and to their political vision, yet is also inclusive and coalitional—they seek to locate the we in *I*, and the I in *we*, recognizing that their liberation depends not only on negotiating this balance between first-person singular and plural, but also in drawing together (*bridging*, in Anzaldúa's terms) other collective identities in shared struggle—a struggle for *our* liberation.

Furthermore, for both thinkers, there is a level of *givenness* to collective identity, yet that givenness is neither static nor beyond their influence. To be Black or to be *mestiza*, for example, is a contingent and historical feature of the worlds in which they each function, and with respect to which they must necessarily situate themselves. Liberation lies not in denying or evading these features, nor in simply accepting them as given, but rather in re-working them in a way that is empowering rather than alienating. Their respective turns to modes of *consciousness* reflect their shared sense that these modes of identity are always in fact *in progress*. It is the *modus operandi* of oppression to treat them as static and fixed (the politics of purity), and to deny them altogether capitulates to this substance-ontological vision of identity.

Biko and Anzaldúa, in their different ways, call on us to take responsibility for these collective identities as ongoing processes. This assumption of responsibility entails a moment of "conscientization"—a taking stock of the reality of these identities and their impact on our sense(s) of self. From this critical encounter with the world and our place within it, we are then called to act. For Biko, one may choose the path of the "non-white," who maintains the normative centrality of whiteness and seeks only to secure advantage within the white-supremacist order of things, or one may choose the path of Black Consciousness, and seek to displace and disrupt the operations of white normativity (both in its material and in its more spiritual/cultural manifestations). Anzaldúa, as we have seen, captures this decision point in her distinction between *conocimiento* and *desconocimiento*. What emerges for both thinkers is a collective identity (a we-subject) proper to a dynamic and relational ontology. The *I*, the *we*, and the *they* are all in an ongoing state of negotiation and contestation, and inasmuch as the mode of oppression seeks stasis, (en)closure, and fixity, the mode of liberation affirms dynamism, openness/ambiguity, and change.

At the same time, the commitment to openness that these thinkers emphasize cannot be understood as total and all-encompassing—as, in other words, *pure* openness. If there are no distinctions whatsoever, then there is nothing to be open to, there is no *other* with whom a subject (individual or collective) can stand in relation. A dynamic and relational ontology, in other words, must see difference and distinction as provisional, ambiguous, and relational, but it does not eschew them altogether. The response to pathological reifications (ossifications) of difference (and identity) cannot be to reject distinctions, exclusions, and boundaries altogether but rather to radically alter our understanding of them and their operation. Just as the response to the politics of purity, as we have seen, must not be ~(purity), our response to the oppressive articulations of identity and difference cannot be a reification or purification of either term. Identity, whether collective or individual, necessarily entails relations of exclusion to some degree. The key move here is the appeal both to the degree and the character of these articulations of difference. The politics of purity would have identity and difference as all-or-nothing relations, but the lesson that both Biko and Anzaldúa are imparting is one in which difference is never *radical* or total(izing). The embodied practice of identity toward which each of these thinkers is leading us, in their different ways, is an ongoing practice of both inclusion and exclusion situated by historical and contemporary cultural and political contexts. The goal toward which they are aiming is one of coalition and solidarity, where differences are acknowledged and affirmed, even as shared goals, practices, and senses of belonging are (re-)negotiated and (re-)articulated among them. Anzaldúa refers to this as "bridging," and in the context of recognition theory, we might refer to it as reciprocity. The key point is that bridges connect *different* ends, and reciprocity is always between different terms/participants.

Here again, the sonic metaphor proves highly fruitful. Who one is emerges not as a thing but as a dynamic process, like a sound wave. This means in the first instance that its defining features must be understood as characteristics of movement, but never in isolation. The characteristics of the movement, the "identity," is a function of the interaction or friction of different elements (again, no friction, no sound—no difference, no identity) within and through particular media (spiritual and material conditions), shaped in turn by the specific relationship(s) with the listener(s). Oppression attempts to present a world in which such movement is arrested or curtailed, but this is only ever in bad faith. In reality, oppression does not arrest movement, but rather works to obfuscate or disavow it in oneself and/or in others. It creates a kind of standing wave, where a relatively constant and stable form of movement can be apprehended *as if* it were static. Sonically, we might think of this oppressive phenomenon as an effort to drown out difference and change—it is a kind of *white noise*. Just as a constant and otherwise overwhelming sound can become so commonplace and normalized that it no longer registers *as sound*, oppression seeks the constitution of a world in which movement no longer registers as such, or at least emerges only on the margins and as a form of decay or disruption—as *wounds*, we might say, following Anzaldúa.

This is why, as I suggested briefly in the previous chapter, the first move in liberatory praxis often involves an emphatic assertion of difference and distinction—an effort to generate *dissonance* within an oppressive soundscape. In the context of white noise that renders one inaudible (while denying all along that there is anything going on to drown you out), the first stirrings of finding one's own voice will inevitably appear as a moment of dissonance. It will manifest as a disruption of the ongoing soundscape that at once establishes one's presence within that soundscape, calls out to others and elicits similar expressions of dissonance (which will be *resonant* with respect to each other), and reveals the dominant white noise as precisely an ongoing *praxis* (movement) that functions to inhibit certain modes and expressions of productive friction (sound). Those committed to Black Consciousness in Biko's sense, or those who are *nepantlerxs* in Anzaldúa's sense, are engaging in this praxis of generating dissonance within a white noise context that functions to drown them out or absorb them into their "proper" role within the normative soundscape. What emerges is in part a kind of sonic interference that aims at once to create moments of resonance with other efforts to disrupt the white noise (coalition, solidarity, and the emerging we-subject), and seeks moments of dissonance with respect to the larger normative soundscape and those who participate in maintaining its normativity.

Importantly, even the aim of resonance does not eschew difference, for resonance just is a certain kind of interaction between *different* sonic elements (and again, even at the most fundamental level, all sound is generated by *friction*—by the interaction of different elements within a medium). At the same time, the aim of the moment of dissonance may ultimately be the generation of new forms of resonance, but this, too, can be achieved in different ways. For instance, the emerging dissonance can come, over time, to be understood rather as a previously misapprehended form of resonance (as when, in one's first encounter with a radically different musical tradition, what at first sounded "off" or "cacophonous" eventually comes to be grasped as harmonious and resonant as one "trains one's ear" and becomes more familiar with the previously alien tradition or musical form). In other words, those participating within the dominant white noise soundscape can come to an awareness of the particularity of their distinct mode of sonic production, and eventually find ways to re-attune their participation and perception such that what was once dissonant becomes resonant. This can, in its turn, require an alteration or even a complete re-creation of that dominant soundscape (this is one way to understand the *decolonial* move). And finally, insofar as all of these processes remain fundamentally dynamic and relational, the emerging shifts in the soundscape, in terms not only of the modes of productive friction being practiced, and in terms of the media in and through which the soundscape is expressed, may elicit variations in the initial dissonant modes that gradually (and necessarily reciprocally) elicit shifts more conducive to overall resonance. In short, a source of dissonance can elicit alterations in the medium, in the dominant sonic paradigm, and eventually in itself—the dissonant intervention, having served its purpose, can be altered and brought into a more resonant relation (which resonance may not have been possible prior to the dissonant intervention).

Recall that there is a distinction to be made between the descriptive physical phenomena and the phenomenon of sound where "resonance" and "dissonance" are at play. The former deals with instances of "constructive" or "destructive" interference, where waves interact in ways that either enhance or diminish what emerges from the moment of interaction. In the context of sound, "resonance" and "dissonance" are in part a matter of the norms of perception, and consequently the historical and cultural context that conditions one's "ear" matters a great deal. My appeal to the concepts of "dissonance" and "resonance" is thus a deliberate effort to emphasize precisely that larger sonic context (the "soundscape") that enables the physical phenomenon to appear in one of these modes. What I am calling an "oppressive" soundscape is one in which the governing norms are such that instances of destructive interference (which, as we will see in the next chapter, can be thought of as moments of "disempowerment") are apprehended by those who accept these governing norms as instances of "resonance." In other words, it "sounds right" for some voices/sounds to be drowned out or diminished (through destructive interference). Conversely, instances of constructive interference (empowerment) are often apprehended as "dissonant"—they sound *wrong*. The aim is to create conditions (which must include an alteration of this larger oppressive soundscape) in which constructive interference can appear, in the phenomenological sense, as *resonance*.

With this in mind, the move to articulate the we-subject of liberation can be understood as a moment of dissonance with respect to the dominant/colonial soundscape (of white noise), and a moment of resonance between the individuals and subgroups within that emerging we-subject. This moment of resonance builds a collective intervention that is more than the sum of its parts precisely because of the resonant relation (a mode of "constructive interference"), and is thus better equipped, in the moment of dissonance, to make a more powerful intervention in and disruption of the surrounding white noise. The emerging we-subject, in other words, derives its strength not from some monophonic unity, like a single note voiced by all, but precisely through the drawing together in a resonant (that is, mutually or reciprocally supporting/constructive) relation of different elements working together to enrich and enhance each other (and thus enhancing them*selves* both individually and collectively). It is thus creolizing in the sense that it is an ongoing moment of productive friction seeking new modes of difference/friction in an open-ended process of dissonance and resonance. In this way, the we-subject has a history that precedes the moment of consciousness in the sense that we are drawing on shared-yet-different experiences and antecedents/ancestors. The Black subject for Biko, or *nepantlerxs* for Anzaldúa, do not emerge *ex nihil*, but draw on and alter or reinterpret a shared *historicity* in a way that articulates and supports who *we* are, and what we are *becoming* in and through this unfolding and dynamic interpretation (conscientization) of a shared situation. Importantly, this "sharing" of situation need not be understood as monolithic—"we" do not share it all in the same way, but retain our particularity even in our shared response. This is particularly clear in Anzaldúa, where the reclamation and rearticulation of a precolonial past plays a distinctive and crucial role in the path of *conocimiento*—the coming to know (in the dynamic/practical sense) oneself individually and collectively on the healing path to a liberatory future. Crucially, within the context of a creolizing account of freedom, this liberatory future is not an end point or final (static) realization, but is itself an ongoing evocation of productive friction.

CONCLUDING LESSONS

Ultimately, the articulation of a we-subject as a moment of resonance/dissonance requires the drawing of distinctions and relations of exclusion. Every "us/we" requires a "them"—every *nos* demands its *otras*. The creolizing move, therefore, does not entail a final resolution where "all are creolized."

We would in such an instance be left with a monolithic condition of (~purity), which is, as I have argued, still enmeshed in the politics of purity. This can be clearly seen when we consider struggles for indigenous sovereignty within settler-colonial states. The creolizing imperative can, under these conditions, appear to enact what is in the final analysis a further moment of genocide, where efforts to protect and preserve a distinct sovereign identity (we-subject) under constant colonial threat become further threatened by a theoretical framework/method that appears to disavow and critique the kinds of exclusionary moves necessary to preserve and develop that identity. Put bluntly, criticizing Dene or Lakota or Aymara efforts to protect the integrity and sovereignty of their communities from centuries-long genocidal efforts as falling prey to the "politics of purity" just seems not only misguided, but profoundly cruel. What is needed, it seems, is *more* "purity," not less, if the future is going to be one that includes these communities. How can the account I am offering here respond to this vital worry?

The first important point to make is that the problem lies primarily in the *way* in which different communities or individuals assert their identity and sovereignty, rather than in the mere assertion of identity (and thus exclusion of the other) as such. As Glen Coulthard (Yellowknives Dene) reminds us, "no discourse on identity should be prematurely cast as either inherently productive or repressive prior to an engaged consideration of the historical, political, and socioeconomic contexts and actors involved" (2014, 103). The colonizers, on the one hand, assert an identity, the function of which is to prevent any productive interaction (friction) with any others. It either absorbs all alterity, cordons it off (into reservations and ghettos, for example), or seeks to destroy or drown-it out (via white noise) utterly. The end goal is always a world in which productive friction with those "outside" of the colonial identity (or identities) is evaded. Such evasion is not a complete break from relation, however, as any project of purity must maintain some relation to the 'external' other insofar as this is necessary to maintain the myth of purity which animates it (cf. Monahan 2011, 163–65). That impurity "out there" toward which one may point is necessary in order to maintain the myth of purity "in here." Of course, colonial identities—those oriented toward purity—will typically disavow the necessity of this relationship to the impure other, positing a pre-given and fixed identity that must be protected from corrupting influences and threats. It aims, therefore, toward a world in which there are effectively no genuine others, or at least none with whom they must stand in a relationship of reciprocity, even as it maintains this sense of self through a constitutive relationship with this other that is explicitly disavowed (in bad faith). This is the world of the *not-self/not-other* Fanon described as the "zone of nonbeing" (and, as we will see in the next chapter, is a key element of Wynter's argument). Assertions of identity in this colonial mode seek an absence of friction/relation in a totalizing yet mythological drive toward and celebration of purity.

It is possible, however, as Biko and Anzaldúa (among many others) make clear, to assert an identity from the position of the colonized, the function of which is the (re)building of communal integrity and power in a way that fosters and is open to (though this certainly need not be the explicit goal) a more genuinely reciprocal relationship with others. Here there may be an emphasis on or a turn toward exclusion, coherence, and stability the goal of which is the conservation/preservation of collective identity (a we-subject) in the face of often overwhelming forces bent on denying or undermining coherence and stability. Preserving and asserting the integrity of one's community under such circumstances may often demand employing practices, including practices of theorizing, that may appear to be instantiations of the politics of purity, on the surface, at least. Asserting sovereign rights to land or traditions, which entails the demarcation and enforcement of the *borders* of that land and what counts as that tradition, will necessarily entail the demarcation of who may or may not be included in the relevant we-subject, and under what conditions that subject may be understood to properly persist, survive, and flourish. The question here involves how to maintain and enhance the distinctive *voice* of the we-subject when it is under constant threat of being choked-off outright, or at least washed-out by the constant din of what I have been calling *white noise*.

Jodi Byrd (Chickasaw) makes similar appeal to a sonic metaphor in their framing of this problematic: "As a result, the cacophony produced through US colonialism and imperialism domestically and abroad often coerces struggles for social justice for queers, racial minorities, and immigrants into complicity with settler colonialism" (2011, xvii). Within the context of the politics of purity as I have been developing it so far, the problem can be stated as follows. The "cacophony" or white noise of colonialism and imperialism is a result of the assertion of a collective identity that has a clear *telos* of purity expressed both spiritually (in the account of history, of culture, and of civilization/law) and materially (in embodied habits, in access to resources, and in the relation to the [home]land), that sees itself as under threat from a variety of "impurities," and arrays its forces so as to assimilate, eradicate, or cordon them off and thus preserve its (alleged) purity. Is the only response to this very real threat (which in many cases, and certainly those that concern Coulthard and Byrd, is an existential threat) to assert a kind of counter-narrative of purity (a variant, perhaps, on "strategic essentialism")?

In keeping with the emphasis on ambiguity at the center (more or less) of the articulation of freedom and liberation I am offering here, the answer to this question is "yes and no." It does demand an assertion of purity in precisely the ways I was gesturing toward above. Effort must be made to articulate, circumscribe, and defend a collective identity in ways that can resist and thwart the efforts toward assimilation or eradication being mounted against it. Those who seek to weaken the integrity and coherence of the colonized we-subject must not be allowed to dictate the terms of interaction or of membership. In the near term, this will require a rather robust "policing" of the boundaries of the we-subject both spiritually and materially (in the senses described above). Concern about the "purity" of the group or its cultural practices may thus, in such (all-too-common) circumstances, be entirely warranted.

Nevertheless, such efforts to maintain group integrity and coherence may be undertaken in ways that do not necessarily collapse into the politics of purity. Creolizing practices of liberation, including decolonial practices, do not aim ultimately at a world without difference—ongoing creolizing practices require *different* elements in and through which processes of creolization may take place. Assertions of identity on the colonial model work to fix a static identity that denies or disavows difference internally, and in denying any sort of productive relationship with difference externally, ultimately seeks a world in which "we" are the only *real* subjects. As Anzaldúa made clear, however, one can affirm one's difference and distinction, one's identity, in a way that is open to productive relations with others. Drawing boundaries and affirming identities need not require the fixation of those boundaries and the ossification of those identities, but can work toward and be open to the kind of *reciprocity* that emerged in my prior discussion of Fanon. Importantly, the reciprocity to which I am referring here is impossible for a colonial identity, since the *essence*, so to speak, of a colonial identity is precisely the foreclosure of reciprocity. This rules out as an instance of genuine reciprocity the aim of gaining "reciprocity" with or "recognition" from the colonizers on *their* terms, since their terms are fundamentally incompatible with reciprocity as such. This point is indeed at the heart of many indigenous critiques of "recognition" (cf. Coulthard 2014; Povinelli 2002). Yet being open, even as coherence and stability are strengthened, to possibilities for *genuine* reciprocity need not fall prey to these critiques, for seeking reciprocity in this sense requires that the colonizers abandon their own commitments to stability and purity (the "world" of the colonizer, and the "white noise" it generates, must be abolished). What is most important with respect to the politics of purity is that assertions of sovereignty and stability *can* create the conditions where productive friction and reciprocity are possible, even as they require the drawing of boundaries. There is thus no contradiction in being critical of the politics of purity and affirming, for example, movements for indigenous sovereignty.

By way of an illustration, consider, in the US context, the various white "nativist" movements that have appeared in different guises from the nineteenth century to their present "Make America Great Again" instantiation. Settler colonists re-cast themselves as the "native" Americans under threat from dangerous alien invaders, thus simultaneously disavowing the existence of the truly "native" peoples of the continent who live under a genuinely existential threat from their colonizers, and articulating a mythologized we-subject who are the *real* proprietors of the *homeland*. The threat has certainly changed over time in various ways—from mid-nineteenth-century fears of Irish, Italian, and Jewish immigrants, to early twentieth-century concerns about Eastern European immigrants, to the contemporary clamor to close the southern border to "invaders" from Latin America. In each case the nativists have maintained yet disavowed the very relationship that informs their self-concept as the rightful inheritors of the continent. *Being* "American" is thus maintained in bad faith as a kind of fixed and given essence that maps onto the natal "homeland" in a way that at once disavows and justifies the history of violence, betrayal, and genocide by which that land was seized. Since the act of conquest was the fulfillment of a destiny or the expression of inherent "fitness," it becomes, in effect, either morally irrelevant (because inevitable), or evidence of the justice of the ongoing occupation of this land (through a "right" of conquest). Consistent throughout, however, is a we-subject constituted through a fixation on the invading "impurity" threatening the body-politic—the other against whom *we* must organize, and a mythologized origin-story that legitimizes ownership of the continent, and thus the right to protect it from the various invaders. There are two important observations to make about this form of "nativism." First, it is quite clearly an expression of the politics of purity, positing a fixed and given identity which is distinctly distinguished from those whom it posits as its "others," and who are in fact, as I have already discussed, *not-self/not-others*. Second, the appeal to the colonial subject as "native" places actual Native Americans outside of the dialectic entirely. If, for the nativist, "good" immigrants are the other with whom ethical and political *relations* are possible, and "bad/invading" immigrants are the not-self/not-other with whom no constructive relations are possible, then the indigenous peoples of the continent become, as Byrd puts the point, "the transit through which the dialectic of subject and object occurs" (2011, xxv).

In terms of the question of identity and the we-subject, this dilemma is made worse by the ways in which, as Anne Waters (Seminole) has pointed out, "historically creating a genocidal definition of who counts as indigenous individuals and indigenous nations, has been carried on as part of extermination practices by the USA through its legislature" (2004, 191). Practices of genocide and forced removal, in other words, have been and continue to *impose*, not just employ, "native" identity categories. As a result, questions of sovereignty, of recognition by the US state, and of identity are especially fraught, and always conditioned by the kinds of relations to state juridical and discursive power one is willing and able to take. My suggestion here is that it may be possible to follow Anzaldúa's claim that the task is not "to move beyond a nationalistic search for indigenous roots but rather to undertake transformative work that processes and facilitates *evolving* as a social group" (2015, 75, emphasis mine). In other words, one need not identify or appeal to fixed and static essences or traditions in the vital effort to affirm a distinct we-subject of decolonial struggle. To assert difference/distinction in the face of a colonial politics of purity can make appeal to shared "roots" that nevertheless understands those roots, and the we-subject who shares them, to have always been dynamic and evolving processes, rather than fixed and static objects. Traditions are always living, in other words, and communities and peoples have always been fluid and porous (even when, as in the case of the colonial subject, such ambiguity and dynamism is disavowed). As Adam Arola puts the point in the context of his own Anishinaubae tradition, "any identity is itself always a process, a *between*, something that is perpetually incomplete, but also perpetually in the process of being generated through our interactions with the world" (2011, 4). The danger posed by the politics of purity lies in the assertion of a fixed and static identity oriented toward the maintenance of all-or-nothing boundaries. The assertion of an incomplete (that is, ongoing and at least somewhat open), dynamic, and relational identity is not only consistent with a creolizing theory of liberation, but in fact a crucial component, since liberation-as-creolizing requires *different* elements to bring together in moments of productive friction.

What follows from the work of these indigenous thinkers, as I read them, is an understanding of appeals to indigenous sovereignty, and of efforts to conserve and protect the integrity of indigenous communities and traditions, as another set of quite particular and context-specific efforts to nurture and project moments of decolonial *dissonance*. Far from collapsing into the politics of purity, they are instantiations of resistance (even when, as I will emphasize below, such resistance is not the explicit *goal*) to the white noise of the colonial milieu and the subjects (individual and collective) who inhabit and animate it. Understood as living and dynamic communities and traditions, rather than as static and ossified historical artifacts, such appeals to coherence and integrity enable, rather than thwart, the conditions for the possibility of a more genuine reciprocity (one that, in the final account, demands the abolition of the colonial subject *qua* colonial). In this way, they are quite consistent with creolizing practices of liberation, despite their surface appearance to the contrary.

Importantly, such articulations of a we-subject in the face of a colonial politics of purity need not, indeed *must not*, be understood strictly in terms of opposition or resistance. As Lindsey Stewart points out so powerfully: "When we reduce agency to resistance, we act as if our reaction to oppression is the only thing that defines us" (2021, 9). Stewart rightly points out not only that "a narrow focus on resisting our oppressors can actually cause us to emulate them" (97), but also how "if we focus too much on gaining political recognition from our white counterparts, we may fail to develop an independent sense of self" (98). Focusing as she does on Black life in the US, she identifies Conjure and root work as one significant source of this independent sense of self that is not reducible to resistance to oppression (103–12). As I read Stewart, she is offering an important reminder that we-subject affirmation under conditions of oppression and colonization always appeals, as Anzaldúa reminds us, to shared roots (*root work* indeed!) in an evolving and relational identity, but that the relation to the oppressor is, of course, never the only relation that matters. These expressions of shared agency may, in other words, often be indifferent to the oppressor, either deliberately, as a form of *studied* indifference, or incidentally. To be sure, these cultivations and expressions of Black (and, by extension, though not equivocation, Indigenous) agency are indirect forms of resistance to the dehumanization of oppression, insofar as they disrupt the *telos* of purity (white noise), but Stewart's point remains—the we-subject of liberation need not, and indeed should not, have a myopic focus on the oppressor.

The collective subject of liberation should thus be understood as an ongoing *praxis* of drawing out and re-working common *roots* in an effort to cultivate and affirm a shared sense of self(-consciousness). The appeal to roots drawn from Anzaldúa is instructive here, in the way they point toward a kind of resilience in the face of an all-too-hostile environment (imagine a tree root breaking through a wall or sidewalk), and in the way they appeal to a diffuse and evolving set of relations and connectivity. Likewise, the collective (Black) *consciousness* to which Biko appeals is in an important way never something generated *ex nihilo*, nor is it ever a *fait accompli*. It draws on shared traditions and experiences (roots) even as it reworks them into a collective agency capable taking up the project and practice of liberation. This marks what Anzaldúa calls the path of *conocimiento*, where one at the same time articulates and comes to know (in the sense of familiarity, not the sense of "knowing that") who one is both individually and collectively, and how the individual and the collective are co-constitutive—that is, relational.

Drawing on the sonic metaphor, we can recognize that this requires moments of stability and coherence, like a standing wave, but this should never be confused with a static essence or a totalizing identity (bereft of difference). It is itself, in other words, only in and through the movement and relation of its various parts, which can be relatively stable, but falls prey to the politics of purity the moment turns toward stasis. The goal here is, as I have been stressing, a kind of productive friction. Within the always-emerging collective subject of liberation this takes the form of the kinds of constructive interference that lend it coherence/harmony, while in relation to the hostile and totalizing colonial/white world (the context of "white noise"), it takes the form of destructive interference. It seeks to disrupt the stability of those oppressive relations and identities that will, because they are enmeshed in the politics of purity, tend to see such disruptions as a profound threat. Such destructive interference need not always be, as Stewart reminds us, the explicit focus of the praxis of the we-subject, but as the "sound" of the collective subject of liberation becomes more stable and coherent, as it *strengthens*, it will inevitably emerge as a disruption of the white noise of the status quo—it will appear (aurally) as an intrusion of dissonance in what had been a "peaceful" soundscape. Importantly for the question of the resistance to settler colonialism, the effort to shore-up and stabilize a collective identity under threat from the "white noise" of coloniality can and must make efforts to insulate itself, which will require the marking and protecting of certain kinds of borders, but understood under the model of the standing wave, this need not commit one to the politics of purity, and can ultimately even be understood, taking the long view, as a creolizing move.

As both Biko and Anzaldúa make clear, the aim of the liberatory consciousness of the collective subject is to create the conditions in which something like genuine reciprocity becomes possible amongst the various modes of collective and individual identity in which we participate. Certainly, to seek acceptance or legitimacy from and on the terms of the oppressor is a profound failure—it is indeed to capitulate to the pernicious understanding of the politics of "recognition" that was the subject of earlier chapters. "Reciprocity," in the sense I intend here, thus demands that *all* those entering into the relation are open to and affirm the ways in which they are altered in and through the relation. A colonial subject, insofar as it remains committed to exclusion and stasis, can thus never be a *reciprocal* participant. Such alterations of the participating subjects are always taking place (this is the underlying reality of creolization), but are all-too-often disavowed (this is the politics of purity common to the colonizing subject). To fully elaborate this sense of reciprocity is the task of the next chapter, where I will frame it in terms of the tension between particular and universal, and the question of the possibility of *the human* within liberatory theory.

Chapter 6

On *Human* Liberation

As was apparent in the earlier discussion of recognition, a central tension in struggles for liberation, at the most abstract level, is that between the particular and the universal. On the one extreme, the reification of universality—we are all the same, *qua* human beings or citizens—leads to a kind of alienation, where profound and significant aspects of one's identity are deemed morally or politically irrelevant, and makes possible the emergence of a dominant, normative form of particularity (white, male, bourgeois, etc.) that can position itself as a *false* universal. This latter danger has plagued many of the Western canonical approaches to freedom, and is thus part of why the creolizing project is so vital. On the other extreme, the reduction to particularity—I am or we are absolutely distinct in my/our unique particularity—results in a kind of absolutizing of difference, where every individual's experience is mutually unintelligible (the "epistemology of provenance"). As I argued in prior chapters, at root these two extremes are expressions of the politics of purity. If what is universal about us is all that matters, then the goal is to purify ourselves, and the body politics, of all particularity. If what is particular about us is all that matters, then the aim must be to purify ourselves and the body politic (which concept must itself be rejected as perniciously universalistic) of all appeals to universality. Furthermore, at the most abstract level, purity with respect to the particular and the universal is unintelligible. The claim that we are all absolutely distinct is a *universal* one, and the claim that we are all the same is a claim about *particulars*. To be unique *like everyone else* is just another way of saying that our deep particularity is in fact a universal feature, and to try to purify one term or the other is tantamount to a kind of conceptual violence. It forces us into molds that simply do not fit.

As I pointed out at in my introduction, any serious look at the work of oppressed people from Sojourner Truth's famous declaration of her shared womanhood to Frantz Fanon's appeal to "set afoot" a new humanity, reveals a consistent theme of oppression as *dehumanizing*. In other words, oppression functions in part as a denial of a profound universality, which is why any liberatory project must in turn make appeal to the universal. Yet the European and Anglo-American theorizations of freedom and liberation that have dominated global discourse for the last few centuries or more all too often fall prey to a universal*ism* that expresses a triumphal coloniality. In other words, the "human" takes on the quite particular characteristics of the self-concept of the colonizers. This is part of why it is necessary to take on a creolizing methodology in this project. In furtherance of that methodology, the goal of this chapter is to take seriously the important critiques of appeals to universality, especially in the context of colonial/European "humanism," without abandoning the universal altogether and thereby falling prey to the politics of purity. Is there a way to appeal to "humanity" or "the human" that does not open itself up to these important critiques? If oppression is indeed *dehumanizing*, then what would it mean to articulate an account of liberation as genuinely *humanizing*?

In the creolizing spirit that animates this project, into the ongoing conversation involving Hegel, Fanon, Biko, and Anzaldúa, I will introduce Sylvia Wynter and Lewis Gordon. Wynter's body of work over the past four decades has offered a challenging and sweeping diagnosis of the colonial condition. Drawing from key works in history, anthropology, literary theory, psychology, philosophy, and cognitive science, her ambitious project is to articulate an account of the rise to dominance of "European Man" as a particular "genre" of our species, one that must ultimately be displaced in order to secure a future for what she takes to be a more genuinely universal conception of the human. Gordon's texts deal consistently with themes of dehumanization and liberation, offering a profound diagnosis of the colonial condition and advancing a liberatory vision of the *praxis* of freedom that is, in his words, "a *universalizing* practice that is never *the universal*" (2021, 37).

My approach in this chapter will be to offer detailed, yet focused accounts of the work of Wynter and Gordon, attending in particular to their accounts of "the human" and of the struggle for freedom under dehumanizing conditions. I will then be in a position to unpack their contribution to the creolizing theory of freedom and liberation, exploring the ways in which those contributions *resonate* with the account of freedom as creolizing that I have been developing so far.

SYLVIA WYNTER ON THE OVERREPRESENTATION OF "*MAN*" AND "THE HUMAN PROJECT"

At the foundation of Wynter's argument is a particular philosophical anthropology—a view of human beings as organisms whose defining feature is our capacity to symbolically structure our relation to the world and each other. This latter capacity sets the conditions whereby we come to embody particular modes of attraction and aversion—a culture-specific account of *normal* behavior that actively shapes, and is not merely a product of, our neurophysiology. We therefore cannot be reduced purely to neurophysiological features, because the motivational function of such features—what attracts and what repels us—is always ineluctably conditioned by our culturally specific *sense of self* (Wynter 2001, 55–58). In Wynter's view, we are, as a species, a "uniquely hybrid" combination of *bios* and *logos* (1995, 43). This means that who "we" are is always a matter our "discursively instituted programs whose good/evil formulations function to activate the biochemical reward/punishment mechanism of the brain—as a mechanism that, while common to all species, functions in the case of humans in terms specific to each such narratively inscribed and discursively elaborated descriptive statement and, thereby, to its mode of the 'I' and correlated symbolically/ altruistically bonded mode of the eusocial 'we'" (Wynter 2003, 273–74; cf. 2006, 134; and 2001, 49). She refers to this process as *autopoetics* (Wynter 1984, 44). Importantly, Wynter's point is not simply the idea that we are both "nature" and "nurture," so to speak, but rather that nurture (*logos*, or in some of her writings, *mythos*) comes to shape or condition our nature (*bios*), though often, significantly, in ways that escape our notice and critical attention. We can, she tells us, "*experience ourselves as human* only through the mediation of the processes of socialization effected by the invented *tekhne* or cultural technology to which we give the name *culture*" (Wynter 2001, 53), but all too often this *tekhne* is attributed to divine providence, or more recently, to natural selection or the laws of economics, and thus not understood as a product of human agency (Wynter 2006, 134). Her overall methodology, as a consequence, is to bring to the fore the ways in which our meaning-making faculties function to articulate different senses of "the human" and of "reason" itself, attending particularly to the ways in which their specific articulations have changed and developed over time, and how they distinguish themselves from other senses of being human.

While this *bios/logos* hybridity is species-wide (universal), Wynter's work is concerned with the way in which the particular Western bourgeois autopoetic *tekhne* of modern Europe and its cultural descendants came to "overrepresent" itself as *the Human* simpliciter (Wynter 2003, 260). In Wynter's account, the medieval European order articulated a *genre* or *kind* of human as *Christian* (2006, 117), where what is now "Europe" was thought of principally in terms of *Christendom*, as distinguished from pagans, heathens, and idolaters. This genre was gradually replaced by the secularized notion of *homo politicus* (122) or the "rational self" (2003, 266) of "European *Man*."[1] In essence, this transition was one from a world view in which redemption from original sin was offered through subordination to the Church and its representatives (the priesthood, certainly, but also the divinely-ordained aristocracy), to one in which redemption from our more base, animalistic, or irrational inclinations and drives could be achieved through subordination to the rational state (Wynter 1995, 13–14). The *True Christian Self* is in this way replaced by rational *Man* as the *genre* of the human specific to European modernity (Wynter 2001, 43). Rational *Man*, or as she also formulates the term, *Man$_1$*, in turn comes to be replaced, with developments in the natural sciences (especially Darwinian evolutionary theory), by a self-image, "*Man$_2$*," in which natural selection comes to replace divine providence and rational mastery of the natural world (2003, 266; 2006, 123). Linked as this process was, historically, to an age of colonial expansion, genocide, and chattel slavery, a crucial feature of the development of European *Man* was the fact that "this ethno-class or Western bourgeois genre or mode of being human" came to represent itself "*as if* it were . . . the human itself" (Wynter 2006, 129).

The genre *Man* thus came to gradually "overrepresent" itself as if it were the human *per se*, and the chief mechanism or strategy of this overrepresentation was the positing of all other genres of our species as standing in a relationship of *lack* with respect to the full (*pure*) humanity of European *Man*. Wynter's own summary of this "strategy" is worth quoting at length:

> [this strategy] was one by means of which Western intellectuals were to be enabled to reinvent the terms—as well as the real-life referent categories that had functions for medieval Latin-Christian Europe as *its* theocentric metaphysical category of Otherness and, therefore, of symbolic death, to the symbolic life embodied in their Judaeo-Christian matrix as the *True Christian Self*, and as a category of Otherness whose real-life referent categories were those groups classifiable as being, *inter alia, heretics, infidels, pagan, idolators*, or *Enemies of Christ* . . . —into new, and now secularizing, terms. That is, as a category of Otherness or of symbolic death, now defined as that of *Human* Others to the True *Human* Self of Western Europe's self-conceptions as *man*, and, as such Others, logically classifiable and thereby only seeable and behavable toward as the *Lack* of this ostensibly only possible conception of what it is to be human. (Wynter 2006, 124, emphasis mine; cf. 1984, 42; 2003, 282)

In positing European *Man* as the most *pure* instantiation of the human, where all others[2] appear as mode of lack or *impurity*, there emerges the general category of what Wynter refers to as "the Human Other to *Man*" (125). Significantly, she argues that this category of human Other to *Man* is necessary to the larger strategy of overrepresentation. To be *Man*, and thus fully (purely) human, is to *not* be numbered among those who are *Other to Man*. It functions, in other words, as a kind of negative definition. The human Other to *Man* in this way serves a vital function. Because it is the human *Other*, it stands as a critical form of contrast—it reveals an already-transcended "primitive" past, or a kind of evolutionary dead-end, and brings into focus, by way of contrast, the unique status of *Man* as fully realized human. At the same time, because it is the *human* Other to man, it adds specificity and content to the meaning of this "full" humanity, since it is not merely contrasted with the "animal" or "nonhuman."

The crux of Wynter's account is the argument that European modernity gave content to its own genre of "the Human" (and a corresponding *humanism*) in and through the relegation of the vast majority of the globe into this ironic intermediate category—more human than beast, but not quite *fully* (purely) human. A defining feature of this full humanity is a particular account of *rationality*. From her earliest articulations of this argument, Wynter made clear that "the ordering principle of the discourse [constituting European *Man*] was the same: the figuration of an ontological order of value between the groups who were markers of 'rationality' and those who were the markers of its Lack-State" (1984, 42). Wynter is consistent on this point, continually drawing attention to the way in which the overrepresentation of *Man* is at the same time an overrepresentation of European norms of reason. This point follows from her historical narrative. The shift from the medieval to the modern self-concept was one marked by the valorization of rationality as the source of redemption (understood as the domination and control of that which is irrational—including not only forces of nature, but those irrational elements within our own psyches and within the body politic). The move to Man_2 inaugurated by the Darwinian revolution simply equated superior rationality with genetically superior "fitness," and saw the rise to global dominance of European peoples and cultures as clear evidence of their "selection" and the "dysselection" of those being dominated (Wynter 2003, 310 and 324). The argument here is not that reason *simpliciter* is somehow colonial or Eurocentric, but rather that the *logos* side of the European *bios/logos* hybrid articulates a particular account of what appears to be "reasonable" or rational, as does every particular *logos* (culture). However, because European modernity posited its particular account of what is rational as *the* universal (overrepresentation as the rational *as such*), it came to view all those who occupied the various categories of human Other to *Man* as marked by a deficiency in their rational faculties. The move to Man_2, leading as it did to a robust account of biological *race* governed by natural selection, saw this fullness or deficiency of reason (and thus humanity) as marked in the flesh.[3]

In sum, the emergence of the genre *Man*, beginning gradually in the sixteenth century, saw the development of a distinctly European sense of self ("we the rational") that understood its particular genre of humanity as isomorphic with the human as such (the universal). This was made manifest necessarily through the generation of the category of the "human Other to

Man," understood as standing constitutively in a relation of lack with respect to the genre *Man*, and representing, within this dominant symbolic order, a kind of "Ultimate Chaos" (Wynter 1984, 37) that requires the control of those who represent (embody) order and reason. As I have argued elsewhere, this self-concept as the bearers of rationality, and the understanding that reason is expressed through domination or control of what is irrational (nature, drives, "the masses"), paired with an understanding of non-Europeans as *lacking* rationality, generates in effect an imperative to colonize (Monahan 2011, 164). The all-too-familiar trope of the "white man's burden" can thus be understood within the framework that Wynter provides as a clear expression of the role that reason plays in the self-concept of the genre *Man*. All of this has, of course, profound material and spiritual/psychological consequences, as Wynter makes clear.

> This misequation [of a particular genre with the universal of the species] then functions strategically to absolutize the behavioral norms encoded in our present culture-specific conceptions of being human, allowing it to be posited *as if* it were the universal of the human species, and ensuring thereby that all actions taken for the sake of the well-being of its referent model continue to be perceived *as if* they were being taken for the sake of the human-in-general: *propter nos homines*. This belief . . . was called in question by Pope John Paul II, in his recent audience with the Amazonian Indians, where he spoke of the "vicious cycle of joblessness and poverty" in which land-hungry immigrants to the Amazon Basin were as trapped as the Amazonian Indians themselves, in a "picture of pain." (Wynter 1995, 43–44).

The result of the overrepresentation of *Man*, in Wynter's diagnosis, has been environmental and human degradation on a global scale. What, then, is to be done?

In an essay reflecting on the legacy of 1492, Wynter frames the problematic, interestingly, in terms of *autonomy*. She argues that the "mutation at the level of human cognition" inaugurated by the turn from a theocentric worldview and the willingness to challenge the boundaries and limits of the Christian episteme of late-medieval Europe gave rise, ultimately, to the natural sciences (38). "This in turn," she goes on, "led to the *autonomy* of such cognition (that is, outside its earlier role as an imperative function of verifying each order's mode of 'subjective understanding') with respect to the earth and physical reality in general" (38, emphasis mine). She counts this as a kind of "partial victory," as our autonomy with respect to the natural world touches only on the *bios* half of our hybrid being, while we remain heteronomous with respect to our *logos*. Wynter draws in this essay, as she would repeatedly in her essays of the mid-1990s on, on a reading of Fanon's concept of *sociogeny* as a way to elaborate her account of the *logos* portion of our "Janus-faced" nature. "What Fanon recognized was the central role played in our human behaviors by our always linguistically constituted criteria of being (that is, our human *skins*, represented *masks*)," Wynter writes (45). So long as the dominant self-concept, European *Man*, understands its "linguistically constituted criteria of being" to be a simple expression of (false) universal "human nature," and its culturally-specific account of reason and meaning to be normative for the species as such, then the "victory" must remain complete. We must, to complete the victory, close "the dangerous gap that now exists between our increasing human autonomy with respect to our knowledge of the physical and organic levels of reality, and our lack of any such autonomy with respect to knowledge of our specifically human level of reality" (49). The inner-workings of the physical world, in other words, are increasingly apparent, while the "specifically human" level of *mythos/logos* (that is, meaning-making) remains always in operation, but behind our metaphorical backs. Because our current sociogenic/symbolic order is so profoundly (self-)destructive, yet presents itself as a kind of inescapable-because-inherent necessity, we stand in a mode of species-wide crisis so long as this "dangerous gap" remains in place. Autonomy with respect to our *logos* must be seized if we are to avoid species-wide catastrophe.

The key to realizing this "complete victory" of autonomy across the entirety to our hybrid being will require, in Wynter's view, a new *poetics*. Because the problem lies in a symbolic order that presents itself as a natural-order, we must confront that symbolic order as a contingent, culturally or *genre*-specific practice of world-and-self-making. As she puts the point:

> Thus, the task before us will be to bring into being a new poetics of the *propter nos*. Such a new poetics would, in the wake of Fanon's formulation [of sociogenesis], have to engage both in a redefinition of the relation between *concrete* individual men and women and in the socializing processes of the systems of symbolic representations generated from the codes that govern all human purposes and behaviors—including those of our present globally hegemonic culture, as at present instituted about [*sic*] in its model of being "Man" ... Such a poetics, as the expression of the universalistic conception of the *propter nos*, will therefore, in the wake of Fanon, look for the explanation of our human behaviors *not* in the individual psyche of the ostensibly purely bio-ontogenetic subject, but rather *in the process* of socialization that institutes the individual as a human, and therefore, *always* sociogenetic subject. (47)

We must, in other words, attend critically to the self-concept of European *Man*, and especially its account of *reason* (40), precisely as the contingent and genre-specific self-concept that it is. Recognizing ourselves as at once its authors and its products, the "new poetics of the *propter nos*" would require taking responsibility for that authorship, and opening the door to re-writing it (and thus ourselves). Thus here, as with the discussion of Biko and Anzaldúa in the prior chapter, we find the theme of *responsibility* emerging in a prominent way.

While the powerful critique Wynter mounts here focuses on the ways in which a particular genre of the human has overrepresented itself as the universal human, she does not reject the idea of the human *as such*. On the contrary, she consistently makes clear her commitment to a *genuinely* universal account of the human. Nearly a decade after the "1492" essay, for instance, she writes that her

> argument proposes that the struggle of our new millennium will be one between the ongoing imperative of securing the well-being of our present ethnoclass (i.e., Western bourgeois) conception of the human, Man, which overrepresents itself as if it were the human itself, and that of securing the well-being, and therefore the full cognitive and behavioral *autonomy* of the human species itself/ourselves. (Wynter 2003, 260, emphasis mine)

Here we see not only her appeal to "ourselves" as a single *human* species, but also her characterization of this struggle as one for "autonomy." She refers to this struggle for autonomy at various points as the "Man vs. Human struggle" (261) and "The Human Project" (2006, 164). This struggle involves two key elements: a need to *"relativize Man"* (161) and an understanding of the Human (as opposed to *Man*) as a *praxis*.

Wynter has thus offered a clear and compelling diagnosis of the global crisis engendered by European modernity and its underside, coloniality. Namely, she argues that a particular genre of humanity, *Man*, with its genre-specific "modes of knowing, feeling, [and] behaving," has assumed a hegemonic position, affirming itself as the human as such, and all other genres as a mode of lack with respect to the fullness (purity) of their own humanity (157). The result is a model of reason, norms for "development," and series of we-subject constituting mythoi designed to represent the present world order, with its endemic degradation of human beings and our environment, as a necessary and inevitable expression an inner essence, whether divine, rational, or biological (or, quite often, all three). This is why Wynter emphasizes the need for autonomy. If these we-subject constituting mythoi (the genre-specific *logos* of European *Man*) are encoded within those very mythoi as simply given and natural ("lawlikely," in Wynter's terminology [2003, 273]), rather than as the all-too-human (thus dynamic and open-ended) creations that they are, then those who see themselves as part of that we-subject will be unable to posit an alternative path (unable to take *responsibility*), and so long as "we" remain in control of the vast majority of the world's resources (as "we" understand those resources), the rest of the world will be dragged down with "us." As a species, we (and here Wynter's "we" is not intended as genre-specific) face a "human cognitive dilemma," which is "how . . . we can be enabled to free ourselves from our subordination to the one culture, the one descriptive statement that is the condition of us being in the mode of being that we are" (295). The generation of a new poetics in the form of the "Human Project" must, therefore, become an explicit undertaking if we, as a species, are to bring about "the fullest possible realization of our autonomy as humans, beyond the limits of Man's Project and, therefore, of our still ongoing 'wrongness of being,' of *désêtre*" (Wynter 2006, 164).

The first key aspect of this liberatory "Human Project" is to "relativize *Man*." In a 2003 essay, Wynter suggests this maneuver, when she points out that the non-Europeans who first encountered Europeans in the early days of colonial exploration and expansion had positions of "Otherness" into which they could categorize these strange newcomers that did not necessarily entail a relation of lack, while on the part of "the Europeans, however, the only available slot of Otherness to their Norm, into which they could classify these non-European populations, was one that defined the latter in terms of their ostensible subhuman status" (2003, 292). Having a particular genre is, in Wynter's account, part of what it means to be human—our hybrid *bios/logos* mode of being in effect requires the generation of a collective "kin-constituting" self-concept by and through which we negotiate the world (1984, 44; 1995, 47; 2003, 273–74; 2006, 116–17; 2015, 198). The hegemony of the genre *Man*, and a principle source of its "wrongness of being," lies therefore not in the mere fact that it is a particular genre of the human, but in the fact that is understands itself precisely as the full or pure realization of the species, and all others as that *lack* of full humanity or *corruption* of pure humanity which must be controlled, displaced, or overcome. Any "new poetics of the *propter nos*" must be directed toward shifting the self-concept of the genre *Man* to one where it understands itself as one genre of the human among many, rather than as the human *per se*—it must be "relativized."

One may, however, quite reasonably understand that sense of self-importance and understanding of itself as the human *as such* to be, in effect, *essential* to the genre *Man*. In other words, any successful "relativization" of *Man* would result in the collapse of the genre altogether. It just would not be *Man* absent a view of itself as the normative center of the universe. Perhaps the result will be a new genre descended, so to speak, from *Man*, rather than a relativized version of the same genre, but the approach is the same either way. Wynter makes this clear in her later writing, focusing on the academic (especially anthropological) study of "other" cultures and peoples:

> This *genre*-specific, Western-bourgeois representation of origins or ethno-class 'legend of descent' thereby makes it normally impossible for anthropologists

and Western academics/intellectuals in general to see themselves/ourselves as in any way *coeval* . . . with other human groups who are their/our objects of study. Indeed, this representation makes it normally impossible for them/us normally to see other human groups as fully—if differently—*co-human*. To breach this projected *Line/Divide* of co-humanity would necessarily call for Western and westernized academics/intellectuals to effect their/our own Autopoetic Turn/Overturn. For such a *turn* would force them/us to accept the *relativization* of their/our own 'part science, part myth' origin-story. (2015, 215–16)

The process of relativization thus entails the autopoetic overturn of the dominant ethno-class *Man*. Rather than seeing ourselves/themselves as the full and complete (pure) expression of the human as distinct from various "deficient" expressions, we/they must re-articulate a self-concept in which *this* way of being human retreats from being *the* way to be human becomes just *a* way of being human among many alternatives. Whether it still makes sense to think of this "overturned" self-concept as *Man* (only relativized), or as some entirely new genre, is an open question, and makes little difference to the autopeotic prescription she offers. Wynter herself is clear in articulating the project as one of relativizing *Man*, and sees this process as central to a fuller realization of our autonomy as a species.

Wynter's prescription, I would like to emphasize, is for an *auto*poiesis, and thus the question of the *self* engaging in the poetic project emerges. She describes "The Human Project" at one point, as "inseparable from the recognition of our individual and collective responsibility for the societal effects to which each such process of genre-instituting leads" (Wynter 2006, 164). Her emphasis on recognition and responsibility very strongly resonates with the existentialist themes that have been appearing consistently in the meditation on liberation throughout this text, and in particular works in concert with the calls for a kind of critical (self)consciousness in the previous chapter's discussions of Biko and Anzaldúa. This is, in other words, another way to think through the process of constituting a we-subject capable of critically appraising and proactively altering its own ongoing practices of self-constitution (or, in Wynter's terms, *autopoiesis*). The challenge before us/them is to refashion our/their narrative practices of "genre-instituting" ourselves/themselves, and so it becomes apparent how Biko, Anzaldúa, and Wynter are involved in a shared conversation and project. This shared challenge is, significantly, a genuinely *universal* feature of our hybrid *bios/logos* mode of being, though the urgency and intensity of the challenge in the case of the genre *Man* is quite particular. This last point brings us finally to an explicit articulation of Wynter's own version of humanism.

From 1984's "The Ceremony Must Be Found" to 2015's "The Ceremony Found" we see Wynter consistently identifying universal features of being, as she puts it in the latter essay, *"ecumenically human"* (2015, 193) while mounting a far-ranging and rigorous critique of the rise to dominance of one genre of the human, *Man*, that takes overrepresents itself as the human per se. The critique, ultimately, is that *Man*'s mistake is to think of being human as having definite *content*—to be human is to be *like* this/us. The truth that Wynter arrives at, and states most unequivocally in that later essay, however, is that "of our *being human* as 'always a doing,' of our *being human as praxis*" (196). Put differently, we might say that "the human" is not a mode of *being* but a *becoming*—and in this way is an always-in-progress *praxis*. The self-concept of European *Man* denies this truth, and thus attempts to account for the human in the mode of static being rather than dynamic becoming. The human is a *praxis* that, in each instance, necessarily articulates itself in and through a specific genre (199–201). For any given *we*, therefore, our humanity is expressed (as a praxis) through a specific *genre*, and this need for genre-specificity can be considered a large part of what is universal about humanity. "*We humans cannot pre-exist our cosmogonies or origin myths/stories/narratives*," Wynter writes, "anymore than a bee, at the purely biological level of life, can pre-exist its beehive" (213). The "Human Project," therefore, must be one not of escaping from our genre-specificity, or arriving at some final all-encompassing "universal genre," but of obtaining some degree of autonomy and responsibility for those myths, stories, and narratives that constitute our genre-specific worlds, our places within them, and most significantly, their relationship to alternative myths, stories, and narratives (to other *worlds*, in fact).

This aspect of the "Human Project" again points toward a moment of *relativization*. All of us are (universally) genre-specific, and we better come to know (in the *practical* sense) this universal when we acknowledge that specificity as one among others (as relative). In this way, it is a call for a kind of *reciprocity*. The Human, as a praxis of becoming enacted only in and through particular genre-specific modes of hybrid *bios/logos*, emerges always through the productive friction engendered by the interaction of these specific genres. When one seeks to deny interaction—to inhibit or disavow this productive friction—then knowledge of the human (and ourselves as human) is impoverished. What is needed is a reciprocity and mutual openness to this kind of interaction. Through the *reciprocal* encounter with difference, the universal reveals itself to us, though never in a complete or fully-present way. And this is not merely a function of our epistemic limitations (tragic), but rather an ontological feature of the human *as praxis*—as an ongoing process of becoming that exists only in and through the interaction of particulars. Wynter's prescription of a "new poetics of the *propter nos*" can thus be understood as a call for responsibility and reciprocity, two themes quite clearly resonant with the account of freedom (autonomy) I have been developing.

Wynter's work, in the later stages of its development, thus appeals directly to the kind of dynamic/relational ontology that has served as the frame for this book. Once we take on an understanding the human as *praxis*, the possibility opens up for a genuinely universal account of the human that does not fall prey to the well-established (and powerful) critiques of European/Eurocentric Humanism. Any account of "the human" that settles on a static and complete or closed content for that concept will necessarily miss the mark, if what it means to be human is to be always in progress (becoming). We can thus say that the "essence" of the human is to always be expressed through *some* particular culturally-specific self-concept, but that the particular *genre* of that expression is always necessarily just one among many possible genres. That horizon of possibility stretches out indefinitely (we have ways of conceiving of our humanity that were unavailable to previous generations) in principle, but the crisis of our present moment rests precisely on the fact that one particularly destructive and short-sighted genre has come to dominate or drown out all others (as a manifestation of "white noise"). The horizon of possibility, in other words, is collapsing as a result of *Man* overrepresenting itself as The Human. Our future viability as a species, therefore, demands the "final victory" of our autonomy and responsibility with respect to those genre-specific *ways* of *practicing* what it means to be human.

LEWIS GORDON AND THE TELEOLOGICAL SUSPENSION OF THE HUMAN

Lewis R. Gordon has identified three central themes or moments in the practice of Africana philosophy. In his words, "Among the pressing themes of Africana philosophy are: (1) philosophical anthropology, (2) liberation, and (3) metacritiques of reason" (Gordon 2011, 99; cf. Gordon 2008b, 92; and 2021, 89–90). Philosophical anthropology, in his account, involves investigations into what it means to be human, and is brought sharply into focus within Africana traditions as a result of the centuries-long processes and relations of *dehumanization* (especially, though certainly not exclusively, as it pertains to race). That is, when one's humanity is consistently called into question, then questions about the scope and meaning of *the human* as a concept can take on paramount importance. This struggle with and against dehumanization, especially through processes of enslavement and colonization, goes hand in hand with the second focus—liberation. The possibilities of freedom, and the ways and means of realizing it, in other words, loom large in Africana philosophical traditions and practices (this is, indeed, what originally drew me to them as an undergraduate). Attention to historical processes of dehumanization, at the same time, reveal that accounts of reason, and what it means to be rational, play a key role. The *philosopher* attempting to grapple with the first two themes, therefore, quickly finds themselves reasoning within a context where reason per se has been understood to be firmly on the side, so to speak, of the dominators over and against the dominated. Thus, the "metacritique of reason" emerges as fundamental to Africana philosophy.

In this section, I will use Gordon's schematic for Africana philosophy as a heuristic guide to lay out what I take to be the key elements of his thought as they pertain to the chapter's central theme—the question of "the human" as it pertains to the theory and practice of liberation. I will, however, take them somewhat out of order, saving the discussion of liberation for last, since that will be the primary way in which this section contributes to the larger theme of this book. As we shall see, however, the three themes are each intimately related, and "starting" and "ending" with any one of them is in an important sense only ever a heuristic convenience. I will begin, therefore, with Gordon's own philosophical anthropology.

One key to understanding Gordon's philosophical anthropology is to frame it within the context of his consistent commitments to existential phenomenology, which is apparent throughout his corpus, from *Bad Faith and Antiblack Racism* (1995a) to *Fear of Black Consciousness* (2022). Significantly, however, his understanding of existential phenomenology is not limited to a particular subset of thinkers and texts in the European canon, but understood rather in broadly thematic terms, which allow him to identify similar methodological commitments in a broad array of texts from around the globe. Thus, while his earlier work did indeed draw heavily on the writings of Husserl (especially in *Fanon and the Crisis of European Man* [Gordon 1995b]) and Sartre (especially in *Bad Faith and Antiblack Racism*), and those figures do continue to appear in his later works, he identifies a broad array of figures who populate his global existential landscape, from Frederick Douglass (2000, 41–61), to Richard Wright (2008b, 133–34), to Ali Shariati (2021, 102), and Anna Julia Cooper (2008b, 71–72). His point here is not that any of these figures were self-identified "existentialists" in the sense often employed within the academy but, rather, that their work evokes, directly or indirectly, many of the themes and raises many of the key problems and dilemmas that can be understood as "existential" in the broad sense. In other words, the claim is not that these non-European figures "fit" neatly into the prescribed definition of "existentialism," or "phenomenology," but rather that they are raising similar questions and pointing toward similar insights into the human condition.

What exactly are those questions and insights? Gordon's discussion of Frederick Douglass offers a very clear account. The theme of the larger text in which his essay on Douglass is situated is "Black existential thought," and he notes early in the essay, reflecting on exemplars like Phillis Wheatley, Richard Wright, Ralph Ellison, and Toni Morrison, that "in black writing is the question of black consciousness, the idea that black people have perspectives on the world" (2000, 42). Since, as Gordon emphasizes earlier in the text, the anti-Black world functions to deny, in effect, that the Black subject has a *point of view* on the world (a position discussed also in the previous chapter), the production of a text, whether an autobiography or some other form of literary work, already constitutes a radical intervention and disruption of that world which Gordon understands in phenomenological terms. If, in the broadest sense, he understands phenomenology as "reflective thought upon what can be called objects of thought," or *phenomena*, then we see that his point about having perspectives on the world is really a gesture toward consciousness, or what the more orthodox phenomenologist would call *intentionality* (73). Or consider his claim that in Douglass's autobiographies (which he reads in conjunction with Angela Davis's later reflections on them), "there is not only the centering of the question of freedom, but also a critique of the practice of using abstract humanity to conceal what existential phenomenologists call 'human being in the flesh'" (43). There is, ultimately, an emphasis on the core thematic that *existence precedes essence*—that human existence, linked inextricably as it is to *consciousness* as an always outward-directed activity (of *intention*), defies what we might think of as a kind of ontological closure. It is always open-ended, incomplete, and insofar as processes of dehumanization function to impose a mode of closure on human beings, then we find that liberation "always calls for a new humanity to emerge out of unfreedom, a new humanity that is paradoxically the guiding *telos* underneath a humanity denied" (54). The point of this exploration of Gordon's existential phenomenological commitments is to make clear the broader framework in and through which to explore his thought generally, but especially as it relates to his philosophical anthropology. With this in mind, I will now follow some of the more specific threads from his earlier work to his more recent.

An obvious point of departure is the concept of *bad faith* (*mauvaise foi*) not only because this originally Sartrean concept is a key focus of his dissertation-cum-book *Bad Faith and Antiblack Racism*, and is a recurring theme throughout his work up to and including his most recent text (Gordon 2022, 59–65), but also because it helps to frame key aspects of his philosophical anthropology. I have already briefly discussed and appealed to the notion of "bad faith," but a more rigorous elaboration is called for at this point. At its core, bad faith "involves the ability to lie to oneself" (59). It captures the complicated condition wherein the liar and the one being lied to are the same person. Its roots in existential phenomenology, however, are crucial for understanding the depth and complexity of the concept. Gordon makes this particularly explicit in *Fanon and the Crisis of European Man*. Starting with the Husserlian insight that consciousness is always *intentional*—that it is always actively directed toward some object—Gordon emphasizes that consciousness is also always *mediated*. That which we intend appears (is "given") *qua* object-of-consciousness ("phenomenon") only by being differentiated from other objects in a complex set of relations mediated by inescapably social webs of meaning (1995b, 15–16). Bad faith emerges when we reflect upon, or intend, our own intentionality. As Gordon puts the point, such an investigation of our own intentionality "is possible only by virtue of a being that can not only question its own being, but may also deny its involvement in the questioning" (16). This possibility of denial is, in turn, a function of the fact that consciousness, as an activity, cannot be captured in any simultaneous act of consciousness. In other words, I may reflect on (*intend* or be-conscious-of) a given act of consciousness (say, my consciousness of the keyboard upon which I write this sentence), but that *act* of reflection is distinct from the act of consciousness upon which it is reflecting (that it is intending as *its* object). According to Gordon, "when I assert who I 'am,' I discover this self instantly eluding me as who I *was*," since the I engaged in the act of assertion is emerging in and through that act as distinct from the content of its assertion (1995a, 14).

Sartre builds upon this phenomenological insight by characterizing this open-ended aspect of consciousness as a form of *negation* or "nothingness" that is *embodied* or situated, but because it is an ongoing activity directed beyond itself, is never reducible to or fully defined by that situation. Because consciousness is always embodied, it is laden with what we might think of as the materiality of *being embodied in this way*, which includes being in this place at this time, and emerging out of this history. It has, in Sartre's terms, "facticity" (1994, 83). But because consciousness is itself an activity, it is manifest not in the mode of *being* at all, but as a negation or nothingness (think here of the "negating activity" Fanon referenced in the prior chapter). Sartre calls this "transcendence" (lxi). "The foundation of human reality is therefore its lack of foundation," as each new act of consciousness generates its own contribution to our facticity, setting the stage for yet further acts of consciousness (Gordon 1995a, 9). Even the act of *intending* a given situation as "not worth altering" is nevertheless an act, and it is in this inescapable condition of always-emerging moments of intention that responsibility rests, for here "we face the fact that we are the ones who must make the choices that constitute our selves" (13). This one way to understand Sartre's sense of *freedom*, and this constant confrontation with freedom entails a kind of deep-seated responsibility linked to what Sartre referred to as "Anguish"

(17). Bad faith emerges as an effort to flee this freedom and its corresponding responsibility though one of two basic modes. Through either "choosing to take refuge in a notion of myself as a reified substance" (*I couldn't help it, that's just who I am*), or by claiming "that what I 'really am' transcends my situation in the world" (*I'm just a human being like any other, and my being 'white' or a 'man' is irrelevant*), one seeks an evasion of freedom and responsibility (Gordon 1995a, 17).[4]

There are many dimensions to and expressions of bad faith that emerge throughout Gordon's writings. Racism expresses bad faith in the way it posits racial modes of *being* that situate human beings along a normative continuum, where one's value or disvalue is simply given in that racial *being*. Gordon refers to this phenomenon, following Simone de Beauvoir, as a "serious" attitude (Gordon 1995a, 95). For the antiblack racist, for instance, being virtuous, civilized, rational, and generally superior is simply a matter of one's *being* "white," or at least their not being "black." One's value is thus a matter of *what* one is, rather than *who* one is (i.e., the choices and actions they take). This is a bad faith evasion of one's active role in generating and perpetuating the racial "reality" to which it appeals. At the same time, denying the ways in which race functions in one's life and conditions the kinds of choices and actions available to them (as in "color-blindness"), is a bad faith evasion of the ways in which race inescapably constitutes the situation (facticity) from and through which we act in the world (97–98; 2022, 58–61).

There is, consistent through all appeals to bad faith, and emphasis on the evasion of responsibility, or, as one might put it, ability to *respond*. If values and meanings are pre-given (by God, or nature, for instance), then no response from me is called for (I bear no responsibility). If the conditions in which I choose are irrelevant (I am "self-made"), then there is nothing to which I am *responding*—I am merely expressing my will. Bad faith can thus be understood as a mode of self-deception aimed at convincing ourselves (and others) that we are either bereft of control (and thus responsibility), or that we have absolute control (and thus are not responsible *to* our situation or to ourselves-as-situated). Either of these modes entails the effort to avoid the "anguish" resulting from our inescapable confrontation with ourselves as consciousness-in-the-flesh, and thus as always *intending* from and through a material and historical context that is both inescapably social and uniquely our own. It is in this sense that "no human being is a subject alone, nor an object alone," and assuming genuine responsibility for ourselves demands a constant negotiation with this fundamental ambiguity (Gordon 1997a, 72).

Bad faith is thus made possible by a particular philosophical anthropology (deeply indebted to phenomenology) in which "human reality . . . is always at a distance from itself" (Gordon 1995a, 52). This is one way in which Gordon captures the existentialist dictum that *existence precedes essence*—for "existence" is a transitive verb, and thus a mode of becoming in the form of intentional consciousness which, in always coming *before* the moment of reflection (reflection on where we have been, where we are, or where we are going—that is, our *situation*) means that human reality is always in an ongoing process of becoming, and thus always at a distance from its *being* (essence). At the same time, because consciousness is in-the-flesh (embodied), human reality is also inescapably conditioned by its being, including especially the fact that its being is ineluctably *social* (Gordon 1995b, 21). This latter feature emerges from the fact that every aspect of our being (facticity/situation), *appears* as such by virtue of the meanings attached to it through diffuse, complex, and always ongoing social processes of meaning-making ("intersubjective constitution"). Even bad faith efforts to evade this sociality (abstract individualism, disembodiment, "color-blindness," etc.) are made possible "through the social dimensions of being" that make these efforts themselves meaningful and, in many cases, *normalize* them (20; cf. Gordon 2000, 78). This constant encounter with a world of meaning in which we actively participate even as it conditions that participation is the source of the ambiguity referenced in the previous paragraph. Who and what I am is always to some extent up to me as an active participant, yet it is never entirely up to me insofar as my participation is always conditioned—hence the ambiguity. When one finds such ambiguity intolerable, one will seek refuge in bad faith, which means we may also link bad faith to the politics of purity—to an effort to avoid indeterminacy and ambiguity.

One way in which Gordon consistently characterizes this ambiguity is as a kind of "openness," such that our existence is always an open-ended process (of becoming) that necessarily defies final definitions and static essences. If we think of an opening as a kind of gap or absence of what would otherwise function to enclose, then we can see how this is linked to Sartrean "nothingness." But Gordon's appeal is richer than mere absence, for an opening can be directional—it *leads* from one place to another. This is evident in his earlier work, for example when he characterizes human existence under racist/colonial conditions (following Fanon) as being "bound, contained, kept at bay, and held secure as a stabilized entity that supports self-delusion" (23). This appeal to openness becomes more explicit in subsequent work. As he writes in *Existentia Africana*: "An impact of social reality, then, is ontological; it transforms concepts—knowledge claims—into lived concepts, forms of being, forms of life" (Gordon 2000, 84). Given our ambiguous position as both generators of the world and generated by it (but never *purely* one or the other), we must understand both ourselves and our world(s) as ongoing (open-ended) works in progress that defy what he refers to as "epistemic closure" (88).

This argument regarding sociality, closure and openness is sustained throughout his work. Consider the following examples:

> As relational, it means that each human being is a constant negotiation of ongoing efforts to build relationships with others, which means no one actually enters a situation without establishing new situations of action and meaning. (Gordon 2001, 78)

> Human beings both create the world we live in and are conditioned by that world. To take on such a complex dynamic, we must then take on the question of "reality" in our thought. That question pertains to the relationship between our embodiment and the social world, and it relates to the question of the ontology necessitated by the emergence of social *reality*. (Gordon 2006b, 45)

> If the human being is in the making, then "human reality" is never complete and is more the relations in which such thought takes place than a claim about the thought. (Gordon 2021, 74)

His appeal to "lived concepts" and "forms of life" in *Existentia Africana* sets the stage for his later account of *decadence*—that which is living is growing and changing, while that which is decadent is ossified (the etymological appeal to bone here is telling) and stagnant—it has become *enclosed*. In the epistemic context, this can take the form of a discipline or method centering itself as complete, rather than as *open* to revision and the pursuit of truth beyond its own boundaries (Gordon 2006a, 13–35).

As we have seen, to be human, according to Gordon's philosophical anthropology, is to be in the inescapably ambiguous position of at once conditioning and being conditioned by a world. In this way we are neither simply reducible to the material and social situations that condition our creative activity, nor are we ever *pure* and unconditioned creativity. Echoing Wynter, therefore, we may say that human existence is a *praxis*, and in this way is a dynamic process of becoming, rather than a static form of being. According to Gordon, "each human being is a constant negotiation of ongoing efforts to build relationships with others, which means no one actually enters a situation without establishing new situations of action and meaning" (2021, 78). Our "negotiating" efforts are thus inescapably conditioned by our embodied and historical reality. The language(s) we speak, the geographical location we occupy, the historical tradition(s) out of which we emerge, the significant features of our physiology—all of these fundamentally sculpt (they both limit *and* enable) what we are able to intend (both in the phenomenological sense of an object of intention, and in the more mundane sense of the plans and projects we are able to formulate), and all of them are themselves shaped by the past and ongoing intentions of other human beings. At the same time, because we remain engaged in that ongoing negotiation, that reality is something that we participate in shaping. This is the deeper sense of "responsibility" at stake, since we find ourselves thrust into a reality that demands from us a *response*, which response will make its own contribution, however minute and diffuse, to that reality. Various forms of decadence and bad faith, as we have seen, thus take the form of avoiding that responsibility by closing off that complicated dynamic and relational process, denying either our active participation in the generation of a shared reality or the ways in which that reality conditions our actions.

The "metacritique of reason" emerges as a necessity in the face of this philosophical anthropology. Note here that the account Gordon is advancing is one in which, in the epistemic context, both the knower and the object of knowledge (human existence) are dynamic processes in a relation of reciprocal co-constitution. This is clearly quite consistent with the larger ontological framework I have been advancing throughout this text, and one that calls for an emphasis on *practical* over propositional models of epistemic praxis. One way to approach Gordon's call for a metacritique of reason, is thus to account for his emphasis on "openness" and relationality as a warning to avoid variations on what Gordon refers to as "disciplinary decadence." I have already made reference to his appeal to decadence as a turn toward stasis or "ossification." Decadence in the context of disciplines "is the ontologizing or reification of a discipline," when "we treat our discipline as though it was never born and has always existed and will never change" (Gordon 2006a, 4). In the broadest terms, this entails a valorization of *method* as a kind of closed or complete system which, once fully articulated, need only ever be applied. If reality were static, and the epistemic agent (as well as their particular method) were not *part of* (standing in relation to) that reality, such closure and completeness might be possible (or at least function as a regulatory ideal). This impulse toward decadence, Gordon argues, is driven by a kind of commitment to purity and a corresponding intolerance for ambiguity. "This quest for purity," he writes, "turns disciplines away from reality in their quest for controlled outcomes" (Gordon 2021, 39). For such *decadent* disciplinary practices, "reality becomes problematic," as a result, "because it is, quite simply, 'impure' and resistant to complete control" (39). Gordon's critique of decadence is thus predicated upon the kind of ambiguous, dynamic, and relational ontology that has been at the center of my investigation throughout this text.

In response to the challenge posed by decadence, understood as an appeal to purity in the form of closure, completeness, and stasis, Gordon calls for a "teleological suspension." In *Disciplinary Decadence*, he offers the following account of a "teleological suspension" of disciplinarity:

> Recall that by this I mean Kierkegaard's move of teleologically suspending the universal/ethical through a leap of faith to the Absolute in *Fear and Trembling*. That which is absolute is greater than that which is universal . . . when one initiates a teleological suspension of a discipline, it could initiate a new relationship to that discipline: one of a higher level of understanding. In philosophical thought, for example, its suspension paradoxically *is* philosophical, but not in philosophy as previously understood. (2006a, 44)

Gordon reminds us that epistemic pursuits, and the disciplines that emerge from them, are always engendered by efforts to understand and confront problems and challenges posed by a reality that is, given his philosophical anthropology, always a dynamic *human* and *social/relational* reality. Decadence is manifest when the problem that led to the generation of the discipline fades to the background, and the discipline assumes a position as self-justificatory—as the "universal" which captures reality in a complete and closed (pure) way. In the process of teleological suspension, we "bracket" that commitment to completeness and universality, returning to the problem or challenge that motivates the investigation, thus allowing ourselves to be *open* to transcending the bounds and norms of the discipline *for the sake of* (this is the "teleological" aspect) addressing that problem. By emphasizing "a commitment to questions greater than the discipline itself" we find that it is necessary not to abandon disciplinary rigor altogether, but rather to preserve an openness and flexibility better suited to an ambiguous and dynamic reality (34).

Given his understanding of philosophy as a "form of radical critique" (1997b, 26), it is clear why Gordon holds the teleological suspension of philosophy *as a discipline* to be more fully philosophical than the all-too-common decadent approaches that dominate the field in the academy. He tells us that, "when philosophers do this—attempt to think beyond philosophy to greater commitments—they ironically breathe life into philosophy's gasping lungs" (2006a, 34). The exercise of reason as a radical critique in a world where there is a dynamic reciprocity between the investigator and the object of their investigation, in other words, precludes the collapse of reason into a closed and complete system that needs only be applied. Reason, in order to raise important self-critical questions about its own scope and practices, must therefore suspend or transcend itself as a way, ironically, to be more fully *reasonable*. This is precisely what is meant by the "metacritique of reason" in its most general sense. For Gordon, this marks the distinction (one I discussed in chapter 1) between *rationality*, which focuses on "instrumental concerns of control and predictability," and *reason*, which "sets the basis for evaluation and self-reflection" (127; cf. Gordon 2011, 97).[5] There is a reification of rationality dominant in much of the discipline of philosophy which takes the valorization of rationality to such an extreme that it becomes *unreasonable* (Gordon 2021, 46). Importantly for the purposes of this chapter, Gordon suggests that one *telos* for which disciplinarity needs to be suspended is that of *freedom* (2006b, 46), which insight brings us directly to the third thematic focus identified in the beginning of my discussion of Gordon's work, liberation. Having briefly described philosophical anthropology and the metacritique of reason, we can now turn to his understanding of liberation as a practice directed toward freedom.

From the outset, it is crucial to bear in mind that there are two distinct, yet interrelated modes in which freedom operates in Gordon's texts. The first mode is a kind of primordial or, one might say, *ontological* freedom that has its roots in his engagement with existential phenomenology. This ontological sense of freedom is bound to the phenomenological mode of *intentionality* discussed above, which picks out our ever-present (so long as we remain alive/conscious) activity of intending/choosing in and through our embodied context/situation.[6] It is the incompleteness, "transcendence," or "nothingness" that plays such a significant role in our fundamental ambiguity as human beings. This is the sense of freedom that makes it possible for us to be always in the process of making ourselves and our world (open-ended processes of becoming). The second mode of freedom is more complicated, and more significant for the purposes of this chapter. For while this first "ontological" sense of freedom is ever-present (and so often, as we have seen, the source of "anguish" and the impetus for bad faith), it remains the case that ontological freedom is profoundly conditioned by our historical, material, and social situation, and the character or quality of these conditions can vary greatly. What really *matters* to us as human beings (who are "condemned," as Sartre would put it, to be free in the ontological sense) are the *ways* in which we are able to exercise or manifest this freedom. It is only in terms of this latter sense that we can understand *oppression* as a phenomenon and liberation as a practice, which Gordon explicates in terms of a distinction between "choice" and "options."

Choice, in this context, emerges as the upsurge of our ontological freedom (our "negating activity") that places us in the position of confronting the necessity to *choose* from and through our embodied situation, which choice then shapes the situation conditioning our next inevitable moment of choice. Again, this is a feature of the dictum that our existence precedes our essence. What matters to us (where "mattering" is revealed through the choices we make) is not always so much *that* we choose, but rather the character of the *options* available to us in a given situation, and in particular whether among our options exists a possible choice that not only "determines something about the chooser," but that is also able "to transform the material conditions imposed upon the chooser" (2000, 76). This latter capacity is, according to

Gordon, a function of *power*, which he understands in basic terms as "things that are able to put other things into being" (86), or "the ability to make things happen with access to the means of doing so" (2021, 21). Some power, in the context of human action, is individual, such as my power to hoist my suitcase into the overhead compartment. The kinds of power that are most relevant to this chapter, however, are kinds of *social* or institutional power where one can affect change in the world indirectly—that is, beyond the extension of one's own body. If I can deprive another of their livelihood by sending an email to my subordinates in Human Resources, or convince millions to purchase my hamburgers through the ubiquity of my advertising, then I have precisely this sort of social or institutional power. Options are a function of the power one has to exercise choice in ways conducive to one's long-term goals. Oppression, for Gordon, emerges as one's social power is minimized and one's options are constricted to the point of collapse. "When people lack power," Gordon writes, "their spheres of influence move inward to the self to the point of *implosion*," and this inward collapse is what he understands as *oppression* (2006b, 45).

Oppression is thus quite compatible with the persistence of ontological freedom, which is another way of saying that oppression inhibits or negates our political or social freedom, not our ontological freedom. For the oppressed, the majority of their choices, and especially the most significant and meaningful choices, focus on *"how to relate to the exhaustion of options"* (Gordon 2006a, 104). Consider a single mother employed as grocery store clerk during a time of global pandemic. She may choose to continue to work, which puts her own life and the life of her loved ones at risk, but enables her to continue to provide food and shelter. Or she may choose to protect the health and safety of her loved ones by staying home, but this will deprive her of income, and open the possibility to become unhoused, putting herself and her loved ones at the dubious mercy of the social safety net. Both options lead to precarity and risk, where her future options will likely be even more bleak and restricted then before.

Suppose further that she chooses to continue working, but becomes infected, and the resulting sickness rampaging through her under-insured family, paired with her lost wages due to prolonged illness, cause her to lose her home. Her options in that moment have become "exhausted." Her freedom, as Simone de Beauvoir put the point, is placed in a situation where it must "consume itself in vain" (1948, 82). Whatever choice she may make at this point is directed entirely toward the staving-off of yet further catastrophe, as opposed to creating a future with better and richer options. This illustrates how oppression places one under conditions where all *choice*s are directed toward delaying a series of looming disasters, rather than building toward a flourishing future. It does not negate or deny *choice*, Gordon argues, but constricts and narrows *options*. Oppressors "have options available to them to avoid implosion," according to Gordon, while "oppressed people do not" (2006b, 45). The teenage child of a wealthy family working that same job as our single mother in order to save money for a trip to Europe with a group of friends clearly has viable options that will open to future flourishing. In Gordon's view, therefore, oppression is a function of the *kinds* of options made available to one within a given context, and not simply a matter of whether one "has a choice" or not. But what is the normative standard by which we evaluate different sets of options? To understand the measure of those qualitative distinctions among available options, we must return to the normative sense of *human* within his philosophical anthropology.

Consider a recurring theme in Gordon's writing: racism. According to Gordon, "that racism involves dehumanization situates it as a form of oppression" (2000, 86). Oppression is thus "a human act of denying the humanity of other groups of human beings" (85). The act of oppression is "a human act" insofar as it is a freely-determined commitment on the part of the oppressor,[7] and it "denies the humanity" of the oppressed insofar seeks to collapse their options to the point of implosion. This is enabled through a bad faith appeal to *seriousness*, or to "the presentation of values as material, determined features of the world" (Gordon 1995b, 22). Insofar as the social order or culture is structured so as to normalize and facilitate this mode of seriousness, it becomes not only possible, but quite normal or ordinary for oppressors to engage in a bad faith evasion of their responsibility for ongoing relations of oppression. Gordon refers to this social/institutional facilitation of bad faith as "weak" or "institutional" bad faith (1995a, 45–48; 1995b, 21–23). Thus, within the context of weak bad faith that makes up (and is made up by) the antiblack *world*, the problems faced by Black people are "thrown out of the sphere of human problems into the sphere of necessity premised upon pathologies" (Gordon 2000, 69). In other words, the antiblack world conceives of such problems not as the collapse of options (*enacted* by human beings in ways direct, indirect, individual, and diffuse) constituting oppression, but as emerging from the "nature" of Black people such that "they cease to be people who might face, signify, or be associate with a set of problems: they *become* those problems" (69).

There is thus a clear appeal to a normative concept of the human at stake in Gordon's consistent appeals to "dehumanization." In *Fanon and the Crisis of European Man*, for instance, he writes: "Oppression is the imposition of extraordinary conditions of the ordinary upon individuals in the course of their effort to live 'ordinary' lives" (Gordon 1995b, 41). Later he characterizes oppression as demanding of the oppressed that they "take extraordinary measures to live ordinary lives" (Gordon 2000, 88), and as "a function of the range of 'normal' actions available before the process of implosion begins" (Gordon 2006b, 45). But what does he mean by "normal" and "ordinary" here? He is not so naïve as to take it to appeal simply to what is normative, or posited as "normal" within a given society (within the sonic metaphor I have been developing, this would be the sonic milieu that sets the conditions for "resonance" and "dissonance"). Indeed, he is quite sensitive to the fact that, within an antiblack context, the "normative" condition for both the oppressor and the oppressed is one of profound pathology and alienation. The *appearance* of a Black person as a fully realized human being, within an antiblack world, will always take the form of a *pathology* (Gordon 1995b, 11). In other words, it is not *normal* (in the sense of being the "norm" for that society) for a Black person in to function as a normal (in the deeper normative sense) human being in an antiblack world. In sonic terms, relations of "destructive interference" with Black subjects "appears," within the sonic milieu of "white noise" as a kind of "resonance"—it "sounds right" to inhibit the self-expression of Black agents, and their resistance to that "resonance" will "appear" as a kind of "dissonance." We face here a puzzle. On the one hand, the social norms that give content to the dominant sense of the "ordinary" within a deeply racist/colonial world are, as Gordon understands them, *dehumanizing*. To be both genuinely human and Other to "white," according to this norm, is to be pathological. On the other hand, when existence precedes essence, and human existence is understood as fundamentally incomplete and "open," what could possibly count as "normal" for the human being *per se*? How do we give content and force to this deeper sense of the *normal* in a way that is not essentialist or decadent?

To resolve this puzzle, we need to return to Gordon's understanding of human existence as a dynamic *praxis* that is always *relational*. In the context of his discussion of power, for instance, this is clear in the way he differentiates between "positive" and "negative" exercises of power.

> Where power is positive, it enables others to make things happen that affect their lives and others in the form of flourishing. The now banal term for this is "empowerment." Where power is negative, it is hoarded and results in the disempowering of others. Colonialism, enslavement, racism, sexism, and varieties of other forms of dehumanization and exploitation are forms of disempowering of others through the concentration of powers in special groups. (Gordon 2021, 22)

Much of the work in this account of power is done by the term "flourishing," and again, the content of this term is not some static end point, like the notion of a "successful" life dominant in contemporary neoliberal cultures.

Rather, flourishing is linked here to *freedom* in the second sense—not as ontological freedom, but as the always socially-situated and embodied process of making and remaking ourselves and the world we share. Freedom in this sense is, he tells us, "a meaning-constituting activity" that is a "constant demand on human existence" (Gordon 2006b, 45). Freedom in this sense, then, is neither a fundamental condition of our existence, nor a static state to be achieved (or at least toward which we must aim as a regulatory ideal). Rather, it "involves cultivating the ability to make things happen, which means it requires power as empowerment and processes of growth" (Gordon 2021, 22). In this way, the call for freedom or liberation "is the rallying of creative resources of possibility" (23), and because such power and such resources are always socially constituted and enacted in relation to others, this means that a "flourishing" or "normal" life in the relevant sense is one in which one's power is always waxing, but emphatically *not* as part of a zero-sum competition where some are "excluded from the production and appearance of and contributing to knowledge" (24). It is, in other words, a kind of "constructive interference," where interacting waves result in their mutual enhancement. Oppression is "dehumanizing," therefore, in the sense that it seeks to constitute a world in which the possibility of participating fully in the ongoing constitution of that world is diminished or foreclosed (as a result of "destructive interference," where the interacting waves, to a greater or lesser degree, diminish each other), which means that what is "normal" or "flourishing" is a matter first and foremost of that active participation, and not reducible to manifesting some prescribed characteristics or dispositions in the form of fixed and stable essences.

One final element of the puzzle of Gordon's account of freedom as human flourishing is his consistent appeals to growth and maturity. Again, there is a common but misleading way to understand these terms. For example, one may hold that being "mature" means behaving in certain ways (bound up often, in the global North, in bourgeois family structures and more broadly in formal and informal rituals of "manhood" and "womanhood") where, to the extent that one evinces these characteristics or behaviors, one has "achieved" adulthood/maturity. Euromodern discourses of colonization often appealed, through the notion of a "civilizing" mission of "development," to a similar concept of maturity on a larger scale, where being a developed/civilized—that is, "mature"—culture meant being *like* the colonizers in the relevant ways. This is not at all what Gordon has in mind here. Rather, his account of maturity or adulthood is contextualized by his existential phenomenological framework in which "the adult world carries the burden of a godless freedom" (1995b, 80).

The world of the child, as Beauvoir points out, is a *serious* world in which parents and authority figures stand like gods dictating and determining the course of their lives and the values to which they must cling (1948, 35–37).[8] The adult world is a world of open-ended responsibility and ambiguity where there are no ready-made ethical recipes to follow, and one must find a way to live with the "antinomies of action" (96). In bad faith, for Beauvoir, the "serious" person retreats to or attempts to recreate the child-like world of ready-made solutions and all-or-nothing answers. Maturity, in this context, is not the arrival at some "finished" state, but rather is a matter of the way in which "one, in [Sartrean] anguish, avows responsibility for one's values while acknowledging the comforting allure of seriousness—an allure to which one may often resist succumbing, but where eradication of *the allure itself* is impossible" (Meagher 2021, 57). Note, importantly, that the claim to have achieved "maturity" *as a mode of static being*, is necessarily a manifestation of *im*maturity in this sense, for it evades one's ongoing responsibility for *continuing* to manifest maturity. Each successful expression of maturity, in other words, only plants the seeds for a future failure, and a sure sign if immaturity is the claim that one *is* "mature" in some final sense.

Gordon's appeal to maturity, which is necessary to understanding his normative account of the human (and thus his account of freedom), functions in this existentialist vein. It therefore avoids the pitfalls of the colonial notion of "development" or any other appeal that entails arrival at some final or complete realization. Maturity, as was the case in our discussion of "pure" recognition in chapter 4, is a matter not of *content* but of *form*. It is a mode of *becoming*, in other words, not static *being*. When he writes, for instance, in his discussion of Fanon's account of anticolonial violence, that "it reveals the implications of a humanity that attempts to evade the challenge and responsibility of growing up," he is appealing precisely to this existential notion of maturity, linking it explicitly to the praxis of liberation (Gordon 1995b, 83). At another point, in a discussion of racism and the blues, he makes this point quite clearly: "Racism attempts to force black people to the developmental level of animals at worst and children at best, freeze them there, and denigrate black self-value. The blues, by contrast, encourages maturation and growth, and is life affirming" (2006b, 22).

In Gordon's view, racism, like all forms of oppression, operates in large part by appealing to and imposing static forms of being and *serious* values, such that, to the extent that racism is the dominant norm, "whites are the presumed standpoint of human maturation" (2006c, 241), such that "implicit in not being developed, then, is the condition of childhood at worst and adolescence at best, but in neither instance is there the condition of full responsibility—namely adulthood" (2006a, 93). Human flourishing or "normality" is thus never a matter of *being* a particular way, but precisely this ongoing *praxis of maturation* in the existentialist sense. Oppression is therefore also a failure to manifest maturity on the part of the oppressors, precisely because of their appeal to their own achievement and realization of a faux maturity in the static/colonial sense. Those who, in the racist/colonial context, posit themselves as the realization of the "mature" human being are thus evincing a profound *immaturity* in this sense. Oppression functions, through the constraint of options to the point of "implosion," to impose an immaturity on the oppressed even as it expresses an immaturity on the part of the oppressors. Freedom at this level, and liberation as the praxis of manifesting this sense of freedom, is thus linked for Gordon to this existential notion of maturity.

We are now in a better position to understand Gordon's appeal to "dehumanization," the "normal," and "flourishing" in his discussion of oppression and liberation. Since, in his view, maturation is an open-ended and ongoing avowal of responsibility, human existence, as a *praxis* of becoming (and not a substantive mode of *being*) serves a normative function in Gordon's politics insofar as one *practices* humanity well when one is *responsibly* engaged in processes of maturation linked to mutual empowerment.[9] This is another example of what I have referred to as a "telos without a terminus"—it offers normative purchase without requiring a fixed and static end point toward which we all must aim. In this way, the notion of the human to which Gordon appeals is "a *universalizing* practice that is never *the universal*" (2021, 37). What we all share qua humans is precisely this ongoing *praxis* of engaging in meaning-making in a world (or, more often, worlds) that at once conditions that praxis and is in turn conditioned by it. There is a universality, but it is a universality that eschews any particular substantive *content*, and works instead through appeal to shared condition of forming our own content.

Oppression, in Gordon's work, functions to dehumanize the oppressed by foreclosing options conducive to processes of maturation and flourishing, and by working to constitute a world in which the oppressed do not appear (in the phenomenological sense) as *conscious* agents. This latter theme runs from his earliest work (Gordon 1995a, 97–100) to his most recent articulations of Black *Consciousness* as a liberatory project (Gordon 2022). In effect, oppression disavows, in bad faith, the humanity of the oppressed at the ontological level, denies or disrupts the *praxis* of humanity at the political level. Two further observations must be made at this point. Firstly, that this denial or disavowal of humanity is always *ironic*, insofar as the *act* of denial implies the realization, if only implicitly, of that which is denied (Gordon 1995a, 41–43). Dehumanization, in Gordon's sense, is thus an ongoing *project*, and never a *fait accompli* (2021, 75). The oppressed are *dehumanized* in the sense of being subject to an ongoing project (often diffuse and institutional) of dehumanization, but they are not dehumanized in the sense of literally being deprived of their humanity. That humanity persists, as the history, for example, of slave resistance and maronnage so clearly teaches, in even the most brutal conditions.[10] Secondly, dehumanization is always a profoundly *social* project (Gordon 1995b, 21), both in the sense that what is denied in the disavowal of the consciousness of the oppressed is their full participation in social life, and in the sense that the project is enabled through diffuse social institutions (culture). The denial of the humanity of the oppressed, in other words, is made *intelligible* by virtue of a cultural framework (Lifeworld) that *empowers* the oppressors at the expense of the oppressed. To use the anti-Black context as an example, since the very categories of "white" and "Black" are a matter of the intersubjective constitution of white and Black people per se, it follows that every instantiation of racism, from the overt white nationalist to the often-unspoken norms that guide housing segregation in the US, is only possible by virtue of these shared meanings and norms. Liberation, therefore, involves the project of *rehumanizing* a social world that normalizes dehumanization, and this is why, as the previous chapter demonstrated, it requires a *collective* response.

This rehumanizing project in Gordon's account, as with Wynter's "Human Project," is predicated on reciprocity. Importantly, reciprocity here is not only compatible with difference, but indeed requires it. Gordon makes this clear:

> Racism, it is said, emerges through an anxiety over the Other. The Other is supposedly a mark of inferior difference. The problem with this view is that it fails to deal with the meaning of *Other*. Implicit in *Other* is a shared category. If one is a human being, then the Other is also a human being: here *I* am and there is *another human being*. Dehumanization takes a different form: here one finds the self, another self, and those who are not-self and not-Other. . . . The struggle against antiblack racism is such, then, that it involves an effort to achieve Otherness. (Gordon 2000, 85)

On Gordon's view, then, the problem with oppression is not that it "others" the oppressed, but rather that it *denies* or evades the "otherness" of the oppressed. In a genuine social relation, I stand before the other and am called to account (responsible) in their presence. Oppression generates situations in which, through bad faith evasions of all evidence to the contrary (Gordon 1995a, 76; 2006a, 6; 2006b, 27–28), the oppressors do not take themselves to stand before the oppressed in a way that holds them responsible, as they would for a genuine *other*. As with the fable of the emperor's new clothes, this evasion is facilitated, as "weak" bad faith, by like-minded fellow-travelers (actual *others*) who will happily affirm your claim (and thus their own) that the oppressed are beneath the status of "other."

For Gordon, this "effort to achieve Otherness" is a necessarily *political* struggle. Recall that human existence is a *praxis* of meaning-making from and through an embodied situation/perspective in an ineluctably social (intersubjectively-constituted) world. The "political," therefore, is not simply a matter of generating and attending to rules that constrain our behavior, but is rather a matter of one's participation in that social, and thus shared, praxis of human existence. The oppressed do not *appear* as participants in the realm of the political in this sense. They may appear as "problems" to be understood and controlled (Gordon 2000, 69–72), but where one is not accepted as having the status of *other* to a political agent, one is effectively held beneath the level of the political as such. He elaborates on the concept of *the political* as "the power of speech in the production of power through which human beings are able to govern their existence" (Gordon 2021, 21). By "speech" here he means broadly the capacity to *appear* (sonically, I should point out) as a participant in the ongoing negotiation and contestation of our shared world. Given his understanding of "power," it is clear that active participation that is *recognized*, we might say, within political life, is absolutely essential for one's *humanity*, understood in-itself as a form of *praxis*. Put differently, "in every moment of posing of the self as other is an implicit appeal to others through which and with which to communicate" (2006b, 18). Liberation thus involves participation in the political in a way that enhances power reciprocally (via "constructive interference"). Not, that is, through the zero-sum "hoarding" of power at the expense of others (who *appear* as "non-others"), which Gordon refers to as "decadent" or "coercive power." Regarding these contrasting approaches to power, he writes:

> As that model [of power as decadent or coercive] is the acquisition of power through the disempowering of others, one should ask what would eliminating disempowerment entail. What would that be other than empowering the once disempowered? This means imaginative and political work should be about extending the potential of flourishing forms of power. It is, in other words, a teleological suspension of power, where decadent power (coercive power) is transcended for the sake of open power (empowering freedom). (Gordon 2021, 66)

This passage brings together the key concepts we have seen recurring in Gordon's thought. Humanity as such is the necessarily social and relational *praxis* of self-creation and self-expression, and that praxis is going well, it is flourishing and maturing, when it is "opening" into new possibilities for self-creation and expression. But since those possibilities are necessarily linked, through our fundamental sociality, to the possibilities of others, this process of "opening" demands a reciprocal opening for others, through a process of *empowering* where my capacity for flourishing is enhanced *by enhancing* that of others. "Freedom," therefore, "always calls for a new humanity to emerge out of unfreedom, a new humanity that is paradoxically the guiding *telos* underneath a humanity denied" (Gordon 2000, 54). This aim (as a *telos* without a terminus) toward "flourishing" and the "normal" is therefore the effort to stand in relations with others characterized by reciprocal *empowering* relations of constructive interference.

UNIVERSALITY, DIFFERENCE, AND THE HUMAN

"When I search for Man in the technique and the style of Europe," Fanon wrote, "I see only a succession of negations of man, and an avalanche of murders" (1963, 312). The argument developed in this chapter, following in the path of Wynter and Gordon, is that the "technique and style of Europe" is the technique and style of *purity* and stasis. It is an effort to fix a set content to the concept of the human, and, through rituals of purification, to demarcate and enforce the border between the full presence of that concept, and those who stand in a relation of *lack* to it. For Fanon, this is a *negation* of the human precisely because it evokes a "substantification"—it strives to treat a dynamic process as a static substance (36). The response to this "negation," not only for Wynter and Gordon, but also for Fanon, is emphatically *not* to abandon the concept of the human altogether, but rather to reject precisely this technique and style of Europe. Indeed, for Fanon, in the decolonial struggle "there must be an idea of man and of the future of humanity," otherwise, "if it is not enriched and deepened by a very rapid transformation into a consciousness of social and political needs, in other words into humanism, it leads up a blind alley" (203–4). The goal of this chapter has been to articulate an account the human that is, in this Fanonian tradition, genuinely universal without recapitulating the technique and style of Europe.

The core of this effort has been an ontological claim—the human must be understood as a *praxis*. As a dynamic and open-ended practice of becoming, humanity as such is not about *content* but *form*. One universal feature is that it always takes on a particular content—it always occupies a specific *genre*, in Wynter's terms—but cannot be simply equated with any particular content. Another universal feature is that human beings are always actively participating in the shaping and re-shaping of content to the concept of humanity to which they belong. Thus, both the human as a *form* of praxis and the particular *content* of that universal praxis are dynamic. We practice our humanity by living a particular expression of that humanity (one among many), and in so doing breathe life into that particular expression as itself an ever-changing process. Furthermore, since these particular expressions stand in constitutive relations with other particular expressions, the vibrancy of those particular expressions, and thus our universal humanity, requires what I have been referring to as an ongoing relation of "productive friction." The encounter with different ways of taking up the praxis of the human opens new possibilities for that praxis, and thus new ways of *becoming* human. Of course, as Wynter, Gordon, and Fanon all made very clear, one way in which this praxis of the human can be undertaken is, ironically, as a project of *dehumanization*. We can practice our humanity in ways that deny or disavow its existence as a praxis in constitutive relation with different practices (i.e., reciprocity).

Dehumanization or oppression, therefore, takes the form of a denial of dynamism and of relation. It seeks to impose a static content to the human and disavow difference in a pernicious form of universal*ism*. This is a politics of purity, and the response to it must be creolizing. It must affirm dynamism, difference, and ambiguity. Liberation as "humanization" means bringing particular dynamic practices of the human together in relations of productive friction. In the face of colonial and universalistic accounts of the human "in the technique and style of Europe," liberation can, as we saw in the previous chapter, require an emphasis on difference as a mode of resistance to assimilation or erasure (resistance to "white noise"). We cannot engage in productive friction when one participant is engaged in the active project of denying that we are a genuine "other" with whom they can interact at all. This is precisely what Fanon is describing in his account of "national culture" (206–48), and what animates struggles for indigenous sovereignty across the globe. When one participant understands themselves to be the complete, closed, and static (that is, pure) manifestation of the human, then there can be no *other* with whom they can or should interact in any productive/reciprocal way. This is a problem not with the idea of the human as such, but with this *particular* expression of the human, and so, in the first instance, the struggle for humanization must take the form of preserving one's particularity in the face of its overwhelming denial. But the goal in the long term is, as we have seen in this chapter, a mode of *reciprocity* in the form of a productive friction in which different practices of humanity are able to interact in, to appeal to Gordon's terms, "mature" and empowering ways (where "mature" picks out an open-ended practice of responsibility, and not a fixed content).

Fanon recognized this, as well, in his essay "Racism and Culture," where he wrote: "universality resides in this decision to recognize and accept the reciprocal relativism of different cultures, once the colonial status is irreversibly excluded" (1967, 44). Within the sonic metaphor, "colonial status" can be understood as a kind of "white noise." It is a totalizing effort to drown out and disavow all difference in a kind of "destructive interference," prohibiting genuine reciprocity and productive friction, and thereby arresting or inhibiting humanity as a dynamic praxis enacted and enriched through that productive friction. The white noise of coloniality and racism works to generate a sonic field in which the destructive interference it engenders *appears* (in the phenomenological sense) as a kind of "resonance." That is, it "sounds right" when different sets of "waves" are drowned out by the ever-present and overwhelming white noise.

Of course, those different waves are not completely negated, and the soundscape of white noise requires constant maintenance and reinforcement (precisely because it remains a dynamic praxis even as it presents itself as a static mode of being). Liberation under such conditions takes the form of the introduction of *dissonance* into that soundscape, disrupting its pernicious resonance and weakening the destructive interference of white noise. As we saw in the previous chapter, the power of that dissonant eruption/interruption comes from the ways in which it draws on different elements (into a we-subject) that stand in relations of resonance with each other precisely to enhance their dissonant impact on the larger sonic field, and in this way liberatory praxis manifests resonance and dissonance simultaneously. The success of liberatory praxis is a matter of its ability to alter the larger soundscape as itself a dynamic praxis, which causes it to *appear* within that soundscape in the mode of difference and particularity—it weakens, disrupts, and alters the white noise. Those who are *responsible* for and to that larger colonial soundscape may either double their efforts to drown out that appearance of dissonance, or alter their praxis in a way that puts it into productive friction (reciprocity) as a new mode of resonance. This latter move would require a modification of both of the normative soundscape and the normative perceptual practices of those responsible to it in the relevant ways.[11] Importantly, this new mode of resonance does not assimilate or annihilate difference, but rather alters its own pitch and frequency to generate "constructive interference" where the different sound waves, now in a relation of reciprocity, are *mutually enhancing* in their difference, yielding an overall soundscape that is more than the sum of its parts (this is, as I read him, what Gordon means by "empowerment").

This reciprocal relation of constructive interference, where the praxis of humanity at the universal level is enhanced through the mutual enhancement of its different expressions at the level of the particular, is *freedom* in the creolizing sense I have been struggling to articulate throughout this text. As an always-dynamic process, there will be constant and ongoing alterations in those expressions (though, like standing waves, they may be quite stable for a time), leading to recurring renegotiations of dissonance and resonance. When these relations of productive friction are going well, when they are mutually enhancing, then new possibilities for expression (new possibilities of the human) will be opened as a result. In this way, it is possible to distinguish between freedom-conducive relations and oppressive relations without needing some static and final account of what it means to *be* "free" or to *be* human. It offers a telos without a terminus.

Coda

An Opening and an Invitation to a Living Practice of Freedom

In her essay "Scratching the Surface: Some Notes on Barriers to Women and Loving," Audre Lorde notes that different modes of oppression (racism, sexism, heterosexism, homophobia) are "forms of human blindness" that "stem from the same root—an inability to recognize the notion of difference as a dynamic human force, one which is enriching rather than threatening to the defined self, when there are shared goals" (1984, 45). Lorde's observations here, that human difference is *dynamic*, and that it can in fact enhance, rather than threaten, identity and the self, clearly resonate with the insights from Biko, Anzaldúa, Wynter, Gordon, and the overall account of freedom as a creolizing *praxis* that has been the subject of this book. There is more than a little serendipity in her admonition to "recognize" here as well, a reference that is not limited to this single instance. In her essay "Age, Race, Class, and Sex: Women Redefining Difference," she writes that it is not the very real differences that inhibit coalition amongst women, but "rather our refusal to recognize those differences, and to examine the distortions which result from our misnaming them and their effects upon human behavior and expectation" (115).

What does she mean by "recognition" in these passages? A further clue can be found in "The Master's Tools will Never Dismantle the Master's House":

> Interdependency between women is the way to a freedom which allows the *I* to *be*, not in order to be used, but in order to be creative. This is a difference between the passive *be* and the active *being*. Advocating the mere tolerance of difference between women is the grossest reformism. It is a total denial of the creative function of difference in our lives. Difference must be not merely tolerated, but seen as a fund of necessary polarities between which our creativity can

spark like a dialectic. Only then does the necessity for interdependency become unthreatening. (111)

The "recognition" of difference, as opposed to its mere toleration, is thus a celebration of human interdependence which generates, "like a dialectic," creativity as an active and enriching mode of being. It allows us to become (for a given "us") more than the sum of our respective parts. Again, the *resonance* of Lorde's words with the project of this book is unmistakable.

My point in introducing Lorde at this late stage of the project is not to show that she can be "assimilated" into the framework I am developing here. Nor is it to show that she is in any sense "Hegelian." Indeed, I would much rather suggest the productive potential of a *Lordian* reading of Hegel than the abuse that would be a Hegelian reading of Lorde. No, my appeal to Lorde in this concluding "coda" is intended as an opening or invitation. Lorde may in some significant ways "resonate" with this text, but it is in her differences—her deep critique of the dichotomy between thinking and feeling (ibid., 100–101), and her prioritization of affect and the *erotic* (53–59), for instance—that the opening her work provides to yet further moments of *creolization* become apparent. The point, in other words, is that, while this "coda" may function as a concluding moment for *this text*, the whole thrust of a creolizing theory of freedom is that each conclusion must also be a beginning—an opening and an invitation to yet further moments of creolization. There are so many openings to explore and paths to follow, and my greatest hope for this text is that others will take those paths, and thus this project, in ways not conceivable, or perhaps even possible, for me as I write this. Like the person who claims that they *are* "mature," any claim to have finally and completely defined or theorized freedom only shows that you don't really know what you're talking about.

Historically, creolization has been at one and the same time a violent imposition—the result of sexual violation, cultural genocide, enslavement, exile, and colonization—and a creative response to those coercive and dehumanizing forces. People found ways to communicate across vast divides by developing creolizing linguistic practices, to carve out a new spiritual home through creolizing spiritual practices (finding roots through "root work"), and to form new identities through creolizing "autopoetic" practices. The real goal of this text is to demonstrate that these latter, life-affirming practices of creolizing are best understood as practices of *freedom*.

The "opening" I hope to inaugurate here is both prospective and retrospective, since the practice of freedom not only opens up new futures, new understandings of where and who we are and where we can go, but also new understandings of where we have been. In his biography of the Haitian revolutionary Toussaint Louverture, the Martinican philosopher and poet Aimé Césaire wrote:

> When Toussaint Louverture came on the scene, it was to take the Declaration of the Rights of Man at its word; it was to show that there is no pariah race; that there is no marginal country; that there can be no excepted peoples. It was to incarnate and particularize a principle; that is to say, to vivify it . . . his was a combat for the *recognition* of man, and that is why he inscribed himself and the revolt of the black slaves of Saint-Domingue within the history of universal civilization. (Quoted in and translated by Nesbitt [2004, 29]; original text Césaire [1960, 344])

The French name Toussaint adopted, "*L'ouverture*," means "the opening," and this is illuminating of precisely this point about freedom as a creolizing practice. For Césaire is portraying Louverture, who "vivified" and "particularized" ideals and practices that were at once imposed on him and yet, in significant ways, inherited by him, as engaging in a struggle for universal recognition precisely through that process of particularization. The practice of freedom is this practice of recognizing difference in a way that, in Lorde's words, "sparks a dialectic" (a *productive friction*) and generates new openings to develop and enhance that practice. In so doing, we "vivify" the practice of freedom.

Notes

INTRODUCTION: BEING, BELONGING, AND FREEDOM

1. For my purposes, there is little to be gained by drawing tight distinctions between "metaphysics" and "ontology." To be sure, there is a long tradition in philosophy of doing so in a variety of ways. Achille Varzi offers an insightful overview of different approaches to the distinction coming out of twentieth-century analytic philosophy (2011). And the continental tradition offers its own varieties of the distinction not only between "metaphysics" and "ontology," but also, thanks to Heidegger, between "ontology" and the "ontic." As I use them in this text, both terms carve out claims and inquiries regarding what *is*. To say that, for example, all ontology is ultimately relation or dynamic, is both an ontological and a metaphysical claim. To affirm or deny that identity is a function of essences is both a metaphysical and an ontological claim. To raise questions about what an "essence" is, likewise, operates in this shared realm. This is what informs my claim later in this introduction that even the rejection of "metaphysics" must rely on metaphysical claims (typically about the lack or inaccessibility of some mind-independent reality).

2. Cf. Linebaugh and Rediker 2000; Linebaugh 2019.

3. I recognize that this is not straightforward for everyone. For many immigrants, especially those who emigrate as children, there is a sense in which they are from the country of their birth, but, depending especially on how long they have been in their new "home" country, there is also a sense in which they are from their adopted country. As international travelers, they could thus be away from two homes, or, if visiting the country of their birth, both home and away from home at the same time. This also completely sets aside the question of scope or scale. That one is from a country is a kind of macro-scale by which to answer to the question of where "home" may be, but of course there can be much more fine-grained distinctions *within* a given country, and those are often not straightforward. In my own case as a child of military parents, for example, there is a good deal of ambiguity in how I think of home at the micro-scale beyond merely the place where my mail gets sent and I keep most of my

stuff. In any event, I hope that the reader will indulge the oversimplification here in the interests of drawing out the larger philosophical point.

4. I offer a more in-depth discussion of belonging and freedom in Ortega's work in (Monahan 2019).

5. This is apparent from the appeal to the "alien" in the term *alienation*, and in its English synonym "*es*trange*ment*." The German term *Entfremdung*, which, from Marx, is a key historical source of these references to alienation, likewise makes explicit appeal to the "strange" (*Fremd*).

6. For readers unfamiliar with this term, it refers to the common practice in the colonial Americas in which enslaved persons would flee captivity to form autonomous "maroon" communities.

7. There is, of course, a contrasting view of freedom that is linked to rootlessness and a lack of "ties" to places of people. This is, interestingly, a feature of certain forms of liberalism (political libertarianism in particular), and certain forms of poststructuralist thought (favoring "nomadic" practices, for instance). I would note that these accounts of freedom as rootlessness can still be understood as articulating a relation of belonging or home, it is simply one that is either radically expanded to include *everywhere* or that treats all relations of belonging as illegitimate. I will later argue that this is a pathological and ultimately oppressive account of freedom in part *because* of this sense of belonging everywhere/nowhere, but at this stage, I wish only to note that all accounts of freedom are also accounts of belonging. Indeed, Allison Weir has articulated an account of freedom as a "practice of belonging" (2013, 128–29).

8. Though my own thinking on this point was developed out of Africana phenomenology, readers familiar with the work of Édouard Glissant will see resonances between my claims here and his own account of relation (cf. Sealey 2020, 83–89).

9. As Paddy McQueen puts the point: "By positing the nomad as a subject who freely chooses to become temporarily homeless," the advocate of rootlessness "invokes precisely the liberal, autonomous subject she is at pains to reject" (2015, 94).

10. Cf. Monahan 2011, 183–88.

CHAPTER 1: FREEDOM AND THE POLITICS OF PURITY

1. As with "metaphysics" and "ontology," there have been many different approaches to the distinctions and relations between "freedom" and "liberation." For my purposes, "liberation" picks out practices directed against oppression and toward freedom. In a world without oppression, there would be no need for liberation. Freedom, therefore, is that toward which liberatory practices aim. Of course, what precisely this means is the subject of this text, and we have quite a way to go before I can begin to offer some real content to these terms. For the moment, I wish only to acknowledge that they are distinct yet related terms.

2. This can vary quite a bit. It was and is common for many racists to view all racial mixture as "unnatural" and illicit (in their ideal world, everyone would "keep to their own"), but the greatest concern and highest levels of both judicial and extra-legal enforcement was reserved for protecting the purity of whiteness.

3. I have focused here on the Black/white binary and the one-drop rule as the clearest and most familiar example of this basic absorption strategy within the politics of purity. But there are many other examples. Indeed, over time, this general rule has been adapted to take into account changing views of whiteness. The gradual absorption of Italians, Irish, Eastern Europeans, and Ashkenazic Jews, into the dominant conception of "the white race" from the late nineteenth to early twentieth centuries is a historic case in point. What we find in all of these examples, however, is the overarching drive to re-describe the ambiguous in ways that re-establish the presumptive purity of the taxonomic system. A clear contemporary example both of this larger drive to purity and to the centrality of whiteness can be found in informal distinctions made in the US between "whites" and "people of color." Whiteness is made central insofar as it assumes the position of color-less in distinction from those who "have" color, and it is pure insofar as any infusion of "color" into whiteness only generates another "person of color," so that whiteness remains (allegedly) pure.

4. For a detailed discussion and analysis of this in the context of questions of purity, see Daphne Taylor-Garcia's *Existence of the Mixed Race Damnés* (2019).

5. This is why so much of contemporary moral philosophy involves the generation of counter-examples and "problem cases." Once one can show the incompleteness or inconsistency of a given theory or principle, one has begun to undermine the entire edifice of the theory. Thus, no matter how bizarre and extraordinary such examples are, they serve a crucial role in the work of moral philosophers within certain mainstream traditions. If ambiguity and incompleteness were permissible within what is thought of as "moral reason," however, such counter-examples would be mere curiosities at best, rather than components of "rigorous" philosophical arguments.

6. This last point in turn sets up the basis for arguments against appeals to racial identity based upon the claim that racial identities deny individuality (cf. Appiah 1994). If being a member of the category means one has no particularity with respect to that membership, then there does seem to be a threat to one's individuality.

7. A compelling argument could be made that the "Tale of the Eloquent Peasant," written roughly 1,500 years before Plato, is a written text at least indirectly about freedom, insofar as it engages with the ancient Egyptian caste system and raises significant questions about the responsibilities members of the different castes bear toward each other. Regardless of whether one holds this ancient text to be a work on freedom, it strikes me as utterly implausible to hold that thousands of years of human history prior to the "Golden Age" of Athens saw absolutely no human beings thinking seriously and systematically about freedom (broadly construed—they were indeed unlikely to be thinking of freedom in exactly the same way as European moderns).

CHAPTER 2: RECOGNITION AND ITS DISCONTENTS

1. While this discussion of recognition will play a pivotal role in my larger argument, I do believe that it is functioning here mainly as a kind of heuristic example, and that the same move could be made with other theories of freedom. I have chosen to use recognition both because it is a common trope in writings on race and racism

(a key interest and motive for my work), and because it is a discourse with which I am intimately familiar.

2. This basic commitment is maintained in Honneth's later writings. For example, see 2001, 25–31; and 2012, 201–16.

3. This is not to say that liberal theorists have not made considerable effort to make a space for notions of *group* rights (cf. Kymlicka, 1995).

4. That triumphalism was perhaps best represented by Francis Fukuyama's *The End of History and the Last Man* (1992). To his great credit, the intervening quarter-century has caused Fukuyama to question his earlier views (Fasting 2021)

5. Cf. Markel 2003, 6, 16, 32, 88, 89, 90, 103, 108, 153, 155, and 178.

6. Refuting this understanding of race is the main goal of the first four chapters of my *The Creolizing Subject* (Monahan 2011).

7. Here are Sartre's exact words:

> This means that he [the democrat] wants to separate the Jew from his religion, from his family, from his ethnic community, in order to plunge him into the democratic crucible whence he will emerge naked and alone, an individual and solitary particle like all the other particles . . . The former [the anti-Semite] wishes to destroy him as a man and leave nothing in him but the Jew, the pariah, the untouchable; the latter [the democrat] wishes to destroy him as a Jew and leave in him but the man, the abstract and universal subject of the rights of man and the rights of the citizen. (1948, 57)

CHAPTER 3: RECOGNITION, COGNITION, AND PURITY

1. There is a clear link etymologically and conceptually between recognition and cognition both in English and in its original (via Fichte and Hegel) German (*Anerkennen* and *Kennen*). This is likewise true for the Spanish *reconocimiento* and the French *reconnaissance*. Importantly for the argument I will make in this chapter, however, there is a subtlety to the connotation of the German, Spanish, and French words that is absent from the English. Namely, there is a difference between *kennen/wissen*, *saber/conocer*, and *savoir/connaître*—all words that are typically translated into English as "to know," but with very distinct usages and meanings. I will discuss this distinction in detail later in this chapter.

2. It is worth noting that there is a significant racial component to this particular example. Memphis is a majority Black city, and so there are significant aspects of the city's life that my own whiteness inhibits my coming to know. Indeed, even Black and white native Memphians may "know" the city in quite different ways. One's knowledge of Memphis will always be conditioned in this way (among others, surely).

3. I recognize that contemporary "intellectualists" will reject this claim. I take my elaboration of the difference to stand as an indictment of their case. Ultimately, my argument is that, if my own account of practical knowledge is credible, then the basic position of the intellectualists, that all instances of "knowing-how" can be broken

down into a series of propositional "knowing that" claims, is untenable. It seems difficult, given the phenomenology of practical knowledge to which I am appealing here, to take seriously, for example, the following paradigmatic statement of the intellectualist position: "For every s and F, s knows how to F iff for some way w of F-ing, s knows that w is a way to F" (Stanley 2011, 71). To point out just one issue, my claim about the ways in which the greatest practitioners alter our understanding of the possible "ways to F" make Stanley's account incoherent. The set of "ways to F" simply cannot be known (in the propositional sense) ahead of time.

4. In the martial arts context, for example, the title "Master" connotes not "mastery" in this sense of final and complete cognition but, rather, a depth of commitment to continued study. In the art I study, this is symbolized by giving a white belt (like those worn by beginning students) to newly promoted Masters, indicating that they remain students of the art. Mastery thus describes a depth of commitment to study, not a completion of study.

5. For more detailed discussions, see Williams (1997), Monahan (2006), and Stojkovski (2015).

6. My reference to "empowerment" here is meant to evoke Lewis Gordon's recent discussion of power (Gordon 2021, 21–22) where he points out that power can be used to limit or constrain the power of others, it can also be used to enable and build the power of others. I shall discuss this in much greater detail in the final chapter. My point here is that relatively "pure" relations of recognition generate this latter sort of power for both participants—it is a power that *enhances* the power of others (and oneself), as opposed to hoarding it.

7. It is furthermore an instantiation of what Hegel referred to as the "Understanding" *Vernunft*, which insists on all-or-nothing, either/or distinctions.

8. In Heikki Ikäheimo's apt terminology, what is being developed through recognition is precisely "Personhood" (2010).

9. I make this case in more detail in my introduction to *Creolizing Hegel* (Monahan 2017).

CHAPTER 4: TOWARD A CREOLIZING FREEDOM

1. One ready response to this turn to Hegel, and one toward which I profess a certain sympathy, is to question why it is necessary at all. Could not any valuable insights of conceptual tools present in Hegel's theory of recognition be better developed outside of the context of Hegel's system? Especially given his views on race, gender, colonization, and the centrality of Europe to the historical development of reason and humanity, would it not be better to set Hegel aside (or even spit on him, as Carla Lonzi famously suggests [1996]), rather than engage in an effort to resuscitate him? If he holds that Africa is outside of the bounds of Reason, and women are essentially doomed to a subordinate role in Ethical Life, then even if there is something in the Hegelian corpus worth salvaging, would it not be better him altogether and generate something new? Perhaps we should follow Teshale Tibebu in declaring that *"Eurocentrism is thus essentially a series of footnotes to Hegel"* and set Hegel aside in favor

of more salubrious theoretical resources (2011, xxi). Indeed, if my project involves advocacy for Hegel's system to any serious extent, then surely, I am only serving to further legitimate the larger project of philosophical Eurocentrism and the coloniality of reason/philosophy. The underlying question in this line of interrogation/accusation is "Why, given your alleged commitment to liberation, to the *Damnes de la Terre*, and to 'Shifting the Geography of Reason,' would you spend so much time on racist/sexist/Eurocentric Hegel?"

I take this to be a fair question, and one that demands a response. The most direct answer here is to appeal to the motivations that I described above. I think Hegel has valuable insights to offer with respect to problems of oppression—insights that, in some cases, can even be deployed against Hegel's own texts. My philosophical approach has always been to start with a problem, and determine which theoretical tools are best suited to addressing that problem, and I have found that Hegel has a great deal to offer here, and to pretend otherwise, even if it allowed me to avoid some quite warranted suspicion, would simply be dishonest. What is more, I read Hegel as fundamentally a theorist of relationality—there is no *thing in itself*, the very concept of *this thing* requires a relation to some *other* (this is a fundamental insight of his *Logic*)—and I see this as true even in how we read and understand Hegel himself. That is, he must be read in conjunction with his interlocutors and especially his critics, both contemporary and subsequent. As I have argued elsewhere, what I take to be Hegel's deepest insights reveal that thought itself, including our thinking about Hegel, must be *creolizing* (Monahan 2017). I will make a case in what follows (though, as I suggested earlier, one that might not be wholly satisfying to Hegel scholars), that Hegel offers conceptual tools which allow one to advance critiques of these pernicious aspects of Hegel's own texts in a Hegelian spirit.

Given that my ultimate position is that Hegel himself occasionally failed to be faithful to his own theoretical insights, it is necessary to turn to these interlocutors and critics to best understand what is being articulated in Hegel's own system. In other words, I see it as maximally consistent with Hegel's philosophical insights to place his stated views in relation to (and often conflict with) not only his European critics and supporters, but more importantly with those who grapple with and against his thought from the so-called *underside* of that history. This is in part what I mean by *creolizing* Hegel. I am thus turning to Hegel, and especially to Hegel's *Logic*, in other words, because I believe that it is possible to find productive insights to shed light on the problems of oppression and liberation that are the central motivation of this project as a whole. This means that it is absolutely necessary, in order to gain an adequate grasp of the problems with which this text is concerned, (let alone what I take to be the keys to addressing them), that Hegel not have the last word. My point is not that the solutions begin and end with Hegel (far from it), but rather that giving Hegel his due, which crucially includes taking Hegel to task for his many profound failures, enables us to make significant theoretical advances in the ongoing project of human liberation.

2. I will capitalize "Understanding" whenever I am using it in Hegel's own technical sense.

3. My appeal to "worlds" here very much has María Lugones in mind (2003, 77–100).

4. Again, the musical analogy is instructive here. The claim that one has fully and completely mastered one's instrument is sure indication that they haven't really got a clue what they are talking about. The true master is inspired by the incompleteness of their mastery.

5. Robin James's excellent book *The Sonic Episteme: Acoustic Resonance, Neoliberalism, and Biopolitics*, offers an important diagnosis of the ways in which a shift to sonic metaphors can nevertheless "produce theories that both naturalize the relations of domination and subordination that neoliberalism and biopolitics produce and create those very same relations within theory/scholarship" (2019, 182). My claim is certainly not that a shift to sonic metaphor is in every case sufficient to avoid these pernicious tendencies. I hope, rather, that my appeal to sound functions in the mode that James refers to, following Alexander Weheliye, as "phonographic," which "define [sound] as code- or register-shifting."

6. We can return to the example of travel discussed in the introduction. When undertaken with the right attitude, one that is "playful" in Lugones' sense of the term (2003, 90–96), rather than arrogant, travel can generate precisely this sort of "productive friction." The encounter with difference enriches one's experience of both the "familiar" and the "strange," the "self," and the "other," revealing new insights into the experience of belonging—of being "at home" without needing to eliminate difference/strangeness.

CHAPTER 5: THE (WE-)SUBJECT OF LIBERATION

1. To illustrate this reading of Fanon, consider the following passage:

> Individual experience, because it is national and because it is a link in the chain of national existence, ceases to be individual, limited, and shrunken and is enabled to open out into the truth of the nation and of the world. In the same way that during the period of armed struggle each fighter held the fortune of the nation in his hand, so during the period of national construction each citizen ought to continue in his real, everyday activity to associate himself with the whole of the nation, to incarnate the continuous dialectical truth of the nation and to will the triumph of man in his completeness here and now. (1963, 200)

2. For those unfamiliar with the apartheid racial taxonomy, "Coloured" referred specifically to persons of mixed ancestry (Welsh 2000, 427).

3. Biko was explicit in his analysis and condemnation of these "bantustans":

> No Bantustan leader can tell me that he is acting at his own initiative when he enters the realms of bantustan politics. AT this stage of our history we cannot have our struggle being tribalize through the creation of Zulu, Xhosa and Tswana politicians by the system. These tribal cocoons called "homelands" are nothing else but sophisticated concentration camps where black people are allowed to "suffer peacefully." (Biko 2012, 95)

4. On that echoes, in provocative ways, DuBois appeal to the "spiritual strivings" of Black folks in the North American context (1994, 3–11).

5. I will take up the question of the universal (both false and genuine) in more detail in chapter 6.

6. My emphasis on "activist" here is not meant to be exclusionary, the "feminist visionary" and "spiritual" components are crucial elements of Anzaldúa's work. The foregrounding of her activism is only meant to illustrate how Anzaldúa's work is *political* in the broadest sense of the term.

7. The term "*Los atravesados*" is a very rich one. It is the substantive form of the verb *atravesar*, which means "to cross over" in the sense of crossing a bridge or a street, or to pass through in the way that a street may "cross" an entire city. In its reflexive form (*atravesarse*), it can also mean to cut off, or to annoy or vex. The substantive form used by Anzaldúa, literally "the ones who cross," plays on that latter connotation, in that it is commonly used to refer to mean (vexing) people—those who cause trouble. Thus, Anzaldúa's appeal to *los atravesados* clearly is meant to evoke the sense of those who transgress norms and boundaries. It should thus be understood as a way of interacting and relating (to others, and to the surrounding social milieu) rather than as a state of being. This is in keeping with Pitts's point about Anzaldúa adopting a relational ontology, and clearly resonates in significant ways with Biko's notion of *Black Consciousness*.

8. As we shall see, Anzaldúa's account of *nepantla* alters a bit over time. As Elena Ruíz notes: "In her early writings the term *nepantla* is used to emphasize fricative ambiguity in existence or a sense of cultural displacement. In the later work, it focuses on a third, creative space that rejects dualisms and tolerates contradiction" (2020, 222n5). The meaning of the original Nahuatl term itself is somewhat contentious, as Pitts discusses in their recent work (2021, 41–44). I will follow both Ruíz and Pitts in my reading of Anzaldúa here, where the earlier work (including *Borderlands/La Frontera*) treats *nepantla* as a condition of woundedness and the *destructive friction* brought about by colliding cultures (worlds), while the later work, including especially her articulation of *las nepantleras*, emphasizes a sense of what Pitts calls "abundant reciprocity" or what I would call *productive friction*.

9. This appeal to "creating a new mythos" is very much resonant with Wynter's project, as we shall see in the next chapter.

10. Coyalxāuhqui is a figure who Anzaldúa describes as an "Aztec moon goddess" (2009, 279). After a planned attack on her mother, Coatlique, was betrayed, her half-brother Huitzilopochtli struck her down, decapitated her, and threw her body down the temple stairs, where it broke apart into pieces.

11. The resonances between *desconocimiento* and "bad faith," and especially with Beauvoir's accounts of "seriousness" are quite evident.

CHAPTER 6: ON *HUMAN* LIBERATION

1. The use of the gendered term by Wynter is, of course, quite intentional.

2. These "others" to *Man* included, to various degrees, numerous populations in Europe itself—women, the physically or psychologically "abnormal," homosexuals, criminals, and so forth. As I have argued elsewhere, these "impurities" *internal* to Europe demanded a praxis of purification concomitant to the *external* purifying praxis of colonial conquest (Monahan 2011, 163–64).

3. This is the process the Hortense Spillers refers to as the "hieroglyphics of the flesh" (1987, 67).

4. It is worth noting that, while Gordon appeals to figures like Sartre and Husserl to articulate key features of his thought, he distances himself from being reducible to offering a "Sartrean" philosopher (2000, 31).

5. This also echoes the distinction in Hegel between "The Understanding" and "Speculative Reason."

6. There is much more that could be said here about the complexities of this "ontological" account of freedom, especially as it relates to the Sartrean roots from which Gordon's earliest articulations of it were drawn (see Gordon 1995a, 50–63). However, such a detailed analysis is not within the purview of this chapter.

7. Given the very complicated psychology with which Gordon operates, it is important to recognize that a "freely-chosen commitment" may nevertheless be only dimly present or explicit to the oppressor, or even actively denied (in bad faith, the racist evades taking responsibility for the commitments made *evident* by their actions and dispositions). So the claim here is not that all racists are freely and explicitly aware of their racism.

8. It is important to bear in mind here that Beauvoir's point is not so much a claim about developmental psychology (though it is certainly relevant) but, rather, a claim about particular attitudes and commitments with respect to one's relation to *value*. The key feature of the serious or child-like attitude is that it takes no responsibility *for* values, though it may certainly entail responsibility *to* values.

9. The responsibility here is to oneself, as well as to others, not only in the present, but across past and future generations (Gordon 2021, 70).

10. One may well wonder at this point about moments of genocide, which seem to pose a challenge to the approach suggested here. Projects of literal extermination seem to be instantiations of dehumanization that are not ironic (in bad faith) in the way I am portraying them here. Do not those cases where the oppressors view their victims as a kind of pathogen in the body politic that must be eradicated/exterminated, rather than as an inferior group to be dominated, manifest this kind of implicit recognition of an explicitly disavowed humanity? This is certainly an important question.

The first thing to consider is the way in which maintaining and propagating the absolute denial of the humanity of others requires a significant amount of evasion and disavowal of all evidence to the contrary. That is, one has to work to generate the sort of obliviousness to the humanity of others that animates this question. In historical cases of genocide, there is a concerted effort to condition the perpetrators to view their victims as an existential threat that must be eliminated. In other words, the *project* of bringing people to the condition where genocidal action becomes possible takes work. Consider, for example, Christopher Browning's study of *Einsatzgruppen* in the waning years of the Third Reich, who were recruited and organized for the purpose of murdering Jews throughout Nazi-occupied Europe (2017). Browning discusses at length the kinds of psychological conditioning that were required to turn the titular "ordinary men" of the *Einstazgruppen* into genocidal murderers. Thus, the arrival at the moment of indifference to the humanity of others, historically, requires precisely this kind of ongoing ironic project Gordon is describing. To bring someone to the point where they can see another as "that which must be exterminated" requires a prolonged effort that *is* ironic in precisely this sense of implicitly acknowledging that which is explicitly denied (indeed, it is ironic in two senses, since bringing the perpetrator to this genocidal outlook requires *their own* dehumanization in a profound way).

Second, the all-too-common moments of death up to and including genocide must be understood socially and relationally as systemic, as part of what Julia Suárez-Krabbe refers to as the "death project" of European modernity (2016, 3). In this way, the individual or even collective moments of death may not be, in their realization, "ironic" in this way (though, again, what *led* to those moments certainly is), but insofar as they communicate "this could have been *you*" to those who remain, the implicit recognition of humanity (as one with whom such communication is possible and functional) remains, though clearly not with respect to the victim(s). This is surely little consolation to those lined up before the *Einsatzgruppen*, or thrown from the deck of the slave ship, or targeted by lethal police violence, but the larger point (which surely was never "consolation") remains. "Dehumanization," even in its most extreme and lethal forms, requires *effort* to generate and maintain, precisely because it requires the ongoing and active disavowal of all evidence to the contrary. Cases of death, therefore, can in this way be understood as part of the process of that generation and maintenance, such that even the realization of dehumanization in the moment of death stands as a moment in the ongoing project of dehumanization at this more systematic level—the "death project" is, in this way, always a *project*.

The appeal of the argument that dehumanization can be total or complete lies in the image of the perpetrator or perpetrators as being utterly unaware of the humanity of their victims. My response here is two-fold. First, in most cases, it lets the killers off the proverbial hook too easily. It is not that they are naively unaware of the humanity of their victims, acting in a condition of pristine innocence. Rather, the talk of "vermin" and the threat of "pathogen," even the acts of violence, are the ways whereby the perpetrators attempt to convince themselves (in bad faith) of the lack of humanity of their victims, which convincing is necessary precisely because at some level they understand it to be untrue. One is reminded here of Beauvoir's discussion of the "sub-men," those who do the "dirty work" of oppression, the one who "fears . . . that the shock of the unforeseen may remind him of the agonizing consciousness of himself," and so "loses himself in the object in order to annihilate his subjectivity" (1948, 44–45). In other words, they are exerting *effort* to maintain their "belief" in the lack of humanity on the part of their victims, which effort belies the very claim they are struggling to sustain. Second, even if we imagine, as is surely true in some, if perhaps not most cases, that the perpetrator harbors absolutely no belief, however implicit or diffuse, in the humanity of their victim(s), we can see that this psychology is itself a product of the larger systematic "death project." In this way, the generation of individuals who are no longer capable of apprehending the humanity of their victims can be seen as part of a project which ironically recognizes that which it seeks to deny.

11. What T. Storm Heter refers to as the whiteness of the "sonic gaze" (2022, 1–5).

Bibliography

Alcoff, Linda. 2006. *Visible Identities: Race, Gender, and the Self.* New York: Oxford University Press.
Anzaldúa, Gloria. 2007. *Borderlands/La Frontera: The New Mestiza.* Third edition. San Francisco: Aunt Lute Books.
———. 2009. *The Gloria Anzaldúa Reader.* AnaLouise Keating, ed. Durham, NC: Duke University Press.
———. 2015. *Light in the Dark/Luz en lo Oscuro: Rewriting Identity, Spirituality, Reality.* Analouise Keating, ed. Durham, NC: Duke University Press.
Anzaldúa, Gloria, and AnaLouise Keating, AnaLouise, eds. 2002. *This Bridge We Call Home: Radical Visions for Trasnformation.* New York: Routledge. 149–63.
Appiah, Kwame Anthony. 1992. *In My Father's House: Africa in the Philosophy of Culture.* New York: Oxford University Press.
———. 1994. "Identity, Authenticity, Survival: Multicultural Societies and Social Reproduction." In *Multiculturalism*, Amy Gutmann, ed. Princeton, NJ: Princeton University Press. 149–64.
Arola, Adam. 2011. "Responses to This Is Not a Peace Pipe: Towards a Critical Indigenous Philosophy by Dale Turner: Dialogue and Identity: Worries about Word Warriors?" *Newsletter on Indigenous Philosophy* 10(2), 2–5.
Anzaldúa, Gloria, and Cherríe M. Moraga, eds. 2002. *This Bridge Called My Back: Writings By Radical Women of Color.* Berkeley, CA: Third Woman Press.
Beauvoir, Simone de. 1948. *The Ethics of Ambiguity.* Bernard Frechtman, trans. New York: Citadel Press.
bell hooks. 2000. *All About Love: New Visions.* New York: William Morrow and Company, Inc.
Berlin, Isaiah. 2002. *Liberty.* Henry Hardy, ed. New York: Oxford University Press.
Biko, Steve. 2012. *I Write What I Like.* Johannesburg, South Africa: Picador Africa.
Browning, Christopher R. 2017. *Ordinary Men: Reserve Police Battalion 101 and the Final Solution in Poland.* New York: Harper Perennial.
Byrd, Jodi A. 2011. *The Transit of Empire: Indigenous Critiques of Colonialism.* Minneapolis, MN: University of Minnesota Press.
Césaire, Aimé. 1960. *Toussaint Louverture: La revolution française et le probléme colonial.* Paris: Présence Africaine.

———. 2000. *Discourse on Colonialism*. Joan Pinkham, trans. New York: Monthly Review Press.

Cisneros, Natalie. 2020. "Borderlands and Border Crossing." In *50 Concepts for a Critical Phenomenology*. Gail Weiss, Ann V. Murphy, and Gayle Salamon, eds. Evanston, IL: Northwestern University Press. 47–52.

Coulthard, Glen Sean. 2014. *Red Skin, White Masks: Rejecting the Colonial Politics of Recognition*. Minneapolis: University of Minnesota Press.

———. Cuguano, Quobna Ottobah. 1999. *Thoughts and Sentiments on the Evil of Slavery and Other Writings*. Vincent Carretta, ed. New York: Penguin Books.

Darby, Derrick. 2009. *Rights, Race, and Recognition*. New York: Cambridge University Press.

Du Bois, W. E. B. 1994. *The Souls of Black Folk*. New York: Random House.

———. 1995. *W. E. B. Du Bois: A Reader*, David Levering Lewis, ed. New York: Henry Holt and Company, Inc.

Dubois, Laurent. 2004. *Avengers of the New World: The Story of the Haitian Revolution*. Cambridge, MA: The Belknap Press of Harvard University Press.

Douglass, Frederick. 1857. "West India Emancipation" https://www.blackpast.org/african-american-history/1857-frederick-douglass-if-there-no-struggle-there-no-progress/, last accessed March 20, 2022.

Fanon, Frantz. 1963. *The Wretched of the Earth*. Constance Farrington, trans. New York: Grove Press.

———. 1967. *Toward the African Revolution: Political Essays*. Haakon Chevalier, trans. New York: Grove Press.

———. 2008. *Black Skin, White Masks*. Richard Philcox, trans. New York: Grove Press.

Fraser, Nancy. 1997. *Justice Interruptus: Critical Reflections on the "Postsocialist" Condition*. New York: Routledge.

Fraser, Nancy, and Axel Honneth. 2003. *Redistribution or Recognition?* New York: Verso.

Fasting, Mathilde, ed. *After the End of History: Conversations with Francis Fukuyama*. Washington, DC: Georgetown University Press.

Fick, Carolyn E. 1990. *The Making of Haiti: The Saint Domingue Revolution from Below*. Knoxville, TN: The University of Tennessee Press.

Freyre, Gilberto. 2014. *Casa-Grande e Senzala*. São Paulo: Global Editora.

Fukuyama, Francis. 1992. *The End of History and the Last Man*. New York: Free Press.

Gordon, Lewis R. 1995a. *Bad Faith and Antiblack Racism*. Atlantic Highlands, NJ: Humanities Press.

———. 1995b. *Fanon and the Crisis of European Man: An Essay on Philosophy and the Human Sciences*. New York: Routledge.

———. 1997a. "Existential Dynamics of Theorizing Black Invisibility." In *Existence in Black: An Anthology of Black Existential Philosophy*. Lewis R. Gordon, ed. New York: Routledge. 69–79.

———. 1997b. *Her Majesty's Other Children: Sketches of Racism from a Neocolonial Age*. Lanham, MD: Rowman & Littlefield Publishers.

———. 2000. *Existentia Africana: Understanding Africana Existential Thought*. New York: Routledge.

———. 2006a. *Disciplinary Decadence: Living Thought in Trying Times*. Boulder, CO: Paradigm Publishers.

———. 2006b. "African-American Philosophy, Race, and the Geography of Reason." In *Not Only the Master's Tools: African-American Studies in Theory and Practice*. Lewis R. Gordon and Jane Anna Gordon, eds. Boulder, CO: Paradigm Publishers.

———. 2006c. "Is the Human a Teleological Suspension of Man? Phenomenological Exploration of Sylvia Wynter's Fanonian and Biodicean Reflections." In *After Man, Towards the Human: Critical Essays on Sylvia Wynter*. Anthony Bogues, ed. Miami, FL: Ian Randle Publishers. 237–57

———. 2008a. "A Phenomenology of Biko's Black Consciousness." In *Biko Lives!: Contesting the Legacies of Steve Biko*. Andile Mngxitama, Amanda Alexander, and Nigel C. Gibson, eds. New York: Palgrave Macmillan. 84–93

———. 2008b. *An Introduction to Africana Philosophy*. New York: Cambridge University Press.

———. 2011. "Shifting the Geograpy of Reason in an Age of Disciplinary Decadence." *Transmodernity* 1(2), 95–103

———. 2012. "Essentialist Anti-Essentialism, With Considerations from Other Sides of Modernity." Quaderna: A Multi-Lingual and Transdisciplinary Journal. No. 1. https://quaderna.org/wp-content/uploads/2012/12/Gordon-essentialist-and-essentialism.pdf.

———. 2021. *Freedom, Justice, and Decolonization*. New York: Routledge.

———. 2022. *Fear of Black Consciousness*. New York: Farrar, Straus and Giroux.

Gordon, Lewis R., and Jane Anna Gordon. 2006. "Introduction: Not Only the Master's Tools." In *Not Only the Master's Tools: African-American Studies in Theory and Practice*. Lewis R. Gordon and Jane Anna Gordon, eds. Boulder, CO: Paradigm Publishers. pp. ix–xi

Grimshaw, Jean. 1988. "Autonoy and Identity in Feminist Thinking." In *Feminist Perspectives in Philosophy*. Morewenna Friffiths and Margaret Whitford, eds. Indianapolis: Indiana University Press. 90–108.

Harris, Cheryl I. 1993. "Whiteness As Property." *Harvard Law Review* 106(8), 1707–91.

Hegel, G. W. F. 1969. *Hegel's Science of Logic*. A. V. Miller, trans. Amherst, NY: Humanity Books.

———. 1971. *Philosophy of Mind: Being Part Three of the Encyclopaedia of the Philosophical Sciences*. William Wallace and A. V. Miller, trans. New York: Oxford University Press.

———. 1977. *The Phenomenology of Spirit*. A. V. Miller, trans. New York: Oxford University Press.

———. 1991a. *The Encyclopaedia Logic*. T. F. Geraets, W. A. Suchting, and H. S. Harris, trans. Indianapolis, IN: Hackett Publishing Company, Inc.

———. 1991b. *Elements of the Philosophy of Right*. H. B. Nisbet, trans. New York: Cambridge University Press.

Heter, T. Storm. 2022. *The Sonic Gaze: Jazz, Whiteness, and Racialized Listening.* Lanham, MD: Rowman & Littlefield Publishers.

Honneth, Axel. 1994. Kampf um Anerkennung. Suhrkamp.

———. 1995. The Struggle for Recognition: The Moral Grammar of Social Conflicts. Joel Anderson, trans. Cambridge, MA: MIT Press.

Husserl, Edmund. 1970. *The Crisis of European Sciences and Transcendental Phenomenology.* David Carr, trans. Evanston, IL: Northwestern University Press.

Ikäheimo, Heikki. 2010. "Holism and Normative Essentialism in Hegel's Social Ontology." Unpublished Manuscript.

James, C. L. R. 1963. *The Black Jacobins: Toussaint L'Overture and the San Domingo Revolution.* New York: Vintage Books.

James, Robin. 2019. *The Sonic Episteme: Acoustic Resonance, Neoliberalism, and Biopolitics.* Durham, NC: Duke University Press.

Jeffers, Chike. 2013. "The Cultural Theory of Race: Yet Another Look at Du Bois's 'The Conservation of Races.'" *Ethics* 123(April), 403–26.

Lonzi, Carla. 1996. "Let's Spit on Hegel." Giovanna Bellesia and Elaine Maclachlan, trans. In *Feminist Interpretations of G. W. F. Hegel.* Patricia Jagentowicz Mills, ed. University Park, PA: Pennsylvania State University Press. 275–98.

Lorde, Audre. 1984. *Sister Outsider.* Berkeley, CA: Crossing Press.

Joseph-Gabriel, Annette K. 2014. "Creolizing Freedom: French-Creole Translations of Liberty and Equality in the Haitian Revolution." *Slavery & Abolition: A Journal of Slave and Post-Slave Studies,* DOI: 10.1080/0144039X.2014.888869.

———. 2017. "Mobility and the Enunciation of Freedom in Urban Saint-Domingue." *Eighteenth-Century Studies* 50(2), 213–29.

Kant, Immanuel. 1988. *Kant: Selections.* Lewis White Beck, ed. New York: Macmillan Publishing Company.

Keating, AnaLouise. 2009. "Introduction: Reading Gloria Anzaldúa, Reading Ourselves . . . Complex Intimacies, Intricate Connections." In *The Gloria Anzaldúa Reader,* AnaLouise Keating, ed. Durham, NC: Duke University Press. 1–15.

Kymlicka, Will. 1995. *Multicultural Citizenship.* New York: Oxford University Press.

Linebaugh, Peter. 2019. *Red Round Globe Hot Burning: A Tale at the Crossroads of Commons and Closure, of Love and Terror, of Race and Class, and of Kate and Ned Despard.* Oakland: University of California Press.

Linebaugh, Peter, and Marcus Rediker. 2000. *The Many-Headed Hydra: Sailors, Slaves, Commoners, and the Hidden History of the Revolutionary Atlantic.* Boston, MA: Beacon Press.

Lugones, María. 1998. "Motion, Stasis, and Resistance to Interlocked Oppressions." In *Making Worlds: Gender, Metaphor, Materiality.* Susan Hardy Aiken, Ann Brigham, Sallie A. Marston, Penny Waterstone, eds. Tucson, AZ: University of Arizona Press. 49–52.

———. 2003. *Pilgrimages/Peregrinajes: Theorizing Coalition Against Multiple Oppressions.* Lanham, MD: Rowman & Littlefield Publishers.

———. 2010. "Toward a Decolonial Feminism." *Hypatia* 25(4), 742–59.

Magaziner, Daniel R. 2010. *The Law and the Prophets: Black Consciousness in South Africa, 1968–1977.* Johannesburg, South Africa: Jacana Media Ltd.

Maldonado-Torres, Nelson. 2007. "On the Coloniality of Being: Contributions to the Development of a Concept." *Cultural Studies* 21(2–3), 240–70.

Mangcu, Xolela. 2012. *Biko: A Biography*. Cape Town, South Africa: Tafelberg.

Mangena, M. J. Oshadi. 2008. "The Black Consciousness Philosophy and the Woman's Question in South Africa: 1970–80." In *Biko Lives!: Contesting the Legacies of Steve Biko*. Andile Mngxitama, Amanda Alexander, and Nigel C. Gibson eds. New York: Palgrave Macmillan. 253–66.

Mariátegui, José Carlos. 1971. *Seven Interpretive Essays on Peruvian Reality*. Marjory Urquidi, trans. Austin: University of Texas Press.

Markell, Patchen. 2003. *Bound by Recognition*. Princeton, NJ: Princeton University Press.

Martinez, Jacqueline M. 2000. *Phenomenology of Chicana Experience & Identity: Communication and Transformation in Praxis*. Lanham, MD: Rowman & Littlefield Publishers.

McNay, Lois. 2008. *Against Recognition*. Malden, MA: Polity Press.

McQueen, Paddy. 2015. *Subjectivity, Gender, and the Struggle for Recognition*. New York: Palgrave Macmillan.

Meagher, Thomas. 2021. "Existential Psychoanalysis and Sociogeny," *Sartre Studies International* 27(2), 48–59.

Medina, José. 2013. *The Epistemology of Resistance: Gender and Racial Oppression, Epistemic Injustice, and Resistant Imaginations*. New York: Oxford University Press.

Monahan, Michael. 2005. "Private Property and Public Interest," *Philosophy in the Contemporary World* 12(2), 17–21.

———. 2006. "Recognition Beyond Struggle: On a Liberatory Account of Hegelian Recognition." *Social Theory and Practice* 32(3), 389–414.

———. 2007. "The Practice of Self Overcoming: Nietzschean Reflections on the Martial Arts." *The Journal of the Philosophy of Sport* 34, 39–51.

———. 2011. *The Creolizing Subject: Race, Reason, and the Politics of Purity*. NY: Fordham University Press.

———. 2014. "Review: José Medina, *The Epistemology of Resistance*." *The American Philosophical Association Newsletter on Feminism and Philosophy* 15(1), 24–27.

———. 2017. "Introduction: What is Rational is Creolizing." In *Creolizing Hegel*, Michael Monahan, ed. New York: Rowman & Littlefield International. 1–22.

———. 2019. "Freedom in Motion: Roberts and Ortega on Flight and Home." *Inter-American Journal of Philosophy* 10(1), 44–61.

Moran, Dermot. 2005. *Edmund Husserl: Founder of Phenomenology*. Malden, MA: Polity Press.

More, Mabogo P. 2008. "Biko: Africana Existentialist Philosopher." In *Biko Lives!: Contesting the Legacies of Steve Biko*. Andile Mngxitama, Amanda Alexander, and Nigel C. Gibson eds. New York: Palgrave Macmillan. 45–68.

———. 2017. *Biko: Philosophy, Identity, and Liberation*. Cape Town, South Africa: Human Sciences Research Council Press.

Natanson, Maurice. 1973. *Edmund Husserl: Philosopher of Infinite Tasks*. Evanston, IL: Northwestern University Press.
Nesbitt, Nick. 2004. "Troping Toussaint, Reading Revolution." *Research in African Literatures* 35(2), 18–33.
Nuzzo, Angelica. 2006. "Dialectic as Logic of Transformative Processes." In *Hegel: New Directions*. Katerina Deligiorgi, ed. Bucks, UK: Acumen. 85–103.
Ortega, Mariana. 2016. *In-Between: Latina Feminist Phenomenology, Multiplicity, and the Self*. Albany: State University of New York Press.
Paccacerqua, Cynthia M. 2016. "Gloria Anzaldúa's Affective Logic of *Volverse Una*." *Hypatia* 31(2), 334–51.
Pinkard, Terry. 1994. *Hegel's Phenomenology: The Sociality of Reason*. New York: Cambridge University Press.
Popkin, Jeremy D. 2007. *Facing Racial Revolution: Eyewitness accounts of the Haitian Insurrection*. Chicago: University of Chicago Press.
———. 2010. *You Are All Free: The Haitian Revolution and the Abolition of Slavery*. New York: Cambridge University Press.
Povinelli, Elizabeth A. 2002. *The Cunning of Recognition: Indigenous Alterities and the Making of Australian Multiculturalism*. Durham, NC: Duke University Press.
Quijano, Aníbal. 2007. "Coloniality and Modernity/Rationality." *Cultural Studies* 21(2), 168–78.
Rawls, John. 1985. "Justice as Fairness: Political not Metaphysical." *Philosophy and Public Affairs* 14, 223–51.
Rediker, Marcus. 2004. *Villains of All Nations: Atlantic Pirates in the Golden Age*. Boston: Beacon Press.
Reiff, David. 1991. "Professional Aztecs and Popular Culture." *New Perspectives Quarterly* 8(2), 42–46.
Roberts, Neil. 2015. *Freedom as Marronage*. Chicago: University of Chicago Press.
Ruíz, Elena. 2020. "Mestiza Consciousness." In *50 Concepts for a Critical Phenomenology*. Gail Weiss, Ann V. Murphy, and Gayle Salamon, eds. Evanston, IL: Northwestern University Press. 217–23.
Sartre, Jean-Paul. 1948. *Anti-Semite and Jew*. George J. Becker, trans. New York: Schocken Books.
———. 1994. *Being and Nothingness*. Hazel E. Barnes, trans. New York: Gramercy Books.
Schutte, Ofelia. 2020. "Crossroads and In-Between Spaces: A Mediation on Anzaldúa and Beyond." In *Theories of the Flesh: Latinx and Latin American Feminisms, Transformation, and Resistance*. Andrea J. Pitts, Mariana Ortega, and José Medina, eds. New York: Oxford University Press. 123–34.
Scott, Julius S. 2018. *The Common Wind: Afro-American Currents in the Age of the Haitian Revolution*. New York: Verso.
Spillers, Hortense J. 1987. "Mama's Baby, Papa's Maybe: An American Grammar Book." *Diacritics* 17(2), 65–81. https://doi.org/10.2307/464747.
Stanley, Jason. 2011. *Know How*. New York: Oxford University Press.

Stojkovski, Velimir. 2015. "Recognition and Political Ontology: Fichte, Hegel, and Honneth." PhD dissertation, Marquette University. Paper 525. http://epublications.marquette.edu/dissertations_mu/525.

Suárez-Krabbe, Julia. 2016. *Race, Rights and Rebels: Alternatives to Human rights and Development from the Global South*. London: Rowman & Littlefield International.

Taylor, Charles. 1994. "The Politics of Recognition." In *Multiculturalism: Examining the Politics of Recognition*. Amy Gutmann, ed. Princeton, NJ: Princeton University Press.

Taylor-Garcia, Daphne V. 2019. *The Existence of the Mixed Race Damnés: Decolonialism, Class, Gender, Race*. London: Rowman & Littlefield International.

Tibebu, Teshale. 2011. *Hegel and the Third World: The Making of Eurocentrism in World History*. Syracuse, NY: Syracuse University Press.

Tshivhase, Mpho. 2018. "Love as the Foundation of Ubuntu." *Synthesis Philosophica* 65(1), 197–208.

Varzi, Achille C. 2011. "On Doing Ontology without Metaphysics." *Philosophical Perspectives* 25, 407–23.

Vasconcelos, José. 2007. *La Raza Cósmica*. Cd. De México: Editorial Porrúa.

Vizcaíno, Rafael. 2021. "Secular Decolonial Woes." *Journal of Speculative Philosophy* 35(1), 71–92.

Ware, Robert Bruce. 1999. *Hegel: The Logic of Self-consciousness and the Legacy of Subjective Freedom*. Edinburgh: Edinburgh University Press.

Waters, Anne. 2004. "Indigenous Genocide: The Unites States of North America." In *Newsletter on American Indians in Philosophy* 3(2), 190–93.

Weir, Allison. 2013. *Identities and Freedom: Feminist Theory Between Power and Connection*. New York: Oxford University Press.

Welsh, Frank. 2000. *A History of South Africa*. London: Harper Collins Publishers.

Williams, Robert R. 1997. *Hegel's Ethics of Recognition*. Berkeley, CA: University of California Press.

Wynter, Sylvia. 1984. "The Ceremony Must be Found: After Humanism." *Boundary 2* 12/13(3), 19–70.

———. 1995. "1492: A New World View." In *Race, Discourse, and the Origin of the Americas: A New World View*. Vera Lawrence Hyatt and Rex Nettleford, eds. Washington, DC: Smithsonian Institution Press.

———. 2001. "Towards the Sociogenic Principle: Fanon, Identity, the Puzzle of Conscious Experience, and What It Is Like to Be 'Black.'" In *National Identities and Sociopolitical Changes in Latin America*. Mercedes F. Durán-Cogan and Antonio Gómez-Mariana, eds. New York: Routledge.

———. 2006. "On How We Mistook the Map for the Territory, and Re-Imprisoned Ourselves in Our Unbearable Wrongness of Being, of *Désêtre*: Black Studies Toward the Human Project." In *Not Only the Master's Tools: African-American Studies in Theory and Practice*. Lewis R. Gordon and Jane Anna Gordon, eds. Boulder, CO: Paradigm Publishers. 107–69.

———. 2015. "The Ceremony Found: Toward the Autopoetic Turn/Overturn, its Autonomy of Human Agency and Extraterritoriality of (Self-)Cognition." In *Black*

Knowledges/Black Struggles: Essays in Critical Epistemology. Jason R. Ambroise and Sabine Broeck, eds. Liverpool, UK: Liverpool University Press. 184–252.

Young, Iris Marion. 1990. *Justice and the Politics of Difference*. Princeton, NJ: Princeton University Press.

Zack, Naomi. 1997. "Race, Life, Death, Identity, Tragedy and Good Faith." In *Existence in Black: An Anthology of Black Existential Philosophy*. Lewis R. Gordon, ed. New York: Routledge. 99–109.

Zambrana, Rocío. 2010. "Hegel's Hyperbolic Formalism." *Bulletin of the Hegel Society of Great Britain* 61, 107–30.

———. 2015. *Hegel's Theory of Intelligibility*. Chicago: University of Chicago Press.

Index

acknowledgment, as alternative to recognition, 35, 40–43, 50, 60–61, 63, 65
Africana philosophy, 142–43
agency
    collective, 101, 103–7
    as dynamic, 54, 79, 81, 90
    and freedom, 7, 23, 100, 128, 133
    and recognition, 30, 32, 43, 79, 83, 97
    and sovereignty, 37, 39
Ahmed, Sara, 104
Alcoff, Linda, 86
alienation, 5, 25, 43, 97, 114, 131, 154, 170n5
ambiguity
    in Anzaldúa, 109–110, 176n8
    and decadence, 149
    and identity, 119, 124, 127, 146–47, 151
    and maturity, 156
    and the politics of purity, 6–7, 15, 21, 26–27, 147, 161
    racial, 12, 15–17
    and rationality, 18–20, 74, 171n5
    and sovereignty, 51, 68
American pragmatism, 21, 68
antiblack racism, 98, 100, 146, 158
antiblack world, 102–3, 153–54

Anzaldúa, Gloria, 21, 94, 107–29, 138, 140, 165
    los atravesados, 107, 110–11, 176n7
    conocimiento, 113–14, 117, 119, 122, 128
    Coyalxāuhqui, 114, 117, 176n10
    desconocimiento, 117, 119, 176n11
    la facultad, 110–11, 114
    mestiza consciousness (*la conciencia de la mestiza*), 108–112, 115
    nepantla, 108, 112–13
    las nepantleras, 112–14, 117, 176n8
    new tribalism, 112, 115–18
    nos/otras, 116–17
apartheid (South African), 98–99, 101–3, 105, 118, 175n2
Appiah, Kwame Anthony, 15–16, 38, 171n6
Aristotle, 23
Arola, Adam, 127
los atravesados. *See* Anzaldúa, Gloria
autopoetics, 133, 140, 166
    See also Wynter, Sylvia
autonomy, 26, 36, 68
    of desire, 24

and recognition, 31, 33, 170n9
  in Wynter, 136–42

bad faith (*mauvaise foi*), 41–41, 51, 61, 66, 82–83, 103, 120, 123, 126, 151, 156, 176n11, 177n10
  in Gordon, 144–47, 149, 153, 157–58, 177n7
Beauvoir, Simone de, 51, 146, 152, 156, 176n11, 177n8, 177n10
becoming
  and Black Consciousness, 105
  and freedom, 90, 95, 151, 160–61
  in Gordon, 147–48, 156–57
  in Hegel, 74
  in Markell, 50–55, 63
  and recognition, 62, 66, 76, 78, 96
  in Wynter, 141–42
belonging, 5–7, 117, 119, 170n4, 170n7, 175n6
Berlin, Isaiah, 24–25, 37
Biko, Steve, 94, 97–106, 109, 118–20, 122, 124, 128–29, 138, 140, 165, 175n3, 176n7
bios/logos. *See* Wynter, Sylvia
#BlackLivesMatter, 31
Black Consciousness, 98–106, 119–20, 128, 144, 176n7
blackness, 14, 100–6
boundaries
  in Anzaldúa, 114, 116, 118
  and creolizing, 71, 119
  and identity, 25–27, 29, 32, 44, 46–47, 79, 85, 125
  and purity, 6, 15, 22, 127
  racial, 13
  and rationality, 72, 75
Byrd, Jodi, 124, 126

Cabrera, Miguel, 13
Cartesian *ego*, 24
Cartesian dualism, 59
Césaire, Aimé, 34, 167
choice. *See* freedom
Cisneros, Natalie, 109

Coatlique. *See* Anzaldúa, Gloria
cognition. *See* knowledge
colonialism, 4–5, 39, 94, 96, 124, 129
coloniality, 5, 94, 129, 132, 138, 162, 174n1
  of Being, 4
compatibilism, 22, 24
la conciencia de la mestiza. *See* Anzaldúa, Gloria
conocimiento. *See* Anzaldúa, Gloria
conscientization, 104, 106, 109–11, 118, 122
constructive interference, 88–89, 91, 93, 121–22, 155, 159–60, 162
Coulthard, Glen, 123–24
Coyalxāuhqui. *See* Anzaldúa, Gloria
creolizing
  definition, 21–22
  and freedom, 29–30, 71–72, 84–86, 89–91, 93–95, 97–98, 122, 127, 162, 165–67
  and Hegel, 174n1
  imperative of, 123
  practices of, 1, 125, 127
  as response to politics of purity, 6–11, 129, 131–32, 161
Cuguano, Ottobah, 33

decadence. *See* Gordon, Lewis
decolonial practices, 125, 127, 160
decolonial thought/theory, 35, 100, 109
Deleuze and Gautarri, 115
desconocimiento. *See* Anzaldúa, Gloria
destructive interference, 88–89, 93, 121, 129, 155, 161–62
determinism, 22–25
difference
  and creolizing, 8, 71, 89, 122, 125
  and identity, 4, 68, 72, 81, 84–86, 119–20, 125, 127, 131, 141, 161–62, 165–67
  and knowledge, 80, 175n6
  and liberalism, 32
  and reciprocity, 158

disempowerment, 5, 36, 82, 93, 102, 121, 159
dissonance, 8, 88–91, 93, 103, 120–22, 129, 154, 162
Douglass, Frederick, 99, 143–44
DuBois, W. E. B., 15, 176n4

empowerment, 61–62, 89, 93, 118, 121, 154–55, 157–62, 173n6
epistemology, 3, 5
    in Anzaldúa, 109
    epistemic closure, 147–50
    epistemic friction, 85, 89
    epistemic justice, 3
    epistemic modesty, 4
    of provenance, 79–80, 131
    and recognition, 49–51, 58, 61, 63, 68
essentialism, 37–38, 40, 42–44, 46, 79, 124, 154
Eurocentrism, 1, 80, 96, 135, 142, 173n1
existentialism, 53, 140, 143, 146, 156–57
existential phenomenology, 103, 143–45, 151, 155

facticity, 145–46
la facultad. *See* Anzaldúa, Gloria
Fanon, Frantz, 29, 94–98, 100, 103, 105–6, 123, 125, 131–32, 136–37, 145, 147, 156, 160–61, 175n1
flourishing, 30, 64, 72, 114, 153–57, 159–60
Fraser, Nancy, 33–34, 37–38
freedom
    choice vs. options, 151–53, 155, 157
    and coloniality, 131–32, 171n7
    as creolizing, 71–72, 85–86, 88–90, 93–97, 122, 124, 132, 162–63, 165–67
    and flourishing, 155–57
    and Hegel, 3, 76
    and liberation, 170n1

    metaphysical vs. political, 22–25, 151–52, 177n6
    and the politics of purity, 7, 11, 26–27, 29, 47
    and power, 159–60
    and recognition, 31–33, 69, 77, 82–84, 89
    as relational, 6, 170n7
    and Sartre, 51, 145–46
friction, 8, 85–87, 120–25, 175n6
    productive, 85–86, 89–91, 93–94, 106, 120–23, 125, 127–28, 141, 161–62, 167, 176n8
Fukuyama, Francis, 172n4

genre (of the human), 133–42, 160
Glissant, Édouard, 21, 170n8
Gordon, Lewis, 14 22, 29, 79, 102–3, 132, 165, 173n6, 177n4, 177n6, 177n7, 178n10
    on Africana philosophy, 142–43
    on bad faith, 41, 144
    on flourishing and maturity, 154–57, 159–62
    on oppression, 151–54, 157–59
    on phenomenology, 144–48
    on rationality and reason, 18, 20, 149–51
    on theodicy, 39
Grimshaw, Jean, 24–25

Haitian revolution, 2
Harris, Cheryl, 13
Hegel, G. W. F., 3, 6, 21, 33, 35, 53, 62, 64–65, 71–72, 82–83, 86, 94, 132, 166, 173n1, 173n7, 174n2, 177n5
    Fanon's reading of, 95–97
    logic, 72–76, 78
    on love, 58
    Markell's reading of, 38–40, 43, 47, 66–67
    on "pure" recognition, 54–55, 58–61, 63, 68
Heter, T. Storm, 179n11
home. *See* belonging

hometactics, 3, 5
homo economicus, 18
homo politicus, 133
Honneth, Axel, 30–34, 38, 66, 72, 172n2
hooks, bell, 58
humanism, 33–34, 68, 80, 110, 132, 140, 142, 160
the "Human Project." *See* Wynter, Sylvia
Husserl, Edmund, 17–18, 21–22, 110, 143, 145, 177n4

identity
    collective, 99, 101, 103, 105–8, 112, 115–19
    and difference, 4, 72, 81, 169n1
    as dynamic, 120, 128–29, 165
    individual, 16, 75, 96–98, 131, 171n6
    and liberation, 8
    and purity, 123–27
    and recognition, 31–38, 40–46, 49–50, 53–55, 61–62, 65–66, 83, 85–87
identity politics, 33–34
Ikäheimo, Heikki, 173n8
indigenous sovereignty, 5, 109, 123, 125–28, 161
intellectualism, 172n3
intersubjective constitution, 110, 147, 158–59

James, Robin, 175n5
Jeffers, Chike, 15

Kant, Immanuel, 18–19, 24, 26, 30, 74
Keating, AnaLouise, 107
knowledge, 50–51, 84–87, 96, 117, 147, 155
    propositional vs. practical, 52–58, 63–64, 66–68, 77, 79–80, 113, 172n3
Kruks, Sonia, 79–80

liberalism, 32–34, 36–37, 72, 170n7
liberation. *See* freedom
logic
    of Hegel, 73–75, 78, 174n1
    and purity, 18–21, 46–47, 69
    of recognition, 36
Lorde, Audre, 165–67
love, 33, 58, 113
Lugones, Maria, 5, 107–8, 175n3

Man. *See* Wynter, Sylvia
Mangena, M. J. Oshadi, 104–5
Mariátegui, José, 33
Markell, Patchen, 34–47, 50–51, 53–55, 58–61, 63, 65–68, 72, 76, 97
maturity, 155–57, 159, 161, 166
McNay, Lois, 36, 38, 43, 46
McQueen, Paddy, 170n9
Medina, José, 85–87
mestiza consciousness. *See* Anzaldúa, Gloria
mestizaje, 109, 112–13
metaphysics, 2–3, 7, 16–17, 25–26, 41, 51, 53, 66, 76, 95, 169n1, 170n1
    metaphysical freedom, 22–23, 27
miscegenation, 12, 14
More, Mabogo Percy, 100, 102, 106
myth of purity, 21, 123–24, 126
mythos, 111, 133, 137

nativism, 5–7, 125–26
negation
    in Hegel, 75, 83
    of the human, 160
    as negating activity, 97
    in Sartre, 145
nepantla. *See* Anzaldúa, Gloria
las nepantleras. *See* Anzaldúa, Gloria
new tribalism. *See* Anzaldúa, Gloria
Nietzsche, Friedrich, 21, 68
nos/otras. *See* Anzaldúa, Gloria
Nuzzo, Angelica, 73–74

Oliver, Kelly, 35
the one-drop rule, 12–13, 171n3

Index

ontology, 2, 25, 41–42, 50, 55, 65, 95, 135, 141, 144, 147–49, 157, 160, 169n1, 170n1
    atomistic, 35
    dynamic, 7, 9, 50, 65, 76, 83, 93, 119, 142, 149
    ontological freedom, 151–52, 155
    racial, 15
    relational, 107, 116, 119, 142, 149, 176n7
    static, 22, 79, 81, 85
    substance, 107, 118
oppression, 1–3, 11, 27, 29, 68, 82–86, 93–102, 104–6, 108–9, 114, 116, 128–29, 151–59, 161, 163, 165, 170n1, 170n7, 174n1, 178n10
    internalized, 25–25, 100–2
    and race, 16
    and recognition, 31, 36–38, 43, 50, 65, 89
    and sonic metaphor, 118–22
options. *See* freedom
Ortega, Mariana, 3, 5, 109, 170n4

Paccacerqua, Cynthia, 110, 114
particular (logical category), 19–21, 33, 49, 68–69, 75, 78–81, 85, 129, 131, 160–62, 167
    personhood, 30–31, 43–45
phenomenology, 18, 21, 79, 102, 106, 117, 122, 143–46, 148, 151, 157, 162
    existential, 143–45, 151, 155
    of practical knowledge, 173n3
Pinkard, Terry, 75, 80
Pitts, Andrea, 107, 109, 112, 116, 176n7, 176n8
Plato, 24
poststructuralism, 21
practical model of knowledge.
    See knowledge
pragmatism. *See* American pragmatism.
productive friction. *See* friction
propositional model of knowledge.
    See knowledge
pure recognition. *See* recognition

purity
    and freedom, 26–27, 97
    of the human, 103, 138, 160
    politics of, 1, 6–8, 11–29, 34, 42–47, 49, 53, 63–64, 67–69, 71–73, 76, 78–81, 84–85, 89, 108, 116–19, 123–29, 131–32, 147, 161, 171n3
    and race, 11–15, 170n2, 171n3, 171n4
    and the real, 16–18, 149
    and reason, 18–20, 73
    of recognition, 55
    telos of, 124, 128

Quijano, Anibal, 100

race
    and bad faith, 146
    as dynamic, 79, 115
    eliminativism, 15–17, 38
    history of, 11–14, 69, 135, 170n2, 171n3
    reality of, 19–20, 146
racism, 14, 96, 147, 153–54, 170n2
    antiblack, 98–101
    and bad faith, 146, 177n7
    and oppression, 156–58
    as white noise, 162
rational agent, 18, 20, 26, 39
rationality, 18–21, 39, 110, 135–36, 150–51
reason, 26, 133, 135–38, 150, 173n1
    analytical, 110
    as dynamic, 67, 72, 74–76
    metacritique of, 142–43, 149, 151
    moral, 171n5
    and purity, 18–20
    speculative, 72, 74–76, 78, 177n5

reciprocity, 57, 59–62, 96–97, 103–4, 108, 119, 121–25, 127, 129, 141–42, 150, 158–59, 161–62, 176n8
recognition, 8–9, 27, 29–34, 40–47, 49, 77–89, 94, 107, 119, 125–26,

129, 131, 140, 159, 165–67, 171n1,
172n1, 173n6, 173n8
   cognitive moment of, 49–58
   as essentializing, 37–39
   exchange model of, 34–37, 46
   in Fanon, 95–97, 161
   in Hegel, 59–69, 71–76
   as theodicean, 39
relationality, 77, 80–81, 84–85, 87, 90, 149, 174n1
relational ontology. *See* ontology
relativization (of Man), 138–140
resonance, 8, 88–91, 93–94, 102, 120–22, 154, 162
responsibility, 95, 99, 103–4, 111, 117–18, 137, 140–42, 145–46, 149, 156–58, 161–62, 177n7, 177n8, 177n9

Sartre, Jean-Paul, 40–41, 43, 51, 61, 97, 143–45, 147, 151, 156, 172n7, 177n4, 177n6
Sistema de Castas, 13–14
sociogenesis, 136–37
sonic metaphor, 8–9, 50, 87–90, 93, 119–21, 124, 128, 154, 161–62, 175n5
sovereignty (sovereign subject), 36–42, 50–51, 59–61, 66–69, 72, 97
   See also indigenous sovereignty
speculative reason (*Vernunft*).
   See reason
Spillers, Hortense, 13, 177n3
Stanley, Jason, 173n3
Stewart, Lindsey, 127–29
Suárez-Krabbe, Julia, 178n10
the subject, 3, 7, 24–27, 31–32, 50–51, 72, 90, 112, 123–29, 138, 140, 146, 162, 170n9
   as dynamic, 75–76, 119–20, 122
   of liberation, 2, 6, 9, 94–96, 98, 100, 105, 115, 118, 129
   of recognition, 35–46, 59–61, 65–68, 74, 78–79

"Tale of the Eloquent Peasant," 171n7

Taylor, Charles, 30–35, 37–38, 43–44, 49, 72
Taylor-Garcia, Daphne, 171n4
tekhne. *See* Wynter, Sylvia
teleological suspension, 149–50, 159
telos, 40, 46, 144, 151
   of purity, 12, 15, 19
   of whiteness, 102, 104
   without a terminus, 57–58, 157, 160, 163
theodicy, 39–40, 46
truth, 80, 148
   as dynamic, 67, 72–76, 78
   value, 54, 64
Truth, Sojourner, 131
Tshivhase, Mpho, 64

Ubuntu, 64
the Understanding (*Verstand*), 72–76, 78–79, 177n5
universal (logical category), 19–21, 30–31, 33, 37, 129, 150, 157, 176n5
   and the human, 103–4, 131–32, 135–38, 140–42, 160–62
   in recognition, 44–45, 49, 68–69, 75, 78–81, 85, 167, 172n7
universalism, 31, 33, 80, 132, 161

Vasconcelos, José, 14, 109
visual metaphor, 8, 41, 50, 86–89
Vizcaíno, Rafael, 111

Ware, Robert Bruce, 76
Waters, Anne, 126
Weheliye, Alexander, 176n5
Weir, Allison, 170n7
we-subject, 9, 94, 98, 105, 112, 119–29, 138, 140, 162
whiteness, 13–15, 102–5, 119, 170n2, 171n3, 172n2, 179n11
white noise, 88, 103, 120–25, 127–29, 142, 154, 161, 162
white telos. *See* telos.
Wynter, Sylvia, 9, 110, 123, 132–42, 148, 158, 160–61, 165, 176n1, 176n9

autopoetics, 133, 140
bios/logos, 133, 135–36, 139–41
the "Human Project," 138–41, 158
overrepresentation of Man, 134–36
tekhne, 133

Young, Iris, 36

Zack, Naomi, 15–16
Zambrana, Rocío, 75
zone of nonbeing, 103, 123

About the Author

Michael J. Monahan is associate professor of philosophy at the University of Memphis. His teaching and research focuses on political philosophy, philosophy of race and racism, Africana philosophy, phenomenology, and Hegel. He has been active in the Caribbean Philosophical Association since its first meeting in 2004, having served as vice president from 2008 to 2013, and currently serving as treasurer and minister of spirits. He is the editor of *Creolizing Hegel* (2017), and author of *The Creolizing Subject: Race, Reason, and the Politics of Purity* (2011), along with numerous articles on political philosophy and the philosophy of race and racism. Beyond these professional pursuits, he spends his time listening to music (having stopped playing and performing sometime in graduate school), cooking, practicing martial arts, and watching delightfully terrible movies.

www.ingramcontent.com/pod-product-compliance
Lightning Source LLC
Chambersburg PA
CBHW021355300426
44114CB00012B/1237